CW00956455

England's Seaside Resorts

England's Seaside Resorts

Allan Brodie and Gary Winter

ENGLISH HERITAGE

Published by English Heritage, Kemble Drive, Swindon SN2 2GZ
www.english-heritage.org.uk
English Heritage is the Government's statutory adviser on all aspects of the
historic environment.

© English Heritage 2007

Printing 10 9 8 7 6 5 4 3 2 1

Images (except as otherwise shown) © English Heritage or
© Crown copyright. NMR.

First published 2007

ISBN 978-1-905624-65-2

Product code 51305

British Library Cataloguing in Publication data
A CIP catalogue record for this book is available from the British Library.

All rights reserved
No part of this publication may be reproduced or transmitted in any form
or by any means, electronic or mechanical, including photocopying,
recording, or any information storage or retrieval system, without permission in writing from the publisher.

Application for the reproduction of images should be made to the National
Monuments Record. Every effort has been made to trace the copyright
holders and we apologise in advance for any unintentional omissions,
which we would be pleased to correct in any subsequent edition of this
book.

The National Monuments Record is the public archive of English Heritage. For more information, contact NMR Enquiry and Research Services, National Monuments Record Centre, Kemble Drive, Swindon SN2
2GZ; telephone (01793) 414600.

Brought to publication by Robin Taylor, Publishing, English Heritage.

Edited by Sara Peacock
Indexed by Alan Rutter
Page layout by George Hammond

Printed in the UK by Cambridge University Press.

Frontispiece
Blackpool Tower, Lancashire;
1891–4, Maxwell and Tuke

Contents

Acknowledgements

England's Seaside Resorts is based on a survey of England's seaside resorts undertaken by English Heritage's Research Department between 2002 and 2006. The project has been enthusiastically supported by numerous colleagues, and the authors are especially indebted to the members of the Project Board, John Cattell, Martin Cherry, Colum Giles, Barry Jones and Chris Scull, for their professional guidance.

A project of this scale and scope required contributions from a wide range of colleagues. We would like to thank Alan Bull, Steve Cole, James O Davies, Mike Hesketh-Roberts, Derek Kendall, Bob Skingle and Peter Williams for the excellent photographs they have taken, a small selection of which feature in this book. Mike Hesketh-Roberts also undertook the onerous task of making the project team's photographs compatible with the systems of the National Monument Record (NMR). Damian Grady has provided us with superb aerial photographs and Ian Leonard has kept us supplied with wonderful modern and historic images from English Heritage's electronic archive. The NMR's darkroom staff have printed huge numbers of photographs for us and scanned many more. Tony Berry and Nigel Fradgley were responsible for the graphics in the book. We would also like to thank NMR archive and library staff, particularly Cynthia Howell and Irene Peacock, for their help in accessing the research material. Special thanks also go to Peter Guillery for his advice in the drafting of the book and to Kathryn Morrison for providing us with insights into the retail world of resorts. Ursula Dugard-Craig has provided us with important, invaluable administrative support. Robin Taylor, Rachel Howard and Sara Peacock have been responsible for bringing the work to publication.

During fieldwork and documentary research we have visited countless libraries, record offices and museums. We would like to express our thanks to all those members of staff and volunteers who have assisted us directly, or who have responded to our on-line requests for information. We are especially grateful to Chippenham Public Library, who kept us supplied with an inexhaustible supply of inter-library loans. Our thanks also go to the following individuals and institutions for supplying images: Sue Berry; Brighton Museum & Art Gallery; the British Library; East Sussex Library and Information Service; Essex Record Office; the Guildhall Library; Hastings Museum and Art Gallery; Jernkontoret; Lady Lancaster and John Murray Ltd; Margate Public Library; Society of Antiquaries of London; Science & Society Picture Library and Bryn Mawr College in Pennsylvania. While every effort has been made to trace copyright holders of some images, we apologise to any who may have been inadvertently omitted from the list.

The historic significance of the English seaside is recognised by a number of dedicated academics, historians and researchers. We have been fortunate to get to know some of them well and share our passions. In particular, we would like to acknowledge John K Walton and Lynn Pearson for sharing their knowledge and being prepared to answer a range of inane questions. Sue Berry has supplied us with advice, support, information and images, and undertook the thankless task of going through our manuscript. Roger Billington and Martin Walker kindly spared their valuable time to show us around the Butlins resorts of Bognor Regis and Skegness, respectively; David Cam did likewise at Blackpool Pleasure Beach.

Finally, we would like to thank our families who have had to put up with our absences on research trips (or, as they call them, holidays). Now that our research is drawing to a conclusion, our wives, Toni and Pam, and our children Mary and William, and Janie and Madelaine may now get the uninterrupted seaside holidays they long for.

1

Introduction

The seaside resort is a special place! This is recognised by historians of the seaside as well as the hordes of holidaymakers who flock to England's beaches each year. Visitors know why these towns are special: resorts have sea and sand; they have a bewildering range of entertainment and new things to do; they have new people to meet; and, perhaps most importantly, they provide a contrast to the home town.

While the special nature of the seaside may seem obvious, understanding the distinctive character of the architecture and landscapes of resort towns is, however, not as straightforward as it may seem. The challenge lies in assessing the influences that impinged on resort growth, identifying any broad characteristics of town development that are peculiar to resorts, recognising architectural styles that may be more prevalent at the seaside and documenting distinctive types of buildings. Although there is much that separates seaside towns from inland towns, particularly those that do not cater for visitors, nevertheless they have many things in common and the purpose of this book is to note the similarities as well as to celebrate the special characteristics of the seaside town.

In 2002 English Heritage undertook a national survey of seaside resorts, home to around 7 per cent of England's population, as well as the holiday destination for millions of other people. The survey involved visits to resorts on every coastline, followed by more detailed examinations of some of the larger and more informative towns. The aims of the survey were two-fold: first, to increase knowledge of, and promote awareness of, the built environment of resorts, and, second, to assist English Heritage with the development of policy for coastal towns. To achieve these aims a number of papers have been published and presented, and a book of historic photographs from the National Monuments Record, *Seaside Holidays in the Past*, was published in 2005.[1] The project team also contributed to *Shifting Sands*, a joint publication with the Commission for Architecture and the Built Environment (CABE), published in 2003,[2] which included recent examples of new buildings and restoration programmes that demonstrate how quality in design can contribute to regenerating buildings and, potentially, influence the future prosperity of whole resorts.

This book is the culmination of the research undertaken during the project. It combines evidence drawn from the fabric of towns with a reconsideration of a broad range of original sources. While iconic structures such as Brighton's Royal Pavilion, Blackpool Tower and Bexhill's De La Warr Pavilion feature in this book, as in other histories of the seaside, there is no intention to delve deeply into their story here; other authors have dedicated entire books to them. However, they will be considered as part of the story of how seaside towns have evolved along with a wide range of less well-known buildings and building types, including many not present on the immediate seafront. There is more to seaside towns than the narrow strip beside the beach, though this may be where most of the more spectacular and distinctive buildings can be found.

England's Seaside Resorts begins by describing how seaside towns share some broad, historical themes in their development (chapter 2). In the 18th century they had to cater for the foibles of the gentry seeking cures for almost every medical condition; these visitors expected to have facilities comparable to those they enjoyed when visiting London and spa towns. By the 19th century a wider public was able to visit the sea, still seeking improved health and entertainment, but also as an escape from the hardships of their everyday lives. While a few thousand wealthy people could afford the time and money to visit the seaside in 1800, a century later millions were spending time by the sea. The effect of this democratisation of holidays was to transform the fabric of resorts and create some of the fastest-growing English towns of the 19th century.

In the remainder of the book the form of

Fig 1.1
Eastbourne Pier,
Grand Parade,
Eastbourne, East
Sussex; 1866–72,
Eugenius Birch
Resort seafronts often have buildings with lively, exotic forms, and the seaside pier typifies the spirit of the English seaside resort. It was the structure most often embellished with architectural forms that would not have been employed in more conservative locations. (DP018578)

resorts will be considered through a number of distinct approaches. The broad underlying themes in the physical development of resorts will be considered in chapter 3, including a discussion of how geographical location and the presence of visitors transformed small working towns and previously undeveloped stretches of coastline into the resorts we recognise today. In chapter 4 the appearance of resort buildings will be discussed. Stylistically, new buildings often followed the latest trends of London, or more often its suburbs, or their reflections in the regions. However, many of the houses and entertainment buildings in resorts could be larger and more florid due to the money brought in each year by visitors. Seaside towns have also consistently embraced the more exuberant end of Italianate, Gothic and Art Deco fashions and they made the oriental and Indian styles their own (Fig 1.1). Within resorts the proprietors of entertainment facilities and accommodation were in competition with each other and so

attractive and flamboyant design served as an advertisement for the pleasures lying within. While resorts grew rapidly to entertain and accommodate visitors, they were also working communities, with all the facilities found in ordinary towns – markets, churches, industry and so on. Therefore, rather than searching for a single story of seaside architecture, there is a need to recognise the existence of a number of complementary architectures. Resorts do have the exotic, seafront buildings, but the simple house, shop and industrial building have also made their own distinctive contributions. The working life of coastal towns was, in some respects, as distinctive as the resort facilities: structures such as harbours, lighthouses and lifeboat stations are integral parts of resorts (Fig 1.2). The coastal location of these towns has also put many of them in the front line in wars, which has left behind strong traces, both through the creation of defences as well as the destruction of existing buildings.

Three areas of activity provide much of the distinctive character of seaside towns and these will be described in the next chapters. The first visitors were drawn to the seaside in search of improved health, and a wide variety of activities and buildings evolved to meet their needs (chapter 5). However, visitors to resorts in all periods also came in search of entertainment (chapter 6). Initially, people had to make do with adapted facilities in existing buildings, but by the end of the 18th century new, purpose-built buildings were appearing to cater for increasing numbers of visitors. Often there was little to distinguish the appearance of most of these buildings from those in any other towns, but during the 19th century a range of distinctive seaside buildings and structures began to appear. The increasing specialisation of architectural forms, prevalent throughout England in the 19th century, applied especially to seaside towns, which can boast piers and pools, permanent funfairs, aquariums, and large entertainment complexes that

would have been unsustainable without large numbers of visitors. The third thematic chapter considers how seaside resorts accommodated the people who arrived each summer (chapter 7). Initially housed in the modest dwellings of local working people, visitors soon began to enjoy accommodation in polite Georgian townhouses, then in increasingly grandiose hotels in the course of the 19th century. In the 20th century the earlier forms of accommodation continued, at least in a modified form, but visitors liberated from the hearts of resorts by the motor car could head for caravan sites and holiday camps around the edges of towns.

The sources

Although no previous book has attempted to examine the architectural development of the English seaside town, interest in the history and architecture of resorts, as a type of settlement, began as early as the 1930s. In 1939 EW Gilbert published a short but

Fig 1.2
Harbour, Padstow, Cornwall
Early resort development often evolved around an existing harbour, the focal point of the historic settlement. Harbours, and the work undertaken in and around them, have always been a source of interest to visitors, and often provide the most picturesque of resort settings. (AA052648)

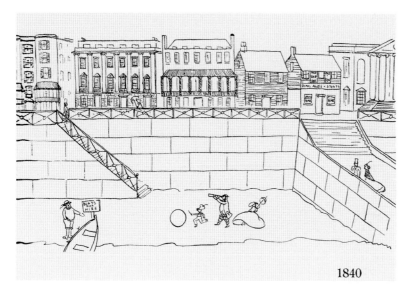

1840

Fig 1.3
Seaside Town in 1840,
from Lancaster 1936
Osbert Lancaster captured
in his own, unmistakeable
style the state of the seaside
in 1840. Terraced houses
for lodging visitors nestled
alongside more vernacular
structures; a seafront
promenade had been
created behind by a sea
wall and a Victorian
family is at play.
(By kind permission of
Lady Lancaster)

significant essay on the historical geography of resorts, providing the first typology of resort development and describing some of the key aspects of the form and character of seaside towns.[3] The most amusing pre-war work on the seaside, and in some ways the most ambitious, was Osbert Lancaster's *Progress at Pelvis Bay*, published in 1936.[4] It began life as a series of six short articles in the *Architectural Review*, published in 1934–5, which charted the architectural development of an imaginary south-coast resort. The text satirically reflects the broad development of the seaside, but it is the cartoons that plot most wittily the evolving townscape and the changing foibles of seaside holiday manners (Fig 1.3).

Where the built environment features in previous publications, it principally occurs as a means of illustrating the history of resorts, rather than examining the buildings and architecture as a subject in its own right. Those publications that do focus on seaside buildings tend to explore the archetypal seaside pleasure buildings, usually the piers and a myriad of seaside pavilions, bandstands and entertainment complexes: for example, Lynn Pearson published a study of the heyday of the florid seaside pleasure building between 1870 and 1914,[5] and Kenneth Lindley in 1973 examined, unfortunately briefly, the whole range of seaside architecture, from the chalets of the holiday camp to the grandest entertainment venues enjoyed by Victorian trippers.[6] In 2006 Fred Gray's *Designing the Seaside: Architecture, Society and Nature* was published.[7] It describes the architecture of health and pleasure at the seaside, with particular emphasis on

the social and visual cultures produced by seaside resorts, both in Britain and abroad. Some more-specialised historical studies link architecture to wider themes. An example is the work of Steven Braggs and Diane Harris, who, while studying the seaside holiday between the wars, devoted a sizeable part of their book to the modernist architecture that became such a distinctive style in resorts before 1939.[8]

While relatively little has been written on the buildings of resorts, the seaside town has been the subject of works by a number of distinguished historians. In 1947 JAR Pimlott's *The Englishman's Holiday* was published, outlining how holidays had evolved, though he seems to have been particularly preoccupied with contemporary discussions about the implementation of the Holidays with Pay Act 1938.[9] He voiced the fear that the right to paid leave, limited for most people to a week in July and August, would create crises in transport and in resort accommodation. The foremost modern historian of the seaside is John K Walton, whose initial research on Blackpool has become the basis for a number of books and articles that have provided the most detailed examination of any resort in England. He also used this research as a starting point for *The English Seaside Resort – A Social History 1750–1914*, published in 1983, and in 2000 he completed the story with the publication of *The British Seaside: Holidays and Resorts in the Twentieth Century*.[10] In both books Walton exploits a wide range of historical sources, including census returns and local authority records, to establish the changing social scene in resorts.

Other historians have also recognised the value of a detailed examination of the history of individual resorts. Sue Berry, formerly Sue Farrant, has written a number of valuable papers and a book on Georgian Brighton.[11] In these she describes how Brighton recovered from being a struggling fishing town to become the most important resort of the 18th century, a process fuelled by aristocratic connections. She has examined how the links between the local aristocracy and the Royal family lured the richest part of society, and its ample wealth, into the resort and created a boom unmatched elsewhere in the late 18th and early 19th centuries. David Cannadine also considered the role of aristocratic landowners in the development of resorts.[12] He focused on Eastbourne, but also examined other resorts where strong leadership helped to create a well-regulated environment, in terms of both physical development and the behaviour of visitors. Some writers have recognised that, through the leadership of strong landowners, resorts could maintain a high social tone, but that the social tone was lowered where development was less regulated. In 1976, HJ Perkin published a short but challenging article where he laid out evidence to support this assertion.[13]

The study of the seaside, as an entity in its own right, may only be a few decades old, but there is a wealth of historic, published material that can be used by modern historians. Most resorts have had their story told, though the contribution of the seaside to the life of the town is still sometimes almost grudgingly mentioned. For example, Margate's history was first examined in Reverend John Lewis' *The History and Antiquities, Ecclesiastical and Civil, of the Isle of Tenet*, which appeared in 1723. The second edition was published in 1736, the same year that a set of seawater baths was advertised in the town, although the new fad of sea bathing was not mentioned in either edition.[14] However, a copy of the second edition, held in the Society of Antiquaries, does have a curious link to the seaside. The antiquary Joseph Ames, a friend of the Reverend Lewis, presented a copy of the book to the Society before his death in 1759. It contained, as an enclosure, a drawing of a bathing machine by James Theobald and a description of how the 'bathing waggons' operated (*see* Fig 5.2). Anthony Relhan published *A Short History of Brighthelmston* in

1761 and although it begins by describing the geography of the town, and its history from the Druids and the Romans, it is essentially a guidebook to the resort and an essay on its air and waters.[15] Sickelmore's *History of Brighton and its Environs*, published in 1827, similarly blurs the distinction between the guidebook and formal history.[16]

These early publications were ostensibly written as histories, but guidebooks, and sometimes the advertisements in them, prove to be some of the most evocative historical sources. The owners of circulating libraries were frequently the publishers of the earliest guides and therefore were sometimes amusingly biased in favour of their own library while being noticeably lukewarm about the opposition (Fig 1.4). The earliest seaside guidebook dates from 1734 and at its heart is a description of the facilities that awaited visitors in Scarborough, along with an extensive list of the aristocracy who had visited in the previous year.[17] Margate's first guidebook, published in 1763, has a frontispiece showing two bathing machines with the distinctive canvas modesty hoods developed by Benjamin Beale in the 1750s.[18] This edition and the subsequent guidebooks published over the next seventy-five years outline in glowing terms the facilities of the resort, with one edition often mercilessly plagiarising a previous one.[19] In some resorts the same guidebook would be published with modifications for many years and the rights to its contents seem to have passed from one library proprietor to his or her successor.

Some national guidebooks were also

Fig 1.4
Detail of the *Long Painting*, Sidmouth, Devon; 1814
An unusual twist to the personal pride of a library proprietor occurred at Sidmouth. The Long Painting *by Hubert Cornish, a view of the fledgling resort, was probably commissioned by the owner of the small, two-storied Georgian library that lies at the heart of the whole painting. In this later, revised engraving in the Royal York Hotel, the print has been altered to depict the library's enlargement. (DP021041)*

published. The earliest, *The Balnea*, was published in 1799 and its subtitle proclaimed that it offered an 'impartial description of all the popular watering places in England: interspersed with original sketches and incidental anecdotes'. The author's impartiality in fact means that he is critical of aspects of most resorts. Margate's High Street 'is a close contracted thoroughfare; many parts of it filthy'; at Scarborough, 'The Assembly-room has nothing to boast of in respect to elegance': and at Weymouth, in the theatre 'the performers are generally of a moderate description, only fit to make the audience laugh, by putting nature out of joint'.[20]

Alongside guides to resorts many books were published extolling the health-giving properties of the seaside. Many 18th-century authors described the merits of their own resorts, while more or less overtly criticising rival towns. The most famous seaside, medical writer was Dr Richard Russell in Brighton, who was followed a few years later by Dr John Awsiter.[21] These early works concentrated on the virtues of sea bathing and drinking seawater, but authors also realised that a mild climate was an essential element in promoting resorts. In 1829 James Clark published *The Influence of Climate* ... in which he examined the impact of climate on health, but he also ventured into more detailed analyses of the microclimate of some resorts.[22] Detailed statistics were included to demonstrate how the temperature, rainfall and hours of sunshine of a specific resort made its climate superior to similar, neighbouring towns. The 21st-century reader might find these medical and climatic works more amusing than scientific, but readers in the 18th and 19th centuries were impressed by a show of expert knowledge, and might be influenced into visiting the town concerned.

From the second quarter of the 19th century trade directories begin to offer outlines of the histories and facilities of resorts. Though the information is usually considerably balder than in some of the more florid guidebooks, directories have the advantage of being published regularly and reasonably systematically. The entry for each town begins with a description highlighting the main facilities and institutions, and although such accounts are often repeated unchanged from one edition to the next, they were usually updated when major alterations or additions took place. Directories also provide further insights into resort life through their street-by-street or alphabetical listings, which often indicate the profession of the resident and the function of the address.

Primary sources for resorts are broadly similar to those for any town, but as a destination for holidays they also feature prominently in collections of letters, novels and diaries, some of which were written by famous socialites and authors, such as Jane Austen or Fanny Burney. Jane Austen set part of *Persuasion* at Lyme Regis, a resort she knew from personal experience, as is evident from her letters to her sister Cassandra, and *Sanditon*, her last, unfinished novel, was set at an imaginary seaside resort. However, some of the most informative writings are in diaries drafted by ladies of leisure with time to document the mundanities of seaside life. East Kent Archives contain extracts from journals written by Lady Mary Coke in the late 18th and early 19th centuries and another diary by Mary Figgins from about 1828, a woman who by the end of her holiday was so relaxed that she was struggling to get up on Sunday in time for church.[23] The diaries of three holidays taken by Daniel Benham, secretary to the City of London Gas Company, have been published by two modern historians, the first two in 1943 and 1944 and the third in 1980.[24]

A wide range of prints, drawings and paintings record the first hundred years of resorts, and are often the only evidence of the form of seaside buildings such as bath houses, libraries and assembly rooms before the middle of the 19th century. The earliest photographs are largely devoid of people, a consequence of the insensitivity of film, but by the end of the 19th century over-dressed Victorian families and horse-drawn carriages dominate every view of the seafront (Fig 1.5). From the 1890s the picture postcard became an essential part of every holiday and saucy seaside postcards, with their visual versions of music-hall jokes, still populate postcard racks outside souvenir shops today. Film also offers important insights into seaside resorts, especially the transient aspects of daily life. Pathé News features, now available online, include a large number of films featuring the seaside from the early 20th century through to the 1960s.[25] The recently discovered and restored films of early film-makers Mitchell and Kenyon show people 'enjoying' a day out at a crowded Blackpool and Morecambe at the beginning of the 20th century. These scenes are dominated by a dazzling collection of bonnets and caps, dark suits and, one assumes, colourful buildings.

Gardens and Pier, Weston-super-Mare

No review of historical sources would be complete without an acknowledgement of how research has been transformed by the internet. Online material was initially limited to electronic access to catalogues, but the arrival of resources such as the *Oxford Dictionary of National Biography* and *The Times Digital Archive* marks the start of a new era in research. Many government papers, statistical reports and Acts of Parliament are also available online. The internet has also provided people with niche interests an opportunity to publish their research on subjects that might never be of commercial interest, though the reliability of such work should always be assessed carefully. English Heritage also has its own electronic resources, such as Images of England,

Pastscape and Viewfinder, which are available to the public.[26]

In 2001 the English Tourism Council stated that 'Seaside resorts have made an enormous contribution to the cultural identity of England and contain some of the finest examples of our built heritage. This is overlooked rather than promoted.'[27] France, Spain, Italy, USA and now the Far East and Africa may provide people with sun-drenched beach holidays, but few places can match the towns of the British coast, with their legacy of nearly three centuries of seaside holidays. This book aims to explain the origins of this legacy, to celebrate the joys of the seaside and to describe what makes England's seaside towns and their architecture so very special.

Fig 1.5
Postcard of Gardens and Pier, Weston-super-Mare, Somerset; *c.*1906–16
Despite the apparent throng of various forms of transport at the hub of this resort, this early 20th-century, coloured postcard appears sedate compared to the modern-day traffic congestion and car parking that dominate many seafronts.
(PC08229, NMR Nigel Temple Collection)

2

A brief history of seaside resorts

Sea bathing has taken place since ancient times, but in the 18th century in England a distinctive seaside culture began to transform the coastline. Initially drawn by the prospect of improved health, the first wealthy visitors demanded a range of facilities similar to those they had enjoyed at spas and the seaside resort was born. Holidays were initially restricted to a tiny proportion of England's population, but over the past 300 years the story of resorts has been one of extending access: rising levels of personal wealth, increased leisure time and improvements in transport opened up previously remote places to tourism. By the early 19th century the aristocracy and gentry were being joined at the seaside by the ever-rising middle classes, while a few resorts were frequented by working people. For the vast majority of the population a holiday was not an option until the end of the 19th century, but it was the advent of paid holidays and motor transport in the early 20th century that made the seaside holiday universal.

In 1980 RW Butler identified a cycle of six stages through which any type of resort evolved. The phases were:

1. the exploitation of a town's unspoilt cultural and natural character;
2. the involvement of local, private initiatives and the provision of some public infrastructure to provide for growing visitor numbers;
3. a development stage where the facilities are reorganised by external interests to improve them for rapidly growing visitor numbers;
4. phase of consolidation where the rate of growth decreases;
5. stagnation; and
6. decline.

More recent writers have pointed out that in place of decline there could be a phase of regeneration, new growth or stability.[1] Considerable debate is under way about which route England's resorts will follow in the 21st century.

Early sea bathing

Health resorts had been established by the Greeks around the Mediterranean by the 6th century BC, and were known as Asklepia after Asclepius, the Greek god of medicine and healing.[2] The Asklepia were theurgical and visitors observed rites including purification, bathing (including sea bathing), fasting and sacrifice.[3] Secular health and leisure facilities were also provided, including baths, gymnasia and theatres. Cities throughout the Roman Empire contained seawater baths, which were prescribed for ailments such as tuberculosis, psoriasis and rheumatism. The emperor Nero constructed baths in his palace and had them supplied with sea water and sulphur water.[4] The Ancient Greeks and Romans also used solaria for sunbathing; Pliny declared 'Sol est remediorum maximum' – 'the sun is the best remedy'.[5]

The roots of the seaside resort in England can be traced back to the upheaval caused by the Reformation. In the Middle Ages people made pilgrimages around England, and Europe, in search of improved physical and spiritual health. Holy wells became identified with specific cures and, as well as being sites for prayer, their waters were drunk, sprinkled on the body and used for bathing (Fig 2.1). Following the Dissolution of the Monasteries in the reign of Henry VIII, when such 'Popery' was strongly discouraged by the Protestant church, these wells gradually ceased to be seen as sources of spiritual cures and began to be recognised as being of medicinal value. A leading Protestant churchman of the time, Dr William Turner, sought refuge in continental Europe in the mid-16th century when Mary ascended to the throne, and there witnessed the benefits obtained from bathing.[6] He returned to England in 1559, following the death of Mary, and in 1562 published a book that questioned the need to travel abroad for remedies, when England could provide similar health resorts if money was invested in them.[7] His writing con-

Fig 2.1
St Winefride's Well,
Holywell, Clwyd;
15th-century well
chamber and chapel
*The medicinal benefits
attributed to seawater did
not immediately remove the
desire for cures using holy
waters. Records of the
healing properties of St
Winefride's Well date from
the 12th century and it
continues today to be a
place of pilgrimage.*
(DP022282)

tributed to a new interest in bathing waters, and by the 1630s springs had been discovered at Tunbridge Wells, Epsom, Harrogate, and significantly, at Scarborough in *c*.1626, establishing a new type of health and pleasure resort: the spa.

Around the time of William Turner's return to England, Thomas Vicary the Sergeant Chirurgion, who died in 1561, was recommending cold seawater baths as a cure for 'fluxes' (dysentery): '... but if it be a Fluxe, and that the patient is not cured, let him stand in a cold bath of salt water of the Sea, three or fower howers or more, and he shall be perfectly holpe'.[8] In 1578 the French Royal Surgeon, Ambroise Paré, advised Henri III to bathe in the sea at Dieppe to cure 'tormenting' and skin diseases.[9] Treatises on the art of swimming appeared in England during the 16th century and in 1581 swimming in the sea was advocated for health reasons: 'The swimming in salt water is very good to remove the headache, to open the suffed nosethrilles, and thereby to helpe the smelling. It is a good remedie for dropsies,

scabbes and scurfes, small pockes, leprosies, falling awaye of either legge, or any other parte'.[10] A treatise of 1610 even recommended the use of seawater, or water combined with salt, for the treatment of impotence in horses.[11]

The first reference to an individual going to the English coast for health reasons may be in Leland's *Itineraries*, dating from around 1540. Leland refers to the judge Finiox, who built a house at Herne in Kent because physicians considered the area to be beneficial to health.[12] Herne is a settlement approximately two miles from the sea and would have been no healthier than any other small Kent village, but perhaps its proximity to the sea inspired the choice. Henry Manship, who published a history of Great Yarmouth in 1619, refers to doctors in Cambridge who sent patients there 'to take the air of the sea.'[13] At Scarborough the discovery of a spring in the cliffs first brought the manners, expectations and money of the spa 'company' to the seaside and seawater was soon being drunk as an additional cure.[14] By 1660 Dr Robert Wittie, a local

Figs 2.2 and 2.3
1754 drawings,
Scarborough, North
Yorkshire; RR
Angerstein

*The Swedish industrial
spy Reinhold Rücker
Angerstein visited
Scarborough in 1754 and
observed that the bathing
and spa industries were the
principal sources of income
for the town, surpassing
that generated by freight
and fishing. Angerstein's
two views of Scarborough
echo the scene depicted by
John Setterington some
twenty years earlier,
including the spa building
and 'bathing houses'.*

*(Both figs courtesy of
Jernkontoret)*

physician at Scarborough, was promoting cold bathing, though he warned that internal consumption of seawater could be injurious to health; in the 1667 edition of his book he noted that bathing in seawater had rid him of his gout.[15] In 1696 Sir John Colbatch employed saline water and steam bathing in a bathhouse he built in Cheshire near the salt deposits.[16] He recalled how a woman from Worcester cured her supposedly incurable tympanitis by immersing her head in sea-water.[17]

By *c.*1700 Sir John Floyer had become the leading advocate of cold-water bathing, publishing several books and papers on the subject. Floyer realised that the sea could act as a huge bath for the nation: 'Since we live in an Island, and have the Sea about us, we cannot want an excellent Cold Bath, which will both preserve our Healths, and cure many Diseases, as our Fountains do'.[18] He recommended the best practices for bathing in the sea: bathing should only last for two to three minutes, it should be undertaken

only before dinner or after fasting, and the bathing programme should be nine or ten dips at least two or three times a week.[19] He also suggested that bathing from June to September would be safest.[20]

Scientists and medical writers had grown enthusiastic about sea bathing, but by the the beginning of the 18th century there are also indications of ordinary people taking to the sea. The *Great Diurnal* of Nicholas Blundell reveals a family with catholic tastes in medical treatment. They were equally content to consult a doctor at Wigan, visit various spas, make a pilgrimage to Holywell and bathe in the sea near Liverpool. Blundell, who lived at Crosby Hall, near Liverpool, recorded several visits to the seaside, some for no specific reason, but on other occasions he was there to shoot game. His first recorded venture into the sea occurred on 5 August 1708: 'Mr Aldred & I Rode to the Sea & baithed ourselves'.[21] As no specific ailments were mentioned, he may have bathed for pleasure during hot weather, although it is possible that he was seeking to relieve his eye problems. A year later, Blundell's children were bathed in the sea on three consecutive days to cure 'some out breaks'.[22] Blundell's earliest reference to sea bathing occurs six years after his diary began. Does this suggest that in 1702 sea bathing was not yet an approved treatment, but by 1708 it had achieved some form of acceptance and respectability?

Before the 1730s references to sea bathing are rare. A bathing house was mentioned in a Liverpool rate assessment as early as 1708, and in 1718 Samuel Jones, a customs officer at Whitby, wrote a poem praising the water of the spa and sea for curing jaundice:

> Here such as bathing love may surely find
> The most compleat reception of that kinde;
> And what the drinking cannot purge away
> Is cured with ease by dipping in the Sea[23]

In Lincolnshire the earliest identified reference to sea bathing appears in a letter dated 2 May 1725 in which Mrs Massingberd of Gunby described how 'Sr Hardolf Wastnage & his lady come in Whitsun week to a farmhouse in this neighbourhood to spend three months in order to bath in ye sea'.[24]

The earliest seaside resorts

These occasional references suggest that early sea bathing was a small-scale, haphazard activity, perhaps, surprisingly, more often practised in the north of England. However, by the middle of the 18th century resorts were developing on most stretches of coast because, although bathing could take place anywhere, towns were needed to provide the accommodation, entertainment facilities and the social scene that genteel visitors expected. The south of England was the first area to feel the full impact of the new vogue, but by the end of the 18th century a network of resorts catering for a range of tastes and pockets had developed, and where resorts had not yet emerged, alternative facilities had appeared.

Three towns vie for the title of England's first major seaside resort: Scarborough, Margate and Brighton. Since the discovery of the mineral-water spring at Scarborough the spa had drawn visitors from 'the Gentry of the North Parts of England'.[25] *Scarborough A Poem*, published in 1732, celebrates a town of 'Health and Mirth' that rivals Bath and records the use of the springs and sea bathing.[26] By 1734 the town consisted of about 2,000 families, in substantial houses 'for the most part, uniform, neat and commodious' around and behind the harbour.[27] It was in these houses that visitors lodged, including in 1733 a number of dukes and earls (Figs 2.2, 2.3, *see* Fig 5.1). Apart from enjoying the spa and sea bathing, the nobility could use rudimentary versions of the facilities found in London and Bath, including a subscription coffee house, a circulating library and a large assembly room.[28]

While Margate could not boast a spa, its position and harbour facilities made it accessible to visitors from London, who arrived by means of a short sea voyage or a stagecoach journey (Fig 2.4). In 1736, the same year as the publication of the Reverend Lewis' history, an advertisement placed by Thomas

Fig 2.4
A View of the Pier of Mergate, Margate, Kent. Joseph Ames, from Lewis 1736

The antiquarian Joseph Ames contributed this plan of Margate to illustrate Reverend John Lewis' The History and Antiquities, Ecclesiastical and Civil, of the Isle of Tenet. It shows the small size of the town at this date and the prominence of its harbour facilities.
(DP017639 Courtesy of the Society of Antiquaries of London)

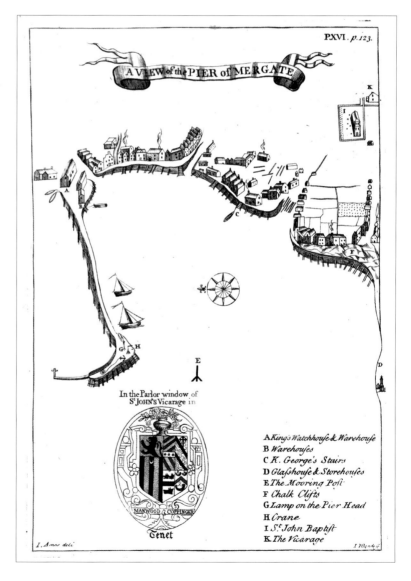

Barber appeared in some Kent newspapers announcing the provision of a bath, the first reference to organised sea bathing in the town.[29] It suggests that sea bathing had been practised 'for several Years' and this might explain why in 1730 Margate was apparently sufficiently busy to attract a theatre company from Canterbury to perform during the summer.[30]

Brighton was also a small working town, but unlike Margate it had no harbour, boats simply being drawn up on to the beach. In 1736 William Clarke described how:

> We are now sunning ourselves on the beach, at Brighthelmstone ... The place is really pleasant: I have seen nothing in its way that outdoes it. ... My morning business is bathing in the sea, and then buying fish: the evening is, riding out for air; viewing the remains of old Saxon camps; and counting the ships in the road, and the boats that are trauling.[31]

Brighton had been in a slow economic decline since the late 17th century and seems to be an unlikely place for wealthy aristocrats to head to the sea.[32] Like Margate, it had to create the type of facilities expected by Georgian visitors, but by the 1750s it already had bathing machines, a spa, an assembly room, a coffee house and library, while the first theatre is mentioned in 1764 and baths in 1769.[33] Dr Pococke in his diary in 1754 attributed much of the resort's success to 'a perswasion that the water here is better than at other places, concerning which a treatise had been written by Dr. Russel'.[34] Dr Russell's writings helped to promote Brighton, but of greater importance was influential local aristocracy with strong national connections. By 1760 visitors to the town included the Pelham family, who had close links to the Royal Family.[35] This led in 1765 to a visit by the Duke of Gloucester, a brother of George III, and in 1783 the first of many visits by the Prince of Wales. It was to be his presence that cemented Brighton's position as the foremost resort in the late 18th century:

> Brighton, twenty years ago a small, insignificant fishing village, is striking proof of miracles brought about by fashion. ... His [the Prince Regent's] presence in or absence from Brighton registered the flow of visitors to the spa. When he was absent, the town was empty and desolate; only when he returned did life and pleasure reappear.[36]

Scarborough, Margate and Brighton were attracting sufficient numbers of visitors by the middle of the century to encourage development in other coastal towns. Most new resorts were in the south-east because of their proximity to London. On the Kent coast visitors were staying at Ramsgate, Dover, Folkestone and Deal by the end of the 18th century, while in Sussex, Hastings, Seahouses near Eastbourne and Worthing were hosting visitors by the 1750s.[37] In East Anglia Old South End, a small hamlet around a farmhouse near the village of Prittlewell, began to develop as a resort in the mid-18th century.[38] A large house, built before 1758, had become the Ship Inn by 1764 and by 1768 South-End was first recognised as a separate entity for rating purposes. The other significant resort in the east of England was Great Yarmouth. Its first baths were built on the seashore by 1759 at a cost of £2,000, a very large investment in a mid-18th-century resort, and a theatre was built in 1778 (Fig 2.5).[39]

Resorts in the south-east and East Anglia were populated by visitors from the capital, but some resorts in the south-west prospered because they were convenient for Bath. Weymouth was apparently being visited for health reasons by 1750, though Dr Pococke, who visited in September 1750, does not mention sea bathing.[40] The trigger for its development as a resort was the ill-health of Ralph Allen (1693–1764), who had made his fortune from postal services and stone quarries in Bath. To improve his health he was advised to bathe in the sea and chose Weymouth, forging an association between the two towns that would last for more than

Fig 2.5
Public seawater baths, Great Yarmouth, Norfolk; 19th century
The Bath House of 1759 was one of the few buildings to be erected east of the town walls before the expansion of the town towards the sea in the early 19th century. The later public seawater baths, advertised on the gable of this short, bow-fronted terrace, was one of many facilities built as the resort developed. (BB83/04754; Howarth-Loomes [WT Fisher])

half a century (Fig 2.6).[41] Allen visited Weymouth regularly until his death in 1764 and during this period he was visited there by the future George III and his brother the Duke of Gloucester.[42] Teignmouth was also attracting visitors by the 1750s, and it is clear from Fanny Burney's visit twenty years later that it was a suitable place for the highest echelons of society, although its facilities were still rudimentary.[43]

Even a more distant resort such as Scarborough welcomed large numbers of visitors from London and Bath. Tobias Smollett in *The Expedition of Humphry Clinker* described how, once the season in Bath had finished, 'all our gay birds of passage have taken their flight to Bristolwell, Tunbridge, Brighthelmstone, Scarborough, Harrowgate, &c'.[44] Scarborough also relied on attracting visitors from large local towns, as it had done when it was primarily a spa town, and other resorts around the coast seem to have exploited a similar local trade. The first advertisement for the baths at Margate in the 1730s appeared in local papers, suggesting this was the market they expected to attract, and in 1750 Exmouth was being visited by people from Exeter in search of improved health.[45] Blackpool was also dependent on visitors from nearby towns and this may be one reason why it was the earliest resort to attract substantial numbers of working-class visitors. The area where Blackpool developed was a modest hamlet with a few farms and fishermen's huts when the first bathers arrived, probably in the 1750s.[46] In 1788 William Hutton described it as follows:

> Although about fifty houses grace the sea bank, it does not merit the name of a village, because they are scattered to the extent of a mile. About six of these make a figure, front the sea, with an aspect exactly west, and are appropriated for the reception of company; the others are the dwellings of the inhabitants, which chiefly form the back ground. In some of these are lodged the inferior class, whose sole motive for visiting this airy region, is health.[47]

Hutton spoke to a gentleman who had been visiting Blackpool since 1761, and recounted how he had seen it change dramatically to begin to cater for affluent visitors who had joined the original, lower-class bathers.[48] Richard Ayton, who visited in 1813 also described the hordes of people still cramming into the few houses of the

village, whereas at Morecambe he met visitors who 'were the manufacturers from the inland towns, come for the benefit of the physic in the sea'.[49] Sir John Floyer at the start of the 18th century stated that cold-water bathing had been initiated by 'the Common People', and in Lancashire there was a widespread belief that the August spring tide would both cleanse the bather and provide protection against future illness.[50] Perhaps the lack of earlier references to widespread sea bathing is due to the Common People being unable to leave their mark in written history.

By the end of the 18th century significant resorts had begun to appear on most stretches of coastline, but in Lincolnshire there were no substantial coastal towns where the gentry could find accommodation and other essential facilities while they bathed. Nevertheless, they were still

Fig 2.6
Ralph Allen's house, Weymouth, Dorset; mid-18th century, altered and raised in late 19th century
Before the expansion of coastal towns into fully evolved seaside resorts, early visitors stayed in existing or new, modest houses. At fledgling resorts, such as Weymouth, the earliest houses were built around the harbour and the river, rather than along the seafront.
(AA042018)

Fig 2.7 *(below left)*
The New Inn, Main
Street, Saltfleet,
Lincolnshire; 17th,
mid-18th and 19th
centuries.
*Originally built to serve
road traffic along the coast,
the New Inn – with this
large, mid-18th-century
wing – was later described
as a 'hotel and bathing
house'. Saltfleet's function
as a resort was curtailed in
the 19th century by land
reclamation that distanced
it from the sea.*
(DP022283)

Figure 2.8 *(below right)*
Plummers Hotel,
Freiston Shore,
Lincolnshire; early
18th century, late 18th
and early 19th century
*Merchants from Boston
came 'to relax their minds a
little from the monotonous
uniformity which a
constant attendance on the
same business naturally
imposes' (Marrat 1814,
173). The Hotel included a
first-floor dining room and
a long room over the stables
with access to the sea bank
behind.*
(DP022286)

determined to avail themselves of the health-giving benefits of the sea. In the absence of resorts the emphasis was on the creation of small facilities, usually just a substantial inn with access to the sea. By 1673, an inn at Saltfleet, presumably the New Inn, was being visited by local gentry who wanted to eat fresh fish.[51] In the mid-18th century, an L-shaped wing was added to it, oriented towards the sea rather than the main road, and this new block included a first-floor dining room with bow windows, which would have provided fine views of the sea, before sea banks and land reclamation intervened (Fig 2.7).

The tiny resort at Freiston Shore was once described, remarkably, as the 'Brighton of the middle classes of Lincolnshire', or, more realistically, as a place where 'a number of tradesmen and farmers resorted with their wives, in hopes of receiving benefit from the use of the salt water'.[52] Visitors could stay at two sea-bathing hotels or at a few lodging houses. Plummers Hotel, built in the early 18th century, probably as a house, was extended during the late 18th century, while the Marine Hotel was built in the late 18th century, specifically for the sea-bathing trade. It was three storeys high, which not only provided a substantial amount of accommodation, but also allowed visitors to view the sea over the sea bank (Fig 2.8).

Some of Lincolnshire's Victorian resorts also began as the sites of sea-bathing hotels. In 1797 Abigail Gawthern spent much of August at Sutton on Sea, probably at the Jolly Bacchus Hotel (Fig 2.9).[53] At the start of the 19th century the village of Mable-

thorpe had a 'bathing house', presumably the Book in Hand Hotel, which was being visited by people from Louth, while Clee-thorpes had an inn established around 1760.[54] A map of 1779 shows that Skegness was a small, inland settlement, but a short distance to the south, and closer to the sea, there was a 'Bathing House and Tavern', which had been built in 1770.[55]

Resort development in the early 19th century

Seaside resorts, along with industrial cities and spas, were among the fastest-growing towns by the early 19th century. However, the rapid growth of some resorts and spas was due to their relatively small size at the beginning of the century, and Blackpool's population actually grew less rapidly in the 19th century than did the population in Lancashire as a whole, a county dominated by the cotton towns around Manchester. Of the first resorts, Scarborough grew slightly faster than the rest of the North Riding, but Margate's population grew by 117 per cent during the first three decades of the 19th century. In 1801 Brighton was the 55th largest town in Britain, but by 1831 it had risen to 22nd.

Most resort development in the 18th century required established towns with an infrastructure, albeit a rudimentary one. However, by the 19th century a few entre-preneurs, witnessing the success of existing resorts, were prepared to invest in new schemes on unoccupied sections of coast-line, or largely uninhabited stretches with a nearby, inland village. Some proved to

Fig 2.9
Jolly Bacchus Hotel,
High Street, Sutton
on Sea, Lincolnshire;
*c.*1805
*The Jolly Bacchus Hotel
provided accommodation
for bathers and offered hot
and cold baths for visitors
who did not want to bathe
in the nearby 'German
Ocean'.*
(DP022287)

be great successes, but others were doomed to failure.

Southport and Bournemouth were among the success stories. Both developed as a result of the entrepreneurial vision of local landowners. Southport grew up on a previously undeveloped stretch of coastline, in a similar way to some of the Lincolnshire resorts. A bathing house was built in 1792 by William Sutton, followed by his hotel in 1798, and a range of other facilities were added during the early 19th century (Fig 2.10).[56] The heart of the initial development was Lord Street, parallel to the sea. Although the form of the resort seems to have the regularity of a planned development, this was largely due to the practice of the two principal landowners, Miss Bold and Mr Hesketh, who leased out to developers parcels of former 'waste land' along the seashore.[57]

Bournemouth is another example of speculative development on an uninhabited stretch of coastline, and again it shows the influence of a small number of powerful interests. Its founder, Lewis Tregonwell, built a house on an uninhabited stretch of coastline in 1811–12, followed by an inn and a handful of cottages to accommodate invalids in search of improved health (*see* Fig 7.11).[58] In 1824, Mrs Arbuthnott wrote that:

> I rode one day to a place called Bournemouth – a collection of hills lately planted by a gentleman of the name of Tregonwell who has built four or five beautiful cottages which he lets out to persons who go sea-bathing. I was so charmed with the beauty of the situation that Mr. Arbuthnot and myself agreed to take one next summer for the sake of a little sea-bathing.[59]

In 1825 it was described as a 'new-built watering-place' with excellent bathing but limited accommodation.[60] Between 1836 and 1840, Sir GW Tapps Gervis, who owned some of the land on the east side of the Bourne, employed Benjamin Ferrey to prepare plans for buildings on his estate, the first of which were Westover Villas and the Bath Hotel.[61] Despite its late origins and its

Fig 2.10
DW Sutton Memorial
Plaque, Duke Street,
Southport,
Merseyside
*This plaque was erected
close to the site of
Southport's first resort
building, which was built
in 1792 by William
Sutton. 'The Founder of
Southport' created the town
amongst ' a wilderness of
Sandhills'.*
(AA058257)

Fig 2.11
The Dome, Upper
Bognor Road, Bognor
Regis, West Sussex;
*c.*1787

Originally called
Hothamton Crescent, this
terrace of three houses was
built by Sir Richard
Hotham, but it failed to
attract large numbers of
aristocrats and royalty to
the new resort of
Hothamton.
(DP022284)

still relatively small size, Bournemouth was featured by AB Granville in 1841 as one of the leading resorts because of its ideal conditions for curing invalids.[62]

Not all landowners, however, met with success in their promotion of new resorts. Sir Richard Hotham, a successful London businessman and former MP, invested up to £160,000 in a prestigious new development for wealthy visitors.[63] Hothamton near the inland village of South Bersted, now part of Bognor Regis, first opened as a watering place in 1791, and in the following years 'it was honoured with the company of several families of the first fashion in the kingdom'.[64] However, the economics of his investment proved unsustainable and on his death in 1799 the estate was sold, leaving his heir a mere £8,000 (Fig 2.11).[65]

In 1816 a large development beside the existing village of Herne Bay was promoted by the local landowner, Sir Henry Oxenden, but in the absence of a pier, steamers between London and Margate could not land significant numbers of visitors at the resort. In 1831 a company was established to build the pier and promote the development of the new town of St Augustine at Herne Bay. The proprietors of the company expected their initiative 'to cause commodious Hotels, Baths, and other public Resorts to be erected, in addition to those already built, for the accommodation of the Nobility and Visitors.'[66] Although the number of people disembarking grew to a peak of 52,205 in 1842, the accompanying developments of the town did not take place (Fig 2.12).[67] Herne Bay had missed the boat.

Fig 2.12
Herne Bay, Kent;
1841
This engraving of the pier and resort of Herne Bay is an idealised view. Few buildings had been completed by 1841 and the outline of the town that was established in the 1830s was only gradually in-filled during the next hundred years in a piecemeal fashion.
(DP022285)

A third major resort development of the early 19th century shared the same characteristics of strong leadership but little success. The first reference to Hayling Island as a seaside resort occurred in the 1820s, when Richard Scott was confident that a watering place would develop on this 'pearl of the ocean'.[68] Plans for villas were prepared by Robert Abraham of London and the foundation stone of a crescent was laid in 1825. It was never finished, but a hotel, library, bathhouse and gardens were completed (Fig 2.13).

The failure of the ambitious scheme at Hayling Island can perhaps be explained by its remoteness, but the investments at Bognor and Herne Bay might have been expected to be successful. Hothamton may have attracted the right type of people but it could never have been large enough on its own to create the vibrant resort atmosphere sought by fashionable visitors. Herne Bay seems to have suffered from a similar problem, though this was probably exacerbated by its proximity to thriving Margate. Within a few years of Oxenden's scheme, railways were opening up the whole of England to visitors, meaning that undeveloped Herne Bay probably seemed an unappealing destination.

As well as the development of new resorts, investment, sometimes on a large scale, could add substantially to existing

Fig 2.13 *(below)*
Norfolk Crescent,
The Beach, Hayling
Island, Hampshire;
c.1825
The construction of a bridge from the mainland in 1825 stimulated the development of the island as a seaside resort. An esplanade, a hotel, baths and library were built, but the visitors never came in large numbers. The half-built Norfolk Crescent serves as a potent reminder of the perils of investing in the seaside in the early 19th century. (DP022288)

seaside towns. At two popular resorts expansion was achieved through the construction of what effectively amounted to large, separate, suburban areas. In 1823, Thomas Read Kemp, inspired by John Nash's development around Regent's Park in London, embarked on the construction of a large estate on his land to the east of Brighton and most of the development was completed over the next two decades. At the west end of Brighton, in Hove, Brunswick Town was built from 1825 on land owned by the Scutt family.[69] Amon Wilds and Charles Augustus Busby were responsible for the design of both schemes, though most buildings in Brunswick Town were probably designed by Busby alone (Fig 2.14).

Kemp Town and Brunswick Town can incontrovertibly be regarded as suburbs of Brighton, but the relationship between Hastings and St Leonards is less clear. In 1828 James Burton acquired part of a farm for the construction of a new town a short distance to the west of Hastings (see Fig 5.12). By 1836 Theodore Hook could write effusively of St Leonards that:

Under the superintendence of Mr Burton, a desert has become a thickly peopled town. Buildings of an extensive nature and most elegant character rear their heads, where but

a few years since the barren cliffs presented their chalky points to the storm and rippling streams, and hanging groves adorn the valley, which twenty years since was a sterile and shrubless ravine.[70]

Burton, as the greatest London builder of the early 19th century, had worked with John Nash on terraces at Regent's Park, and the links between the two are obvious.[71] In scale and location it can be argued whether St Leonards was a suburban development of the existing resort or, as it seems to have been conceived, a separate, high-class settlement for wealthy residents and visitors.[72] As finally built, it consisted of grand terraces along the seafront flanking a hotel with a bathhouse and a library in front (Fig 2.15). Behind, there was an assembly room and, on the hillside, a park was created surrounded by villas. St Leonards provides a succinct definition of what was needed in a Georgian resort, with facilities for health, amusement, a range of accommodation and the society of fellow visitors. The settlement also included two lower-status inland streets to service the needs of the seasonal inhabitants: Mercatoria to house merchants, and Lavatoria for laundry.

By the early 19th century resorts were being created in a number of ways. Resort functions were being grafted on to existing

Fig 2.14 (opposite)
33–42 Brunswick Terrace, Hove, East Sussex; 1824–8. Amon Wilds and Charles Augustus Busby
The Brunswick Estate at Hove was planned as a self-contained resort, isolated from, but close to, Brighton. The high-quality houses faced the sea and the rectangular garden 'square', the next level of housing faced the roads extending back from the front, and working-class houses were tucked in between. (DP017921)

Fig 2.15
36–44 The Marina, St Leonards, East Sussex; 1828. James Burton
St Leonards' centrepiece was a seafront hotel flanked by terraces, rather than an elongated square as at Kemp Town. This was probably influenced by the geography of the site, which was more suitable for linear development parallel to the shore. (DP017995)

towns, functionally and physically, and with growing confidence in the longevity of the seaside, entrepreneurs were also prepared to invest in new developments on largely untouched stretches of coastline. A third approach involved engulfing a small pre-existing coastal village or villages. Among this category were Blackpool, Torquay and Weston-super-Mare, though the last of these also had a small, inland agricultural village near where the resort developed. Blackpool expanded northwards and southwards from a cluster of buildings located on the coast around where Talbot Square now stands. Further south there was a separate, small settlement called South Shore. A few buildings from this village survive, but by the late 19th century they had been surrounded by the new buildings of the resort.

A fourth type of resort development, but closely linked to the third type, was the creation of a new settlement built on coast-lines with small villages one or two miles inland. These were originally agricultural settlements oriented to the countryside rather than the coast and they had established names that were often not adopted by the new resorts that have engulfed them. At Bognor Regis the original village was named South Bersted, and at Southend it was Prittlewell.[73] As late as the 1840s Morecambe was still a small, inland village called Poulton le Sands or Poulton by the Sands. When the railway arrived a short distance to the south, development was clustered around the line and the station, transforming the coast and prompting the change of name. Other examples of this type of development include Bexhill, Clacton-on-Sea and Cleethorpes (Fig 2.16). Although Southend began to be built in the late 18th century, most resorts of this type developed during the 19th century.

Local government in expanding resorts

The rapid growth of the population and building stock of resorts required not only significant private investment but also an increase in the scope of local government.[74] Some seaside towns were ancient boroughs with at least rudimentary institutions that might be able to cope with change, but in the early 19th century many were in a governmental limbo similar to the predicament of new, industrial towns.[75] They had outstripped the parochial governmental structures of the original settlements, but had not yet reached the size or status where the next level of local government applied.[76] As these villages became towns, the need for better roads, sanitation and lighting became acute and the most common solution was to seek an improvement act, a type of legislation that was also adopted by many boroughs. Improvement acts were also obtained for new developments beside or within existing resorts such as the Brunswick Town development at

Fig 2.16
Old Town, Bexhill,
East Sussex

The former village lies on high ground around one mile from the sea and is centred on the parish church and the former manor house. After the Second World War it was enveloped by the growing resort.
(DP017993)

Hove whose Commissioners came into existence after an Act of 1830.[77]

In 1776, Weymouth, an ancient borough, obtained one of the earliest improvement acts for a seaside town.[78] The income from a rate of 6d in the pound could be used as collateral against borrowing £2,000 for works, and further money could be raised by creating turnpikes and levying tolls. The commissioners appointed under the act were responsible for paving and cleaning the roads, providing street lighting, cutting new gutters and drains, and sinking wells to provide water to fight fires. They could also remove nuisances, from piles of waste to whole buildings. This range of powers appeared regularly in acts for other towns, but at Weymouth there were also special provisions to prevent the construction of thatched buildings, and the thatch on any existing buildings had to be removed by 1 January 1784.

The improvement act was also recognised as a vehicle for extending local government in new resorts as well as in ancient boroughs. By the 1820s Bognor had outgrown the capabilities of the parochial government of South Bersted and therefore in 1822 an Act of Parliament was obtained, granting powers to sixteen local gentry with substantial property holdings.[79] They assumed control of the newly built market and obtained powers to stop anyone undressing on the beach or bathing in the nude. By 1824 some street lighting and road improvements had been undertaken and in the following year the Board of Commissioners was enlarged to 33 to bring in capital for projects such as a new road along the seashore, as well as constructing drains and sewers.[80] In 1835 the scope of their powers was again widened to include cleaning the streets, repairing pavements, and erecting groynes and other sea defences.[81]

Towns had various ways to raise money. In addition to rates, funds could be raised by levies on markets and specific commodities, such as coal.[82] Licensing was also introduced by some improvement acts; this was ostensibly to regulate the towns, but it also served as an additional source of income. Bognor had licence fees of 5s for boats and 2s 6d for bathing machines, while council minutes for Folkestone in the 1850s show that hackney carriages, pleasure boats, bathing machines and even slaughterhouses were licensed.[83]

As the 19th century progressed, some improvement commissioners took on addi-tional responsibilities. In all types of town this might include the provision of water, gas and a fire engine. At the seaside, public finance might also be used to provide facili-ties designed to increase the attraction of resorts, such as piers, gardens and harbour facilities. In 1787 Margate's Improvement Act made the commissioners responsible for the pier, though this was removed from their control in 1812.[84] The Town Commission of Weston-super-Mare, founded in 1842, had decided by 1845 to build a pier to connect Birnbeck Island to the mainland, but this scheme was not executed.[85] Often the largest project undertaken by local government was the provision of a sea wall and the creation of an esplanade. At Bridlington a rate was levied in the 1840s to raise £30,000 to construct a wall 700ft (200m) long, and in 1877 Margate borrowed £140,000 for the sea wall and street improvements.[86] However, many private individuals and companies also took on responsibility for sea defences to protect their own investment. At Bexhill, the seventh Earl de la Warr, the *de facto* local government, had the sea wall built in 1883; while on a more modest scale, at Teignmouth, the first sea wall was com-missioned by Mrs Hubbard, who ran the baths.[87] At Southend it was the railway company that invested in the promenade and sea wall.[88]

During the 19th century many resorts that had begun life as bare stretches of coast, or small villages and towns, had become large enough to adopt the new, standard forms of local town government. For instance, Margate's Improvement Commis-sioners persisted until 1857, when a new council was created by a Charter of Incorpo-ration, and Southport was incorporated in 1867.[89] Bognor's Improvement Commission continued until 1867, when it was replaced by a Local Government Board, which was in turn replaced by an Urban District Council in 1894.[90]

Transport and seaside holidays in the 18th and 19th centuries

Surplus income, and the leisure time to enjoy it, was essential for a trip to the sea-side, even a short one, but underpinning any extension of the opportunity for a holiday was the availability of affordable and effi-cient means of transport. By 1750 the major roads radiating from London had been improved and during the next two decades, the era of the so-called 'Turnpike Mania', county networks of major routes began to be created. Most roads were upgraded to promote trade, rather than for passenger travel, and although turnpikes to seaside resorts were uncommon in the 18th century, travellers began to benefit from the generally improved state of main roads.[91] In the 1730s, when Scarborough was already attracting sea-bathing visitors, there were no turnpikes in Yorkshire, but by 1752, when the route from York was improved, passengers could travel to the coast from most Yorkshire towns on roads that had been rebuilt in the preceding 20 years. In Sussex, Hastings had a turnpike from Ticehurst by 1753, but it took until 1765 before it was possible to enjoy easier journeys to Tunbridge Wells, where travellers gained access to the wider network of improved roads in the south-east.[92] In 1750 the average speed of travel in England was 4.7mph, but by 1830 it had reached a giddy 9.4mph. Although turnpikes and technical improvements to road construction generally made travel faster, journeys remained uncomfortable and even dangerous (Fig 2.17). The opening scene of Jane Austen's *Sanditon* involves an accident en route to the seaside on a 'very rough lane' where the surface is 'half rock, half sand'.[93]

Improvements to roads and methods of travelling coincided with a rapid increase in the population and a growth in national wealth. Journeys became quicker and more comfortable, but fares did not rise significantly, leading to a marked increase in the numbers of coaches on the roads.[94] Between 1781 and 1809 the number of coaches from London to Scarborough grew from 12 to 60 each week, and from London to Weymouth the equivalent rise was from 12 to 73.[95] Coaches were the preserve of wealthier travellers, but most resorts also seem to have had slower, cheaper waggon services for luggage and poorer travellers. A substantial part of Blackpool's early clientele came by cart: 'Most of them come hither in carts, but some will walk in a single day from Manchester, distant more than forty miles'.[96]

Margate and Ramsgate had relatively poor road connections to Canterbury and, therefore, London, yet by 1800 they were thriving resorts, as a substantial portion of their visitors arrived by boats along the Thames.[97] An 1810 guide noted that Margate was 'conveniently stationed in respect to the metropolis for conveyance by water or land'.[98] Thomas Lott, who holidayed in east Kent in 1815, travelled from London by coach, but returned on a sailing hoy, a cheaper journey that lasted an arduous 27 hours.[99] Hoys transported grain and fish from Kent to London, and imported other goods, particularly coal and timber, but carried passengers as well.[100] William Cowper, writing in 1779 described a typical such voyage: 'The hoy went to London every week, loaded with mackerel and herrings, and returned, loaded with company. The cheapness of the conveyance made it equally commodious for dead fish and lively company.'[101] In 1763 Lyons' guide amusingly recorded that: 'The Hoy, like the Grave, confounds all distinctions: High and Low, Rich and Poor, Sick and Sound, are here indiscriminately blended together.'[102] However, by the early 19th century an element of social grading had been introduced through charging for different types of accommodation. In 1810 the fare was 7s for passage in the common cabin, 9s for the second cabin and 13s for the state cabin.[103]

The introduction of a steam packet service along the Thames in 1815 resulted in more reliable and faster journeys, as well as lower fares and, therefore, increased visitor numbers.[104] At the beginning of the 19th century around 20,000 visitors arrived annually at Margate by sea and in 1835–6 this peaked at 108,625.[105] More frequent services, at lower prices (a result of increased competition), contributed to changing the character of the visitors who could spend time at North Kent resorts, including London shopkeepers who would set up business there during the summer months. Steamers also made possible affordable day

Fig 2.17
The 3 Browns book'd for Brighton, and only one place; c.1830. Charles Jameson Grant

Grant's satirical lithograph depicts the Brighton coach as it prepares to depart from the Belle Sauvage Inn, Ludgate Hill, London. It is doubtful whether this load could ever accelerate to 9.4 mph, and a long, uncomfortable journey is suggested to be one of the prices to pay for a seaside holiday. (Guildhall Library, City of London)

THE 3 BROWNS BOOK'D FOR BRIGHTON, AND ONLY ONE PLACE.

trips from London to Gravesend, and even to Margate, while by the mid-19th century men from these towns were able to remain in London during the week and join their families at weekends.[106] In Mary Figgins' diary for September *c*.1828 she described how her brother had to return from Margate to London on business for a few days during their holiday.[107] The frontispiece of a book published in 1865 entitled 'Arrival of the Husband's Boat' shows excited wives greeting their husbands on the pier at Margate.[108]

While towns along the Thames had already experienced a limited form of mass tourism, the impact of the arrival of the railway was more far-reaching, transforming the appearance of resorts as well as the types of visitors. Rail travel was cheap, fast, reliable and generally more comfortable than previous forms of travel. Ticket sales soon reflected the growing number of passengers on the network and they illustrate the extent to which working-class travellers were gaining access to the system. Between 1850

and 1870, first-class ticket sales rose by 280 per cent, second-class by 193 per cent and third-class by 584 per cent.[109]

Seaside resorts gradually came within the reach of most working people, even if only for a day. In 1837 stagecoaches are estimated to have brought 50,000 travellers to Brighton, but in 1850 in a single week 73,000 people arrived by train.[110] On 3 August 1863 over 30,000 people travelled by train to the newly opened station at Cleethorpes, with a further 4,000 arriving on horse-drawn vehicles.[111] Blackpool, still a modest-sized resort in 1861, dealt with 135,000 train passengers in that year, and by 1879 this had risen to almost one million. By 1914 around four million passengers were travelling to Blackpool by train each year (Fig 2.18).[112]

The standard, and broadly true, story of resorts in the 19th century is that they remained relatively small until the arrival of railways, but these changes brought contrasting fortunes to England's earliest resorts. In

Fig 2.18
Blackpool, Lancashire;
20 August 1895
As the tide receded, the beach became a playground for masses of visitors and a trading area for scores of stall holders. The beach has always been the focal point of the English seaside resort, and has continued to be a venue for a multitude of activities.
(NMR LMS Collection CC79/00488)

the 1840s Brighton's population increased by 40 per cent and Scarborough's by 28 per cent, but at Margate there was a drop of almost 9 per cent, followed by another decline in the 1850s. The underlying reason was that steamers had brought huge numbers of Londoners to the town, but once the delights of other resorts became an option, people previously restricted to the Thames Estuary could branch out. Daniel Benham, who had taken his holidays at Ramsgate in 1826 and 1829, ventured to the West Country in the 1840s.[113]

Part of the growth in residential populations in some seaside resorts can be explained by the new phenomenon of the commuter. Margate had seen a small amount of weekly commuting facilitated by increasingly rapid steamships. During the second half of the 19th century, Southport began to serve as a dormitory for wealthy Liverpool businessmen, and Brighton came within reach of London through the reduction of the rail journey time to $1\frac{1}{2}$ hours.[114] By the end of the 19th century, commuters to Bradford were prompting the development of their own suburb at Morecambe.[115]

Railways strengthened the relationships between particular resorts and inland towns in their hinterland, but they did not create them. While wealthy visitors had the time and money to travel wherever they wished, less affluent travellers had to take a convenient line to their nearest stretch of coastline and this consolidated existing links. Thus,

the populace of Lancashire towns headed west: AB Granville in 1841 described how 'the Manchester factor and artisan – the rich and the "middling comfortable" visited Southport while "the Prestonians" preferred Blackpool because of the paved road, though the arrival of the railway will make the journey even easier'.[116] The inhabitants of West Riding towns headed east, though Leeds was closer to Blackpool than to Scarborough. Here the directness of the railway lines, and perhaps the rivalry between the two counties, seems to have been more significant than distance on the railways.[117] The towns of the East Midlands had no resorts of their own until railways opened up the Lincolnshire Coast, and comprehensively land-locked Birmingham never acquired its own resorts, but spread its population around the country.

Railways were a vital new facility for Victorian Britain, but not all towns, or more accurately not all of their citizens, were in favour of the railway. In the 1830s Weston-super-Mare was bypassed because of local opposition, but the town subsequently relented, and a short branch line was soon built to link it to the mainline.[118] In 1846 some townspeople at Bridlington also objected to a station near the quay, the more fashionable part of town, and therefore it was built further inland. While some towns and landowners tried to resist what many saw as progress, others were quick to embrace it. Lord Burlington actively

Fig 2.19
Saltburn-by-the-Sea, Cleveland; Ordnance Survey map 1894
The Saltburn Improvement Company was formed in 1860 and held a competition for the development of a resort on land purchased from Lord Zetland. Situated on the cliff top to the west of the historic settlement, George Dickinson's winning plan set out parallel, 'jewel streets' between the cliff-top Marine Terrace and the new railway line. (Reproduced from the 1894 Ordnance Survey map.)

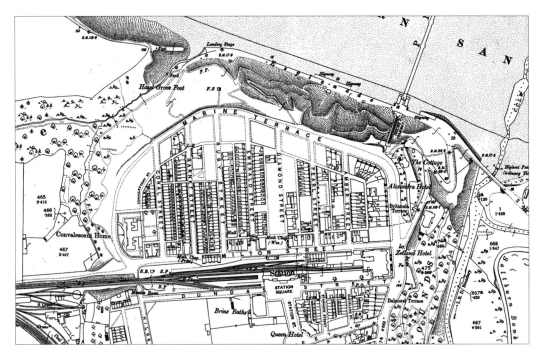

campaigned to get a line to Eastbourne and invested in the resort. On 15 June 1849 he wrote in his diary that 'The railway has certainly improved the prospects of the place considerably'.[119]

In contrast to entrepreneurial landowners, railway companies were predominantly passive agents in the growth of seaside resorts. The three instances where railway companies tried to develop entire resorts were all unsuccessful. Firstly, in 1854 the Hull and Holderness Railway opened a line to Withernsea and established an Improvement Company, but the new settlement never prospered as a resort.[120] Secondly, in 1879 a group of directors from the Furness Railway planned a promenade, a hotel and avenues of houses at Seascale, but a decade later only a dozen houses had been built. Thirdly, the Carlisle and Silloth Bay Railway commissioned an architect to lay out a large resort at Silloth in the 1850s.[121] The company exercised strict control over every aspect of the development and built a terrace in Criffel Street, a hotel, baths, pleasure gardens, the sewers and gasworks. By the mid-1880s, with little else built, the running of the town had passed to a Local Board and a Town Improvement Society, leaving the railway company simply as a landowner.[122]

Large developments involving railway companies were usually partnerships with local landowners, though the precise arrangement varied in each case. For example, at Saltburn Lord Zetland, Henry Pease and the Stockton and Darlington Railway Company were involved in the development.[123] The town was centred on the station, which opened in 1862, and in 1863 William Peachey, the architect of the station, completed the Zetland Hotel (Figs 2.19, 2.20).[124] Similarly, at Cleethorpes, the Manchester, Sheffield and Lincolnshire Railway invested over £100,000 to build an exhibition hall, a museum, aquarium, amusement park and baths, as well as the promenade and

Fig 2.20
Former Zetland Hotel, Glenside, Saltburn-by-the-Sea, Cleveland; 1861–3, William Peachey

Designed for the Stockton & Darlington Railway Company, the Zetland Hotel was the true terminus for the line that was built from Redcar, with its own covered platform at the rear of the building. The hotel has now been converted into flats.
(DP006407)

gardens.[125] The main landowners in the town, Sidney College Cambridge and the Earl of Yarborough, took advantage of this investment by laying out large numbers of building plots for speculative development.[126]

Trips to the seaside in Victorian England

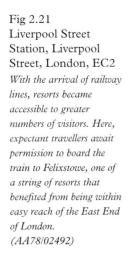

Fig 2.21
Liverpool Street Station, Liverpool Street, London, EC2
With the arrival of railway lines, resorts became accessible to greater numbers of visitors. Here, expectant travellers await permission to board the train to Felixstowe, one of a string of resorts that benefited from being within easy reach of the East End of London.
(AA78/02492)

Railways were the most significant factor in the growth of Victorian resorts, but their impact would not have been as dramatic without an accompanying increase in England's wealth, a long-term relative fall in prices, especially during the late 19th century, and hence a rise in disposable income. However, surplus income was not sufficient in itself to stimulate a growth in holidays; time to travel was also required. Wakes Weeks in Lancashire and the Bowlingtide holidays in the West Riding of Yorkshire were traditional annual holidays that survived the industrial revolution (where workers took a week's holiday at the same time each year, dependent on the town

where they lived), and other local holidays and festivals continued more patchily in other counties.[127] Before the arrival of railways these were often enjoyed at home, where local fairs were held, but increasingly the annual holiday was spent at a nearby resort.

Although traditional holidays survived in some places, the industrial revolution eroded the number of days off enjoyed by most people.[128] In 1824 the Bank of England closed for 39 days' holiday, but by 1871 only Christmas Day, Good Friday, 1 May and 1 November were still being observed.[129] In 1871 the Bank Holidays Act attempted to redress this by creating four additional holidays, including, most significantly for the seaside, the first Monday in August.[130] Additional days were soon appended to these three-day weekends, so that gradually the week-long holiday was established before legislation recognised it in the 20th century in the Holidays with Pay Act of 1938.

Surplus income and increasing leisure time meant that large numbers of less wealthy people began to be able to enjoy day trips or short breaks to the seaside, especially

after the creation of Bank Holidays. The first excursions organised by a railway company occurred in 1830 and by the end of the 19th century all railway companies offered a wide range of day trips (Fig 2.21).[131] Private individuals and a variety of groups also organised excursions. In 1841 Thomas Cook arranged his first trip from Leicester to a temperance fete in Loughborough and was soon arranging visits to seaside towns.[132] Day trips were also provided by mechanics' institutes, organisations of working people and enlightened employers.[133] In 1903 office staff at Cadbury's Factory at Bournville had a hectic day trip to Weston-super-Mare.[134] It included lunch, dinner, a boat trip and a ride on a charabanc, and all this had to be fitted in after they had completed their paperwork at the factory. Political organisations were also responsible for large excursions. In 1919 the annual Joy Day and demonstration of Lancashire and Cheshire Miners' Federation brought tens of thousands of miners and their families to Blackpool on 135 trains.[135]

Religious groups used railways for excursions, but they also opposed undermining the Sabbath. For example, residents of Blackpool, Lytham, Southport and Morecambe successfully petitioned local railway companies to suspend, albeit temporarily, Sunday excursions.[136] However, in the balance of pious protest on one side against the profitable use of idle rolling stock on the other, the profits of the railway companies usually prevailed. Nevertheless, some companies tried to prove that it was possible to combine an excursion with religious worship. The Lancashire and Yorkshire Railway offered 'Sea Bathing for the Working Classes' on Sundays and promised that 'Parties availing themselves of these trains will be enabled to bathe and refresh themselves in ample time to attend a Place of Worship.'[137]

With the growing numbers of residents and visitors it became necessary for resorts to provide larger facilities in place of the circulating library, assembly rooms and small theatres of Georgian resorts. Piers, winter gardens and, in the early 20th century, the multi-functional kursaal and the cinema appeared to cater for the changing tastes of holidaymakers. The beach and seafront were transformed from places for genteel promenading and sandcastle building to a venue for a bewildering range of small stalls and amusements, and a new level of hustle and bustle. In 1895 the Town Clerk of Blackpool listed 316 standings on the foreshore catering for the huge numbers of trippers, and

this probably only represented the more official tradespeople and entertainers.[138] Changes to the entertainment scene in Victorian resorts will be considered in detail in chapter 6.

Seaside holidays in the 20th century

Many of the factors that had shaped the evolution of resorts in the 18th and 19th centuries were still at work in the first half of the 20th century. At their simplest these can be characterised as the ability to provide more opportunities for holidays, through increased leisure time, growing incomes and greater access to affordable transport. The earliest examples of paid holidays predate the Great Exhibition of 1851, and by 1860 the Southern Metropolitan Gas Company was giving its staff a week of paid leave.[139] This practice spread slowly during the later half of the 19th century, and for many people the only opportunity for a 'holiday' was through organised activities such as militia camps, temperance and religious trips, benevolent excursions and working holidays such as hop- or fruit-picking. In 1928 the first statutory provision allowed shop assistants in seaside resorts to have paid leave in lieu of the extra time they had to work during the summer season.[140] Four attempts were made to get another bill passed allowing two weeks' paid leave for more workers, but the recommendations of the Amulree Committee and the subsequent, more realistic Holidays with Pay Act 1938 provided most people with only a week of paid leave.[141] In March 1938 7.75 million (41.9 per cent) of the 18.5 million workers who earned less than £250 per year had some form of paid leave.[142] By June 1939 over 11 million people enjoyed paid holidays and, by 1955, 96 per cent of manual workers were receiving two weeks' paid leave.[143]

Although there was widespread support for the idea of paid holidays, there was concern about how resorts would cope with a sudden influx of new holidaymakers. In the 1930s most holidays were taken in August leading to a surge in rail travel and a scarcity of accommodation.[144] Roland Robinson speaking in a Parliamentary debate in 1938 described how

They [the travellers] are so tired that they require two or three days' holiday to recover from the journey ... . We hear of people sleeping in baths, on billiard tables or in armchairs, because there is no other accommodation available for them. In the day they go on to crowded beaches until at the height of the season the beaches resemble human ant-heaps rather than anything else.

This is the sort of holiday to which the worker in this country is condemned under the present system.[145]

The increased demand for accommodation in the high season, far in excess of what most resorts could satisfy, required a radical solution. An article in the *Architectural Review* in 1936 blamed the demand for affordable accommodation during the school holidays for the spread of bungalow towns and holiday camps.[146] However, in the inaugural edition of the *Holiday Camp Review* in April 1938 one author, unsurprisingly, advocated holiday camps as the solution to a future accommodation crisis, and Pimlott, writing in 1947, also believed that institutions such as Butlins would alleviate this problem.[147]

The train remained the main way to travel to the seaside until the mid-20th century. For example, on one Saturday in August 1935, 467 trains arrived and departed from Blackpool and on 28 July 1945 the LMS carried 102,889 passengers to the resort.[148] However, the beginning of the decline of rail travel was under way: in 1919 there were just over two billion passenger journeys per year, but this figure had halved by 1950.[149] In 1945 Elizabeth Brunner proclaimed, perhaps slightly prematurely, that 'The age of the motor car is superseding that of the railway, and is likely to have a profound effect on holiday habits'.[150] In 1951 around 27 per cent of people went on holiday by car, the same

proportion as those using coaches, while railways still accounted for approximately 47 per cent of travellers. In 2002, 73 per cent of holidaymakers within Britain went by car, 6 per cent by coach and only 12 per cent by rail.[151]

The charabanc and motor coach were the pioneers of motor transport for people heading to the seaside (Fig 2.22). By the late 1920s HV Morton could pronounce that 'The remarkable system of motor-coach services which now penetrate every part of the country has thrown open to ordinary people regions which even after the coming of the railway were remote and inaccessible'.[152] Some previously sedate resorts that had survived the impact of railways were affected by the arrival of coach parties. Robert Roberts described how his family and friends went on trips after the First World War:

> Wealthier members of the proletariat, in their week's unpaid annual holidays, took *en masse* to motor char-à-banc tours round Britain. Middle- and upper-class people, resident in posh hotels and spas and along the south coast, were startled, then amazed to see horny-handed sons of toil and their spouses sitting, diffidently it is true, but sitting in the lounges and dining-rooms of places they had previously considered their own preserve.[153]

Paid leave and increasing access to affordable and convenient transport brought in huge numbers of visitors to resorts. In the late 1930s it was estimated that 7 million holidaymakers visited Blackpool, Southend had 5.5 million visitors, Hastings 3 million and Bournemouth and Southport 2 million.[154] As well as catering for growing numbers of visitors, the resident populations of resorts were also increasing rapidly. In the first half of the 20th century, despite interruptions by the two wars, the population of leading resorts rose by 50 per cent, faster than that of England as a whole (34.5 per cent).[155] Sections of the south coast of England became a magnet for people seeking genteel retirement, earning it the uncharitable nickname of 'Costa Geriatrica', although retired people form a significant part of the population of all resorts around the coast.[156]

By the beginning of the 20th century all the popular resorts had well-established local government institutions providing a range of basic services as well as being involved with some forms of entertainment. For instance,

Fig 2.22
A Charabanc, from Lancaster 1936

Osbert Lancaster's story of the seaside resort included modes of transport used for excursions. The first motor vehicle, 'a two-cylinder, chain-driven De Dion-Panhard', was recorded as having made 'several successful trips along the coast until it finally exploded on the hill going up to Pelvis Magna one hot afternoon in the summer of 1919'.

(By kind permission of Lady Lancaster)

Bournemouth's local authority owned the two piers, the Winter Gardens, a museum, parks, two golf courses and the cliff lifts, and it ran a municipal orchestra and band.[157] In the inter-war years many local authorities took on a greater role in the provision of facilities for visitors.[158] The largest commitment was undoubtedly at Blackpool, where seven miles of promenade were built at a cost of £1.5 million, around £75,000 was spent in 1921–3 on an open-air pool, £250,000 was assigned for improvements to the Winter Garden, and, in 1939, an indoor seawater bath was completed at a cost of £300,000.[159] Considerably smaller Hastings spent over £100,000 on the White Rock Pavilion, which opened in 1927, and in 1931 £180,000 was spent on the promenade, including the new car park, and £100,000 on baths.[160]

The popularity of the seaside continued to increase until the 1970s, though it suffered significant, but temporary setbacks during two World Wars. In the First World War coastal towns suffered some damage, and a few defensive structures from this conflict survive, but the impact of the

Second World War was much more dramatic (Fig 2.23). An article published in *The Times* in 1943 described 'Wartime decay at Margate'.[161] The town's population had dropped to a third of its pre-war figure, 'Half the property in the borough has been damaged to a greater or lesser extent' and 'From being a bright and well-kept background to cheerful holidaymaking, Margate has become damaged and shabby. ... But worse even than the damage done by bombs is that due to premises being left empty and unattended through interruption of the town's peace-time function of a holiday resort.' Before the war there had been 30 first-class hotels, 60 smaller hotels, 150 private hotels, 1,300 boarding houses, 1,500 apartment houses and 3,500 private dwellings that took in visitors. By 1943 there were just two hotels and four or five boarding houses for visitors.[162] In contrast, at the other end of the country Blackpool was reaping some benefit from its location because access was not restricted as it was on the more vulnerable southern and eastern coasts. At one time up to 45,000 RAF recruits were lodged in the town and there were also

Fig 2.23
Waterloo Crescent, Dover, Kent; 1942–3
Many seaside resorts suffered from enemy action during the Second World War. Dover was vulnerable to air raids, and it was targeted by German artillery batteries on the French coast. Over 10,000 buildings were damaged in Dover, of which nearly 1,000 were destroyed. (A43/05436)

substantial numbers of evacuees, not just children, but also civil servants from London.[163] Far from being denuded of its populace, it was estimated that Blackpool's population grew from 128,200 in 1939 to 143,650 in 1945.

The 1950s, the era of 'Hi-de-Hi', seems like a golden age for the seaside holiday, but the peak actually occurred in 1974 when 40.5 million people took a holiday in Britain of four days or longer. However, other statistics show that the annual migration to the Mediterranean sun was already well under way.[164] English seaside towns were now faced with competition from resorts where tourists could find a mixture of the familiar and the exotic, an echo on a grander scale of what the English seaside was like for holiday-makers in the 19th century. Mediterranean resorts were relatively new with a better climate and more modern facilities, whereas British seaside resorts had 'the constraints of decaying infrastructure, designed for one era and not evolving, or not physically able to evolve, to accommodate the demands of another'.[165] Competition from the foreign holiday was not the only factor in the decline in the seaside's popularity; people in the late 20th century could choose from a wider range of domestic holidays and leisure activities. A potentially vicious circle can develop where decreasing popularity leads to less private and public income to invest, which in turn leads to poorer facilities and therefore fewer visitors. Add to this media stories of dirty beaches, crime, and benefit bed-and-breakfasts and the seaside can appear an unappealing option for a family holiday.

Conclusion

RW Butler examined resorts in the widest sense, but his analysis (*see* p 8) applies well to English seaside towns. The first resorts were attractive to visitors in search of health through sea bathing and the seaside climate. Once the first visitors arrived, local entrepreneurs were prepared to invest modest sums to improve facilities and provide accommodation, but by the early 19th century much larger investments were being risked, not always successfully. Effectively the lead role in resort development passed from hotel proprietors, inn keepers and local businessmen to major local landowners and entrepreneurs. Butler suggests that in the middle phases of his cycle external interests become involved with reorganising resort facilities. In a sense the arrival of the railways could be seen as an external influence on the development of the seaside resort, but of equal importance was the contribution of local entrepreneurs or businessmen from large, nearby towns. Butler does not include a role for local government, but it is clear that it had a pivotal role in many resorts. Stagnation and decline are the last two stages in Butler's cycle, and both have been observed at the seaside.

Butler's cycle provides a description of the phases through which resorts have passed, but it does not identify the drivers behind the cycle. These can be grouped together under the heading of 'increasing access'. Increased wealth, more leisure time and improved, more affordable means of transport apply equally in the late 18th century or the early 20th century to explain why the numbers of holidaymakers increased. In the late 20th century the same factors can also be cited to explain the decline of the seaside resort, as they now allow worldwide travel for weeks at a time, relegating the seaside, for many people, to a venue for short breaks, day trips and conferences.

3

The form of resorts

Most market and county towns were centred on a market place and grew slowly, often only by infilling within their initial footprint. Later growth followed a familiar pattern: rings of housing, differentiated by social class and age, surrounded the historic core, industrial suburbs grew along rivers, and over time renewal saw the clearance of inner areas as commerce elbowed out housing. In industrial towns the competition for land adjacent to water led to intensive development along rivers or canals, shifting the economic centre of gravity away from the historic centres of the original settlements. A similar story is found in ports, where access to the waterfront was a primary consideration in their expansion.

Like ports, the development of seaside towns was skewed towards their waterfront, the sea, the geographical factor from which all their peculiarities of form and function arise. Rather than emanating from the heart of long-established settlements, seaside resorts were laid out, principally, in reference to the shoreline, although towns with pre-resort origins have areas where older, irregular nuclei prevail. Because their centres are located at the edge of the town, it might be tempting to think that resorts have their other half missing. However, they contain all the elements of equivalent inland settlements, but in overcoming and exploiting their coastal location, they have faced different challenges and employed different solutions. These can be grouped under two broad, but overlapping headings, the effect of their geographical location and the impact of visitors on the development of the town.

Seaside resorts, like inland towns, spread along features such as hills, river valleys, roads and railways, but they also have distinctive elements in their layout due to their location. The character of the coastline at a particular town defines the direction in which development will spread, either along a relatively flat seafront or on to cliffs and hills above. In many early resorts a harbour from the precursor settlement still serves as a focal point for expansion, as well as providing local colour for inquisitive visitors. From the 19th century until the present day a perpetual battle between man and sea has taken place, with the natural form of the coastline gradually being replaced by ever more substantial sea defences. Secure behind these, a promenade and a major road were usually laid out during the 19th century, parallel to the coast. On the landward side of the road stands the first line of buildings, the main canvas on which seaside frivolity is painted. These buildings, despite regular reinventions of their superficial decoration, retain evidence of the changing fortunes of resorts and serve as a record in cross-section of the outward expansion of the town.

The presence of visitors underpins most development at resorts and, as will be seen in the rest of the book, this led to distinctive forms and styles of architecture, as well as having a profound impact on the overall form of resorts. All towns have areas of housing developed for particular classes of resident and the same applies at resorts. However, this may be more obvious in some seaside towns where special measures were taken to safeguard the genteel resident and visitor from less affluent residents and particularly the hoards of trippers who descended on the towns.

An area where the impact of geography and the visitor combine to influence the appearance of seaside resorts is transport. Improved means of transport brought growing numbers of visitors into resorts during the 19th and 20th centuries, and has contributed to defining some of the direction and alignment of new developments.

The freedom that the internal combustion engine provided during the 20th century allowed visitors to reach every part of the coastline and established new towns, and new types of settlement, including seaside suburbs. Caravan parks occur right across the country, but nowhere so prolifically than on the coast, stretches of which are dominated by vast, haphazard settlements of caravans and holiday cabins.

A geography of the seafront

The narrow strip of land between the high-water mark and the first line of buildings is central to the identity of the seaside resort. It is the key open space that makes resorts special and serves to soften their heavily urbanised character. In major resorts between 2 per cent and 13 per cent of the land area is public space such as parks, nature reserves and the beach at high tide, but this grows more or less significantly as the tide recedes.[1] For example, at Blackpool and Weston-super-Mare the area of the beach is dramatically increased by the low tide, though much of the land uncovered at the latter is not suitable to walk on (Fig 3.1, see also Fig 2.18), whereas at Weymouth and Brighton the effect is less marked as the land drops more steeply into the sea. This contrasts with the public space in the other kinds of settlement examined for this study. In the spa towns just 5 per cent to 8 per cent of their area could be classified as open spaces. Some of the historic towns had up to 20 per cent, often focussed along a river, but where the river was needed by industry, such as in a Lancashire mill town, there was as little as 3 per cent of open space in the central part of the town. This was usually in the form of relatively small, formal parks, provided to

counter poor hygiene resulting from over-crowding and inadequate sanitation.[2]

The relationship between the land and the sea is the key factor that defines the character of the seafront. Where there is a marked slope to the beach and the land behind, seafront development may begin near the high-water mark. In the central and western parts of Brighton, for instance, the principal line of buildings is a short distance from the high-water line, separated from the sea only by the upper part of the shingle beach, a sea wall and a road (Fig 3.2, see also Fig 3.21). On flatter stretches of coastline there may be a broad area of relatively undeveloped land between the sea and the start of the built-up area. This land, some of which may have been reclaimed from the sea, is unsuitable for substantial buildings and may be treated as gardens, car parking or as an area for amusements. The widest example of this type of 'no man's land' is at Southport, where the first line of buildings is over 600m from the beach, the intermediate area being occupied by a lake, amusements and gardens (see Fig 3.39).

At a number of resorts, the seafront is dominated by cliffs, which could have prevented development, but at many of these locations the cliff tops provided relatively cheap land that may have been easier and

Fig 3.1
Blackpool,
Lancashire; 1895

Figure 2.18 shows the beach at low tide, a venue for stalls, amusements and huge numbers of people to gather. At high tide these are driven from the beach, leaving only a few people to paddle. This twice-daily ritual is an important element in the changing character of a resort.
(OP00479)

more economical to develop than rougher seafront land. As elevated cliff-tops provided the best sea views, they were desirable locations for the creation of the highest-status schemes. Developers usually tried to maximise their profits by making their sea-facing blocks as prestigious, and as expensive, as the housing market of the individual resort could bear. Hence the estates on the Leas at Folkestone are grander than the equivalent sea-facing terraces at Cliftonville at Margate, yet both were aimed towards the top of their respective residential and visitor markets (Figs 3.3, 3.4).

Thus in some resorts the focus of development shifted from the historic settlement on the seafront to the cliffs above. At Southend, for example, the first seaside buildings were predominantly at sea level, to the east of the current town centre. A shift of emphasis in the town's plan to the west and up on to the cliffs began in the early 1790s when the Royal Hotel and the adjacent terrace were built. A poem published in 1793 described the contrasting parts of the resort:

Here, without order, sev'ral houses stand,
Scatter'd along the shore, and near the
    strand;
Some built in lofty style, of modern date,
Some long erected, and of lowly state:
And on a gentle eminence in rear,
Three rows of smaller tenements appear.

The recent buildings regularly plann'd,
High on the cliff with southern aspect stand,
Dispos'd with neatness, symmetry, and taste,
In pleasant site, and order aptly plac'd.
Along the front a spacious Terrace lies,
Whence an enchanting prospect meets our
    eyes.[3]

Fig 3.2
Ordnance Survey map, Brighton, East Sussex; 1877
*This map shows the narrow area between the high-water line and the first line of buildings. It also demonstrates how dominant the seafront is as the axis of alignment for the blocks nearest the sea. The area at the north is less regular as the streets were also laid out in relation to the railway line.
(Reproduced from the 1877 Ordnance Survey map)*

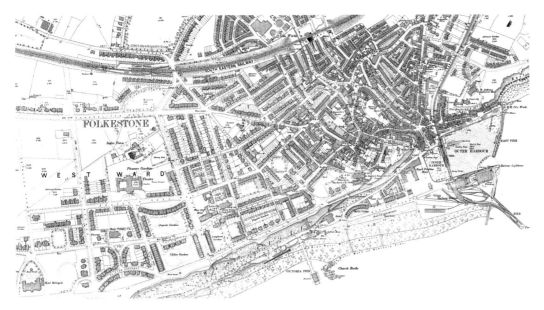

Fig 3.3
Ordnance Survey map, Folkestone, Kent; 1898
*The new estates with large buildings and open spaces on the cliff-top Leas to the west are in marked contrast with the dense, more irregular streets of the old town.
(Reproduced from the 1898 Ordnance Survey map)*

Fig 3.4
1–31 Clifton
Crescent, The Leas,
Folkestone, Kent;
1870s
*This was the most
prestigious development
on the Leas in the 1870s.
A series of large, detached
and semi-detached houses
was built around a self-
contained garden. The gate
and a cautionary sign still
provide residents with some
extra privacy.*
(DP022293)

Similarly, historic Scarborough was located around the harbour. During the 18th century residents and visitors moved into new houses on the hillside between the harbour and the castle, but by the 19th century larger and more prestigious developments were concentrated on higher land to the south of the town, closer to the spa. Exploiting the cliff tops had become a necessity as most of the land near the heart of the resort had already been occupied.

The desire to be by the sea meant that improved or reclaimed land was sometimes exploited as a location for new building. For example, at Teignmouth and Great Yarmouth the main seaside developments were on areas of sandy land known as the Den (*see* Fig 4.5), and the North and South Denes respectively, and Weymouth's seafront growth during the late 18th and early 19th centuries was predominantly on a narrow strip of land beside, and to some extent reclaimed from, the sea (Figs 3.5, 3.6). At some resorts reclamation was undertaken by developers to allow the creation of new buildings near the sea, as well

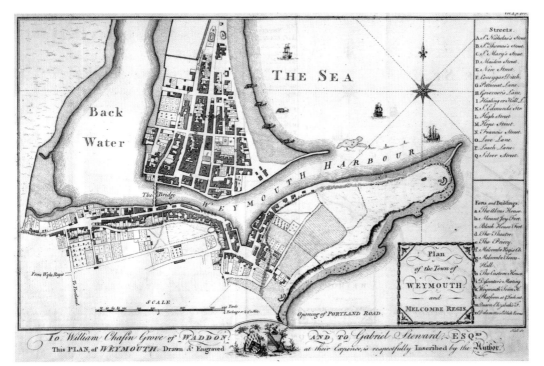

Fig 3.5
1774 map of
Weymouth from
Hutchins; 1774
*The town in 1774 was only
a little larger than in the
Middle Ages. Weymouth on
the south side of the river
was still a narrow strip of
buildings alongside the
harbour, but Melcombe
Regis, the settlement on the
northern side of the
harbour, had begun to
expand northwards a short
distance.*
(DP022292)

Fig 3.6
Weymouth, Dorset
*With the arrival of bathers,
new prestigious terraces
were built in a line along
the seafront. New housing
was also built at the south
end of the seafront, and
during the 19th and 20th
centuries the town
expanded by reclaiming
land from the 'Back
Water', further inland.*
(NMR21660/10)

Fig 3.7
Detail of the *Long
Painting*, Sidmouth,
Devon; 1814

*At Sidmouth, there was no
protection from the sea
when the* Long Painting
*was painted. Ten years
later, a storm damaged
many houses at the resort,
prompting the construction
of a sea wall, which was
built in 1835–8 by the
Exeter architect GH
Julian.*
(DP021042)

as at the heart of the resort, rather than because of a shortage of land in the surrounding countryside. Perhaps this trend was also influenced by the relative cheapness of this new or improved land, compared with prime farmland.

Constructing the seafront

The seafront is the frontline in the battle between man-made structures and the power of the sea, and during the past two centuries the irregular, natural form of the shoreline has been replaced by the regularity of the sea wall and the promenade (Fig 3.7). In the 19th century these walls were often elegant stone structures, but the 20th-century solution usually involves vast expanses of concrete, sometimes shaped to

Fig 3.8
Seafront, Ventnor,
Isle of Wight; late
19th-century
photograph

*Elegant ladies in
voluminous clothing enjoy
a stroll along the
promenade, which was
created when the sea wall
was built. (BB81/03277A)*

reflect the force of waves (Fig 3.8). Whatever their form, however, the walls serve a valuable purpose, thus Jaywick Sands, with its motley collection of chalets and bungalows, owes its continued existence to a tall wall that obscures any sea views from the houses, but would prevent a repeat of the damage caused by the renowned storm of 1953, which caused devastating floods and claimed 35 lives (Fig 3.9). Regardless of when the sea wall was built the effect was the same: the natural irregularity of the shore was replaced by a constructed line that was rigid and unchanging.

Promenades are a by-product of sea defences, providing visitors with a healthy, bracing place to walk and socialise. They are often the location for formal gardens, usually in the form of long, relatively narrow rectangular beds, whose plants are carefully chosen to be colourful and even exotic, yet varieties that are robust enough to weather storms and thrive in the salty atmosphere. In addition to gardens the promenade provides a number of the basic facilities expected by visitors. It is now a location for food kiosks, information offices and a route for transport to take tourists along the beach. There is also a greater preponderance of toilets, benches and shelters on a seafront than appear in the parks of an ordinary town (Fig 3.10). In addition, the promenade is the location for the facilities required by bathers, showers and water taps. These are normally just basic facilities beside the sea wall, but in Bridlington they have been made into features within a comprehensive remodelling of the south

Fig 3.9
Sea wall, Jaywick,
Essex

*In 1953, the greatest storm surge on record for the North Sea brought devastation to the east coast of England and killed 35 people at Jaywick. A tall, concrete, sea wall was erected, but high tides broke over it nevertheless during the storm of 1987.
(DP022290)*

Fig 3.10
Shelter, seafront,
Blackpool,
Lancashire; 1905

*Along the promenade a series of shelters were added in around 1905. Their busy roofline, with exotic motifs, owes an obvious debt to the kiosks and booths on the nearby piers.
(AA053296)*

promenade, while at Blackpool new facilities have been included in the modern lifeboat station (Fig 3.11).

Promenades are also a venue for major works of public sculpture. Among the earliest was the statue of George III at Weymouth, unveiled in 1810, five years after the King's final visit (Fig 3.12).[4] In recent years large works of art have been recognised as a way of enlivening seafronts (Figs 3.13, 3.14). For example, at Morecambe the Tern project has been inspired by the wildlife of the bay and the sculpture that Eric Gill provided in 1933 for the Midland Hotel. At the heart of the scheme is a statue of Eric Morecambe, who attracts many pilgrims in search of a memorable photograph (*see* Fig 8.10). War memorials were often erected on the seafront, performing the role of a market place or a park in other towns.

Part of the area between the seafront and the first line of buildings is usually also occupied by a major road running parallel to the sea. Once a place for polite promenading and coach rides, it can now be as wide as a major dual carriageway, restricting passage between the town and the sea to a handful of crossings (Fig 3.15). Lesser streets are aligned to this road, rather than the central high street of an ordinary town, and if considerations arising from land ownership or geographical features did not intervene, a resort would resemble a fairly regular grid stretching back from the seafront (*see* Fig 3.2). A desire to be by the sea means that the overall plan of most resorts is more linear compared with inland towns of a similar size and the main axes of coastal towns are often parallel to the coast line rather than emanating from a central core. This lure of the sea has meant that development has been drawn along the shoreline with the most prestigious buildings sited on the seafront and smaller, lower-status buildings behind.

Behind the major seafront road there is a line of buildings, predominantly former houses, which once provided lodgings and now contain shops and restaurants. There are also hotels, some purpose-built, others that have been created from grouping together former houses. Major places of entertainment are also prominent features on seafronts. All these seafront buildings reflect the changing tastes of residents and visitors, and record the rate at which a resort

Fig 3.11
Lifeboat House,
Promenade,
Blackpool,
Lancashire; 1998,
Poynton Bradbury
Wynter Cole
Architects Ltd

Following the introduction of a new Atlantic 75 lifeboat, the existing 1937 lifeboat house was too small. This new lifeboat station was built to house three lifeboats, along with improved crew quarters and a visitor centre, as well as the footbath and drinking fountain. Blackpool's first lifeboat station appears in Fig 3.25.
(AA053316)

Fig 3.12 *(left)*
King George III's Statue, Esplanade, Weymouth, Dorset; unveiled in 1810, J Hamilton
George III's statue was commissioned to commemorate the 50th year of his reign and to celebrate his visits to the resort. In 1788 the monarch was struck down with porphyria and was advised to head to the seaside. He arrived in Weymouth in 1789, the first of 14 visits he made up to 1805. (AA037544)

Fig 3.13 *(below left)*
They Shoot Horses Don't They, Promenade, Blackpool; 2002, Michael Trainor
(AA053279)

Fig 3.14 *(below)*
'Desire', Promenade, Blackpool; 2001, Chris Knight
The sculpture on the south beach at Blackpool is some of the most exciting modern sculpture at the seaside and embraces a wide range of styles and materials. These works were created as part of a £20-million scheme to renovate the Victorian promenade.
(AA053278)

Fig 3.15
The Promenade near
the Tower, Blackpool,
Lancashire

*Wide roads dominate most
of the seafronts of English
resorts. Far from being a
suitable place to
promenade, they are now
major arteries of the towns.
(AA053361)*

Fig 3.16
Plan of Brighton,
East Sussex

*Brighton's expansion
echoed that of many inland
towns, namely in concentric
rings out from a historic
core. From the tight
historic settlement, the town
grew very rapidly during
the 19th century, with the
main direction for
development being along
the coastline.*

1788

1822

1880

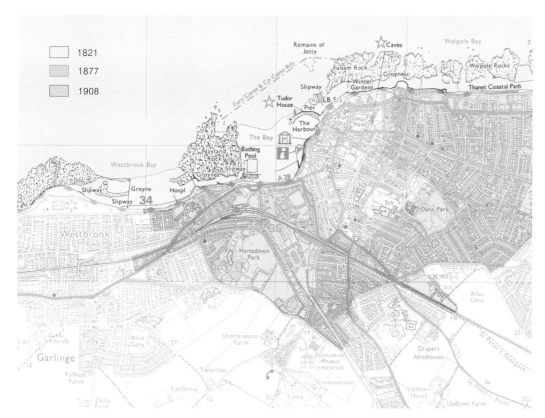

Fig 3.17
Plan of Margate, Kent
*At Margate the first
development was clustered
around the harbour area
and along streets leading
inland and up towards the
parish church. During the
19th century new resort
development was spreading
along the coastline on either
side of the early town.*

*(Both of these maps are
based upon Ordnance
Survey material with the
permission of Ordnance
Survey on behalf of the
Controller of Her Majesty's
Stationery Office © Crown
Copyright. Unauthorised
reproduction infringes
Crown Copyright and may
lead to prosecution or
criminal proceedings.
English Heritage
100019088. 2007)*

expanded. This line is like a cross-section through a town, where the phases of expansion are recorded like tree rings (Figs 3.16, 3.17). A trip along a seafront highlights how the character and age of the buildings changes as the observer travels out from the centre of the resort. To illustrate this, the easiest town to examine is Blackpool, where the sea and the tramline provide a consistent line from which to see its spread. Blackpool is also a good choice as it is relatively flat, meaning that geographical features have had a limited impact on its form.

Blackpool's seafront

The historic heart of Blackpool was centred on Talbot Square. In this area a small number of three-storied buildings of the mid- and later 19th century survive, including the former Roberts' Oyster Bar of *c.*1830–40 and an adjacent late 19th-century house with terracotta detailing (Figs 3.18, 3.19). Of this original settlement, the only other surviving 19th-century buildings are on the north side of the square and in the streets behind; the rest of this area has been repeatedly redeveloped, particularly to the south where large entertainment complexes, including the Tower, have replaced the housing that once existed there

(*see* Fig 4.31). At the southern end of the area dominated by entertainment buildings, a group of buildings around the Foxhall Public House have survived that are smaller and lower in status. These were not replaced by substantial housing in the late 19th century, but were too far from the centre to be replaced during the 20th century by larger entertainment buildings (*see* Fig 8.1).

The next stage of settlement, from later

Fig 3.18
Roberts' Oyster Bar,
Promenade,
Blackpool,
Lancashire; *c.*1830–40
*Opening as Roberts' Oyster
Rooms in 1876, the
restaurant remained, until
recently, a significant
feature near the heart of
historic Blackpool. This is
a rare survival from the
earliest phase of the town's
development, and by the
end of the 19th century
other similar buildings were
already being replaced by
larger buildings.
(AA053238)*

Fig 3.19
Clifton Hotel, Talbot
Square, Blackpool,
Lancashire; 1865–74
*Situated on the south side
of Talbot Square, the
Clifton Hotel evolved from
the original Clifton Arms
Hotel on the corner of
Talbot Square and the
Promenade. Ideally
situated, the hotel provided
convenient access to the
recently completed North
Pier.*
(AA053251)

Fig 3.20
Claremont Hotel,
North Promenade,
Blackpool, Lancashire
*Originally Lansdowne
Crescent, a concave terrace
of 20 houses, this
development formed part of
the North Shore expansion
of Blackpool in the second
half of the 19th century.
In common with the
majority of large terrace
developments, none of the
houses survive as single-
occupancy dwellings,
having been either
converted into flats or
combined with
neighbouring houses to
form hotels.*
(AA053236)

in the 19th century, is characterised by taller houses and terraces, both to the north and south of Talbot Square. The area to the north also contains a group of large hotels (Fig 3.20, *see also* Fig 7.15). On the south side, the tall terraces, originally built as houses to provide lodgings, have often been converted into hotels, either singly or by amalgamating a number of buildings. Moving further northwards and southwards along the coast, the buildings become later in date, but this journey through time is interrupted where an earlier settlement existed. A small village, South Shore, existed by the 1830s a short distance to the north of the modern Pleasure Beach, but by the end of the 19th century it had been engulfed by the inexorable spread southwards of Blackpool.

Blackpool's expansion along the seafront is outwards, chronologically and with distinct zones of development. These include a central entertainment zone, areas of terraced housing, a group of large hotels and, at its outer edges, extensive estates of 20th-century suburban housing. Although no two resorts have the same arrangement, the broad type of development can be found in many seaside towns. For instance, the central part of the seafront at Brighton does not have the same number of large entertainment complexes as Blackpool, but it does have a broadly chronological development outwards along the seafront, with distinct areas of hotels, terracing of various 19th-century dates and modern apartments and housing at the outer edges (Fig 3.21, *see also* Fig 4.36).

Industry and the harbour

At Blackpool and Brighton resort development dominates the seafront, but at many seaside towns industry has a major presence at the heart of the town. The first resorts were created in working towns and this aspect of their story has continued alongside the new leisure industry that now forms the core of their identity. In most towns there is a desire, and usually the ability, to shield visitors from modern industry, but in small, early resorts this was not possible and probably not considered necessary. For example, in the diary of his Ramsgate holiday in 1829, Daniel Benham described the steam engine that opened the harbour sluices and his visit to the gasworks.[5] At some resorts without a harbour, the beach, these days considered the preserve of the holiday-maker, was the base for fishing fleets. This practice can still be seen, for example, at Hastings, where the eastern part of the beach still has dozens of working fishing

Fig 3.21
Brighton, East Sussex
The architectural landscape of Brighton has changed dramatically in recent years. Some of the Georgian and Victorian seafront developments are now dwarfed by a range of taller, residential buildings on and behind the seafront. (DP017946)

Fig 3.22
Net and tackle stores,
Hastings, East Sussex
*The working life of
fishermen has been a source
of amusement for visitors
since the first seaside
settlements attracted
holidaymakers. The rows of
tall net and tackle stores
form an important feature
on the working beach of
Hastings Old Town.
Repaired and rebuilt over
the centuries, the oldest of
these structures probably
dates from the 16th
century.*
(DP018021)

Fig 3.23
Beer, Devon
The steep sheltering cliffs and deep draught of Beer Roads made this picturesque village an important industrial coastal settlement for many centuries. Also famed for its hand-made lace, Beer has become a popular resort. The duality of its identity is illustrated by the zoning on the beach, where working fishing boats are separated from the areas for leisure pursuits.
(DP022289)

Fig 3.24
Harbour, Weymouth, Dorset
At the heart of Weymouth is its harbour. Once the lifeblood of the resort, until the late 18th century it was the focal point for the houses of new residents and their lodgers. However, the charms of the seafront, and the availability of building land, soon prevailed. By the end of the 18th century the most important housing schemes were being built further north (see Figs 3.5, 3.6).
(AA037566)

boats, net lofts and stalls selling fresh fish, or Beer, whose small beach has separate areas dedicated to working boats, pleasure craft and deckchairs (Figs 3.22, 3.23).

Harbours underpinned the economies of many seaside resorts, especially out of season – such as Margate's harbour, which allowed it to become the first resort to cater for a form of mass tourism, as described in Chapter 2, and which served a fishing fleet and a large number of cargo vessels. Harbours were also transport hubs, providing services along the coast and across the channel: in 1794 Weymouth became the departure point for a packet service to Guernsey and Jersey, a steam packet being introduced in 1827 (Fig 3.24).[6] Harbours also attracted visitors embarking on pleasure trips around the bay. Abigail Gawthern on holiday at Weymouth

Fig 3.25
Lifeboat House,
Lytham Road,
Blackpool,
Lancashire; 1864
Some resorts have more than one surviving lifeboat station and Blackpool has two former buildings and the current one on the promenade (see Fig 3.11). This early building was replaced in 1937 by a new one on the seafront with its own slipway.
(AA058341)

Fig 3.26
Former lifeboat
station, East Beach,
Lytham, Lancashire;
1863
Lytham's former lifeboat station, a small ecclesiastical-style building, stands beside the windmill in the heart of the open area between the sea and the resort, near the modern lifeboat station.
(DP022305)

Fig 3.27
Lifeboat station,
Aldeburgh, Suffolk;
1993
The modern approach to lifeboat station design often, though not exclusively, embraces high-tech forms. Aldeburgh's new lifeboat station houses an all-weather boat and an inshore lifeboat in two units flanking the crew facilities.
(DP022306)

described such a trip: 'I and Frank went in a boat with a civil man with a pair of oars about a mile out at sea; a lovely day, much delighted, no wind; walked after on the pier; were on the sea an hour and half'.[7]

A wide range of buildings serviced the needs of the harbour. The most common were warehouses, many of which have now become apartments, but there were also grander public buildings such as fish markets, customs houses, seamen's missions and harbour-master's offices. However, two types of working buildings, lifeboat stations and lighthouses, have been, and remain, popular destinations for visitors.

Charles Cooke, appointed in 1858 as the first architect of the Royal National Lifeboat Institution, was responsible for the introduction of the familiar, almost ecclesiastical appearance of lifeboat stations, his favoured designs resembling a church hall with large doors. In many resorts lifeboat stations closed when new, larger, main lifeboats were introduced and some have been converted to other uses. For instance, Skegness' former lifeboat station (built in 1864) has become the Smuggler's Den souvenir gift shop and Blackpool's first station (of the same year) is a rock shop (Figs 3.25, 3.26, 3.27). Other early stations are still in use, thanks to the introduction of the smaller inshore lifeboat in the 1960s; at Teignmouth the 1862 boat house, which had closed in 1940, was reacquired by the RNLI in 1991.[8]

The lighthouse is a staple motif of gifts in seaside shops, yet, apart from short lights guiding ships into harbours, only a few are now located at resorts. Examples in seaside towns may adopt the classic, tapering, cylindrical form of those found at sea, but some early examples are square or polygonal in plan, and still others are surrounded by loggias (such as the harbour lighthouse at Lowestoft and the lower lighthouse at Fleetwood; Fig 3.28). As well as adding a distinctive element to the townscape and the horizon, lighthouses were often a destination for visitors. John Allen Giles on holiday in Sussex in 1845 set off to see the nearby lighthouse:

During the two months that we spent at Burling Gap, we made an excursion in a picnic party to Beachy Head light-house, and admired the beautiful arrangement of the lights, by which ships coming home up the channel were protected from the danger of losing their way by night in these narrow seas.[9]

The impact of war

Working buildings of coastal towns are obviously contributors to the evolution of the seafront, but wars, and defences associated with them, have also left a mark, especially in the south-east of England. During the 18th century the vulnerability of the coast to a beach landing led to the creation of a haphazard collection of forts and gun platforms.[10] Thomas Turner, in his diary for

Fig 3.28
Lighthouse,
Lowestoft, Suffolk
This short lighthouse takes advantage of the hill on which it stands. It overlooks the buildings at sea level and the site of a modern caravan site.
(AA053470)

Fig 3.29
Martello tower,
Folkestone, Kent;
1805–8

*Martello towers were
around 30 feet (9.1m)
high, with tapering walls
designed to deflect cannon
shot. Their doors were set
approximately 20 feet
(6.1m) above ground level
and some towers were
strengthened by the creation
of a wide, dry moat. This
example was reused in the
Second World War as an
observation point.
(DP022307)*

1762, described a visit to the seaside and for
him the only notable event of the day was
his inspection of two newly built forts.[11]
With the outbreak of war with France in
1793 the need for an enlarged army and
improved defences was recognised. Much of
the increased military presence was concentrated in new or expanded barracks near
seaside resorts: Brighton had cavalry and
infantry barracks and Weymouth's Radipole
barracks, which housed 404 men in 1798,
was soon enlarged to accommodate 912
men and 51 officers.[12] To protect vulnerable
stretches of coastline, small circular forts
known as Martello towers, some situated in
resorts, were built along the south and east
coasts between 1805 and 1812 (Fig 3.29).[13]

Although France was a recurring threat during the 18th and early 19th centuries it was
often resorts on the more vulnerable coast-
lines that continued to grow fastest. People
who might have travelled around Europe
were now forced to stay at home, and the
presence of large numbers of officers and
their families stimulated the social life of the
towns.

Later wars had a negative impact on seaside towns. Some east-coast resorts were
shelled by the German navy in 1915, but
most damage during the First World War
was caused in raids by Zeppelins and Gotha
bombers, such as in 1917, when an air raid
on Folkestone damaged and destroyed
buildings, killing 33 people.[14] Holidaymakers at Ramsgate after the First World War
could send their loved ones a postcard
boasting that the town had suffered 119 air
raids between 1915 and 1918, killing or
injuring 138 people and causing nearly
£108,000 worth of damage.[15]

By the Second World War, advances in
weaponry increased the amount of the damage caused to resorts. For example, more
than 2,700 bombs and shells hit Margate,
destroying 238 buildings, severely damaging
541 and damaging 8,391 others (*see* Fig
2.23).[16] As well as enemy action, the seafronts of resorts were affected by the need to
install beach defences. Contemporary news
footage shows beaches covered with tangles
of barbed wire, concrete blocks and obstruc-
tions built of materials such as scaffolding
poles. Their appearance marked the final
death knell for the bathing machine and other
fragile facilities that contributed to beach life.
Pillboxes were also added to harbours at a
number of resorts such as Lowestoft and
Lyme Regis; some still survive, though most
have been demolished (Fig 3.30). Cliffs were
used for observation points and a number of
the old Martello towers were converted for
this purpose (*see* Fig 3.29).

Visitors and the form of resorts

The presence of large numbers of holidaymakers during the summer has had the most
profound affect on the character of resort
expansion. Some aspects of the impact of
visitors are considered in more detail later in
the book – Chapter 4 explores the appearance of seaside buildings, while Chapters 5,
6 and 7 deal with the architectural manifes-
tations of three types of activity particularly
associated with the seaside: health, enter-

Fig 3.30
Pillbox, Porthminster
Beach, St Ives,
Cornwall

*St Ives has a small pillbox
set into the rocks at
Porthminster Beach.
Because of its position,
shape and materials it
might not have been seen
by an approaching enemy.
(AA052785)*

tainment and accommodation. However, visitors had impacts on resort form and character in other, perhaps less obvious, ways.

During the 18th century, visitors resided within the established footprint of the town, but by the end of the century distinct areas of seaside, residential development were emerging alongside the earlier settlements. This is particularly clear at Weymouth where new terraces were built in a narrow line along the seafront, as a veneer across the northern edge of the historic town (*see* Figs 3.5, 3.6). Similarly, at Great Yarmouth – where the pre-resort centre was concentrated along the river, with the undeveloped seashore to the east – during the 19th century new resort buildings were constructed on land between the walls of the old town and the sea. While Weymouth and Great Yarmouth had their resort area attached to the side of the historic town, at

Brighton and Margate new resort development flanked the original towns (*see* Figs 3.16, 3.17). These contrasts, of course, stem from geographical factors: the earlier towns' orientation to the sea dictated where seafront development was possible, and how it might relate to the shoreline and the hub of the earlier town.

The creation of distinct resort zones continued during the 19th century. For example, Lowestoft in 1844 was still a small hilltop town with a few bathing machines on the seashore below, but a decade later Samuel Peto had built several hundred houses in a separate development on the south side of the river (Fig 3.31).[17] Whitby also has a distinct 19th-century resort zone on the cliff tops on the west side of the town, with the historic centre concentrated along the river below.

Within resorts, the seafront was predominantly the preserve of the visitor, while the

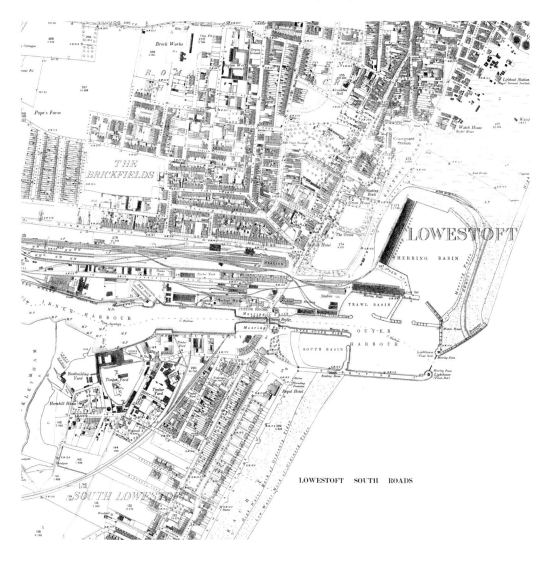

Fig 3.31
Ordnance Survey map, Lowestoft, Suffolk; 1890
The original, pre-resort town was concentrated on the north side of the river, above the harbour. With the arrival of the railway in the 1840s, Samuel Peto, the local MP and lord of the manor, began to develop the area south of the railway. He laid out high-quality, large houses on the seafront, with smaller homes in the streets behind.
(Reproduced from the 1890 Ordnance Survey map.)

inland areas were largely for residents. Where the two groups encountered each other there could be friction. Social tensions existed in the first resorts, as was the case on the Steyne at Brighton: 'the fishermen make a practice of spreading out their nets to dry; and the medley appearance of the rough sons of Peter tending their apparatus by the side of the female anglers, who are baited with all the allurement of fashion and gaiety' made a striking contrast.[18] In the competition to claim space it was the fishermen who lost out. In the 19th century respectable holidaymakers and residents feared and despised the influxes of day trippers to their resorts. William Miller had the misfortune to be at the seaside during a bank holiday and found that: 'The ordinary visitors at Teignmouth were nearly banished by the crowd which surged upon the promenade, the beach, the machines, the river – and ate and smoked on the common and danced on the pier.'[19] A resident of Scarborough said that the railway robbed it of its genteel exclusiveness, as it: 'brought a new host of invaders who were the pale, emaciated inhabitants of murky and densely populated cities seeking to restore their sickly frames to health and vigour by frequent immersion in the sea.'[20]

In large resorts and those with twin settlements, such as Brighton and Hove or Hastings and St Leonards, it was possible to have some level of separation between excursionists and polite residents. However, in other towns more or less formal attempts at social zoning were developed by directing arrivals away from polite residential areas or sometimes more overtly through measures such as enclosing and policing estates. For instance, at Scarborough a separate excursion station was created in about 1900 on the site of former goods sheds (Fig 3.32). Its purpose was to separate trainloads of trippers from the regular rail users and it allowed large numbers of visitors to reach the seafront without having to go through the centre of town. At Blackpool the building company that developed Claremont Park on the North Shore had a toll gate and policed the estate, and similar measures were introduced by Earl Radnor in his estate at Folkestone where some of his developments on the Leas still face closed, private gardens (see Figs 3.3, 3.4).[21]

Commerce

The presence of distinct communities of residents and visitors had an impact on the location and character of commercial buildings, sometimes leading to the creation of two or more centres around which new developments might be clustered. In early resorts the centre was the heart of the original town, but by the second half of the 19th century the focal point for seaside development might have shifted towards the station or a new pier. Many resorts also developed a separate commercial centre, sometimes the old high street or a new shopping street or new arcade, usually conveniently located for residents as well as visitors. For example, the Folkestone Tontine Building Company was established in 1848 to provide a new shopping street up the valley of the Pent Stream, and by 1873 the lower half of the street had been built. Once a fashionable shopping street, it is now populated by small shops and take-away restaurants, the commercial focus of the town now being on Sandgate Road. A similar development can be seen on St George's Parade in Herne Bay (Fig 3.33).

Today there is a clear divide between the shops where residents purchase their goods and those catering for visitors. The main commercial centre of resorts contains the normal range of high-street shops, though for towns of their size they often have a higher concentration of shops catering for a more price-conscious shopper. High-street brands and retail multiples do not often venture towards the beach, though there were seafront department stores at Blackpool and Morecambe. Instead shops along esplanades are usually small, single-outlet retailers on the ground floors of former houses, with the floors above often being vacant or simply used for storage (see Fig 8.1). These shops cater for the requisites of a seaside holiday,

Fig 3.32
Former excursion station, Londesborough Road, Scarborough, North Yorkshire; opened 1908

This undistinguished building was a short distance from the main station in town. From the excursion station visitors could make their way to the beach, not via the heart of the town, but down a valley where fewer genteel residents would be disturbed.
(DP006360)

such as rock, buckets and spades, and a bewildering range of unnecessary souvenirs. The pawnshop may also be more prevalent at some resorts, and is often found near amusement arcades or other types of entertainment designed to relieve visitors of their money.

By the 19th century even a small seaside town had the full range of everyday shops, probably more than in a town of a similar size without a holiday population. A guidebook to Bridlington in 1839 noted that 'The inns and shops are of a superior class; and the number of the latter is much increased by migratory traders, during the summer months'[22] In 1824 Teignmouth, a town with just 4,000 inhabitants, had five drapers, thirteen milliners, four tailors and eight bootmakers;[23] food was provided by five bakers, three brewers, seven grocers and nineteen general merchants;[24] the strong association between the seaside and health was reflected in the three chemists, two physicians and four surgeons listed. Visitors also purchased their own food at local markets: Mary Figgins, on holiday in Margate in around 1828, would go there on most days to purchase food for her landlady to cook.[25]

At Herne Bay in the 1830s it proved cheaper to obtain goods brought from Canterbury by delivery vans.[26]

Bazaars first appeared in London at the beginning of the 19th century and were soon established at a number of seaside resorts.[27] They were large spaces with counters that could be rented by traders offering fancy goods to visitors. One of the most prestigious, the Pelham Bazaar in Hastings, built in the 1820s in front of Pelham Crescent, consisted of two rows of shops flanking a central, top-lit corridor (Fig 3.34).[28] Levey's Bazaar at Margate was described in 1831 as:

> a long spacious room, with a paved floor, which in the summer renders it delightfully cool; it is lighted by windows in the roof, and is very tastefully and neatly fitted up. The length of this apartment is greatly relieved by arches thrown across it, and at the end is a splendid mirror … .This Bazaar is approached through an elegant Grecian archway, with a circular lantern at the top … [29]

Arcades of shops reminiscent of their illustrious predecessors in London also appeared at some seaside resorts. One of the

Fig 3.33
St George's Parade, Herne Bay, Kent
St George's Parade – in front of St George's Terrace, which was built in the 1830s – contained a number of shops as well as a circulating library, assembly rooms and baths. The current buildings provide little more than a hint of the original arrangement. (AA052789)

Fig 3.34
Pelham Crescent,
Hastings, East Sussex;
1820s

*This development contains
two important facilities for
visitors. The long narrow
building in front was the
Pelham Bazaar. Behind is
a rare example of a church
at the heart of a major
seafront development.*
(DP018012)

longest arcades to be built at the seaside was the 'Royal Arcades' at Weston-super-Mare: it was largely destroyed by bombing during the Second World War, but the shorter Royal Victoria Arcade of 1835 still survives at Ryde. The grandest example surviving at the seaside is the 1896 Wayfarer's Arcade, opening off Lord Street in the heart of Southport (Fig 3.35).[30]

Religion

Shops were important features of seaside towns, but notable absentees from most seafronts are churches, though they were included in two significant developments at Hastings in the 1820s, in Pelham Crescent, and in the new resort at St Leonards (*see* Fig 3.34). Their absence is not surprising. In the first resorts, visitors made use of an existing church, which was usually inland at the heart of the original town or in the village a mile or two from the coast. The author of a guide to Herne Bay in 1835 noted that 'The want of a church is much felt, the residents having to walk upwards of two miles to attend public worship'.[31] As

towns grew, new churches were required, but central seafront locations had already been occupied and developers seem to have been unwilling to part with a prime site for something that brought no financial return. A desire to maintain a certain distance from any potential indiscretions taking place on the beach might also have been an influence on the absence of churches. The modern seaside resort has been described as 'a liminal environment … where the usual constraints on respectability and decorum in public behaviour might be pushed aside in the interests of holiday hedonism'.[32] There is evidence that this has always been so: saucy poems about ladies bathing at Scarborough were published as early as the 1730s and a directory for Brighton published in 1770 described how one adventurous man ventured into the ladies' bathing area only to be expelled vigorously by the dippers and the bathers.[33] Clearly 'the usual constraints' were already being challenged in the 18th century.

Formal religious institutions may be absent from most seafronts, but the beach was a place where more informal religious

Fig 3.35
Wayfarer's Arcade, Southport, Merseyside; 1896
This structure, reminiscent of a large winter garden,
provides the grandest setting for shopping at the seaside.
Set on Lord Street, which is lined with shops, it is a far cry
in character and location from the seafront souvenir shops
that dominate the seafronts of most resorts. Its grandeur
seems to owe more to its need to cater for commuters to
Liverpool rather than seaside visitors. (AA002818)

gatherings took place. At Worthing there was a post that until recently bore a sign stating 'STAND RESERVED FOR THE DELIVERY OF SERMONS AND PUBLIC SPEECHES'. On the seafront nearer the pier there is a commemorative stone that records that the Salvation Army had preached the gospel to fishermen since 1896 (Fig 3.36).

Preaching on the beach may have been adequate for visitors, but the growing numbers of residents at seaside towns required new churches. At Herne Bay in 1835 there was only a modest Gothic chapel and another smaller one for 'dissenters'.[34] These were inadequate and as early as 1831 measures were in hand to remedy the situation: 'It is also intended to proceed forthwith to build a New Church, on a piece of ground which has been given for that purpose by Sir Henry Oxenden.'[35] By 1835 another author reported that 'The large church, already

begun, stands on ground marked out for Oxenden Square, Sir Henry Oxenden having, very liberally, granted a piece of ground for that purpose'.[36] Like so many other aspects of Herne Bay this venture was not completed.

Oxenden provided a site at the heart of his new development, and some seaside resorts had churches on similarly prominent, but inland, sites. At Margate most visitors initially attended the old parish church at the top of the town, but a new large church, Holy Trinity Church, was added in 1825–8 in the centre of Trinity Square. During the 19th century a large Baptist church was built on the north side of Cecil Square, while another, Wesleyan, chapel was built on Hawley Square (Fig 3.37). The most striking location for a seaside church is St Peter's at Brighton, which dominates the north end of the Steyne. This grand,

Fig 3.36
Salvation Army gathering, Blackpool, Lancashire; 1946–55. Photographer: John Gay

In their tailored uniforms, on what seems like a stiflingly hot summer's day, the Salvation Army runs a beach mission for children. The song on the chart is that old favourite, 'All Things Bright And Beautiful'. (AA047908)

Gothic-revival church ranks among the most substantial churches of its period, but most churches in resorts seem to be fairly standard in size, style and form. Most are set within the communities they were built to serve, rather than being established for the benefit of visitors, though they would have expected to attract visitors (Fig 3.38). However, the Chapel Royal in Brighton, which opened in 1795, was only open during the holiday season and at Weston-super-Mare the church, which was rebuilt in 1824, had pews that were purchased by lodging houses for the use of their guests.[37] At least one church made more substantial provision for visitors. At Margate, the medieval church of St John the Baptist had to be reordered and additional services provided:

From the great resort of company, and for their accommodation, seats have been erected in the middle chancel, and at the west end of the middle aile; prayers are also read every Wednesday and Friday, and an additional sermon preached every Sunday by the present curate; for which extra duty (and also considering that he hath no other remuneration), it is expected that visitors should subscribe to his book, which is left at different libraries.[38]

There have also been small communities from a number of other faiths in some seaside resorts of which Judaism has left the most concrete and oldest marks. Brighton had its first synagogue in Jew Street in 1792 and at the beginning of the 21st century has the fifth largest Jewish population in

Fig 3.37
Baptist Chapel, Cecil Square, Margate, Kent; mid-19th century
The chapel, seen here from the rear, was a prominent feature on the north side of Cecil Square. Built to cater for the rapidly expanding resort, its central location, opposite the assembly rooms, suggests some accommodation has been reached between faith and fun.
(AA050230)

PRAY FOR THE SOUL OF WILLIAM WALKER.

Fig 3.38
View of Blackpool
Tower, Church of the
Sacred Heart, Talbot
Road, Blackpool,
Lancashire; church
built by EW Pugin in
1857, enlarged in
1894 by Pugin and
Pugin
*This is a rare example of
a church acknowledging
its seaside location. This
window, a memorial to
William Walker, shows
the seafront before late
20th-century developments.
(AA052996)*

England.[39] Bournemouth, which also has a large Jewish population, has also been a popular destination for Jewish visitors. This explains the presence of a large synagogue, founded in 1911, as well as kosher hotels, including the former New Ambassador, which was reputedly the largest kosher hotel in Europe.

The influence of transport on resort expansion

Transport links were instrumental in determining the form of seaside developments because they facilitated sometimes extraordinary levels of growth, fuelled by the rising tide of visitors, and because of the impact the transport routes and hubs had on the geography of the seaside town. The impact on resort development of improved methods

of transport, which brought in growing numbers of visitors, was arguably greater than in any other type of settlement. In all towns, railway lines interrupted existing urban patterns and created new ones, taking over large areas for sidings and yards, and acting as barriers and as axes for the alignment of new developments.[40] In most seaside towns railways either ran broadly parallel or perpendicular to the coast, depending on whether the line continued or terminated at the resort. For example at Southend and Whitstable two separate lines at 90 degrees to each other served the towns: a through-line parallel to the coast and another that terminated in each resort (Fig 3.39). In contrast, Cleethorpes, Walton on the Naze and Hunstanton had lines that ran parallel to the coast, but terminated in the town: this was a consequence of location and economic concerns, each resort being the final place en route that would merit the financial investment necessary to construct the line. Where railways passed through seaside towns, the line generally ran parallel to the coast, usually at a distance from the sea established by geographical features, or at the edge of the town as it existed when the railway arrived. At Dawlish and Colwyn Bay the impact of the line on the resort was secondary to the imperatives of the railway as a whole. At these seaside towns, the cost of engineering the main line was reduced by following the coast and so the course of the railway line is close to the sea, partially cutting off the town from the seafront – an arrangement that could scarcely have improved the resort in the eyes of its visitors.

Most resorts had simple rail layouts, but in towns where there was a need to overcome particular geographical features more complicated layouts were created.[41] At Felixstowe, Folkestone, Lowestoft, Morecambe and Weymouth, the added complexity was due to the need to provide access both to the town for visitors and to the port for freight. The largest resorts, such as Brighton, Blackpool or Weston-super-Mare, developed complex layouts due to the presence of separate, often competing lines, delivering large numbers of visitors to the heart of the resort. At Ramsgate and Cromer there were separate stations on or near the seafront supplementing the main station serving the town, and Scarborough's excursion station was a short distance from the sea and the town centre (Fig 3.40, *see also* Fig 3.32).

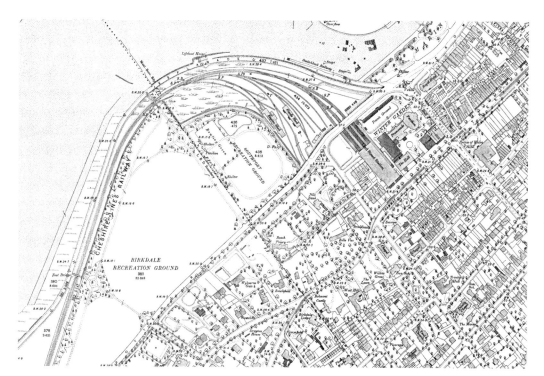

Fig 3.39
Ordnance Survey
map, Southport,
Merseyside; 1894

*Southport's railway line
ran along the coast, but at
the town performed a tight
loop to reach the station.
It was located to be
convenient for the seafront
and Lord Street, the main
shopping thoroughfare of
the resort. (Reproduced
from the 1894 Ordnance
Survey map.)*

Fig 3.40
Ordnance Survey
map, Ramsgate, Kent;
1898

*The seafront station,
Ramsgate Sands, allowed
visitors direct access to the
beach. A second station,
serving the town, was
located a short distance
inland above the seafront.
(Reproduced from the 1898
Ordnance Survey map.)*

Fig 3.41
Station, Saltburn-by-
Sea, Cleveland; 1861,
William Peachey

The railway station was at
the heart of the resort (see
Figs 2.19, 2.20). William
Peachey designed it for the
Stockton and Darlington
Railway and began to lay
out the new town to the
north of it.
(DP006385)

Within towns, railways established an alternative axis to which streets might be aligned. As a result, the plans of some resorts were partly dictated by strong, parallel or perpendicular axes to the coast and the railway, sometimes cutting across the grain of earlier features such as the alignment of former field boundaries or building plots as parcelled up for resort development. At Saltburn and Herne Bay the stations were the focal points for the layout of part of the town (Fig 3.41, *see* Fig 2.19); from around 1900 the streets in Herne Bay emanated from the station, creating a sunburst pattern.[42] At Brighton, Queen's Road was created as a wide, main route from the station towards the sea and the parallel streets around it rapidly filled with new housing.[43] The arrival of visitors *en masse* brought changes to the character of existing streets, where the road connecting the station to the seafront might be transformed, perhaps from a genteel row of villas, into a centre for shops, refreshments and entertainment.

The effects of transport on resort form continued with the spread of the motor car, which created new types of problems and opportunities. The freedom offered by car ownership changed the pattern of travel within towns and allowed more people to travel to, and live in, settlements without a railway station. Towns and cities began to spread rapidly as people were able to live further from the centre, and in degrees of isolation from one another, so creating suburbia. Of course, most towns developed extensive suburbs, but the seaside acquired its own particular variation as a direct consequence of the car, a form of suburbia independent of existing resorts. Plotlands allowed people who could not afford to purchase a property in the heart of a resort, or did not wish to live in the more formal environment of a seaside town, the opportunity to reside, temporarily or permanently, at the seaside. Keeping costs down inevitably brought a poor standard of architecture and design, and although to the modern eye these settlements have a certain charm, some contemporaries felt they were an abomination. Laurie Lee reported how, en route from Gloucestershire to London, he decided to go along the south coast as he had never seen the sea:

[Image content]

The South Coast, even so, was not what I'd been led to expect – from reading Hardy and Jeffery Farnol – for already it had begun to develop that shabby shoreline suburbia which was part of the whimsical rot of the Thirties. Here were the sea-shanty-towns, sprawled like a rubbishy tidemark, the scattered litter of land and ocean – miles of tea-shacks and bungalows, apparently built out of wreckage, and called 'Spindrift' or 'Sprite O' The Waves'.[44]

Plotlands were established, particularly on the south and east coasts, for a variety of reasons and through various mechanisms. For example, Peacehaven was conceived as a commemoration of the horrors of the First World War and was originally to be named Anzac-on-Sea.[45] Contemporary commentators thought it was far from being a fitting memorial: CEM Joad described it as 'a pigsty of hideously coloured bungalows, shacks and even tents, set down, without rhyme or reason, in a fair, green land'.[46] Similarly, at Jaywick and Jaywick Sands, beside Clacton-on-Sea, large plotlands were established, the streets of the latter being named after models of cars (see Fig 3.9).[47] These settlements were populated with more or less haphazard bungalows and cabins, but some plotlands used former railway carriages as houses: before the Second World War they were common at Bungalow Town at Shoreham by Sea, while at Sutton on Sea three houses made from carriages still survive, including a two-storied house (Fig 3.42).[48]

Cars increased opportunity, but they also caused problems. Uncontrolled sprawl exercised planners concerned to protect the character of their towns and their fringes.[49] In 1938 an essay entitled 'Leisure as an Architectural Problem' analysed the planning challenges facing the seaside: 'Bungalow colonies, camps, city refuse dumps and general ribbon development along coastal roads all contribute to the general decomposing process which will soon leave very little of England's 1,800 miles of coastline that is not irreparably damaged.'[50] Another writer in 1936 described the first Butlins holiday camp as 'a remarkable venture', but cautioned against the spread of Elizabethan-style chalets to Dorset cliffs or a Cornish cove.[51] However, on some stretches of England's coast, caravan sites and chalet settlements have merged into vast, seemingly uncontrolled settlements (Fig 3.43, see also Figs 7.27 and 7.28).

Fig 3.42
Marsoville, Lindum and Wavelands, Furlongs Road, Sutton On Sea, Lincolnshire; 1901
These three substantial houses, built from old Great Eastern railway carriages, were to serve as holiday homes and they are still occupied. The first and third houses have an upper storey, formed in the case of Wavelands by two more carriages. (DP022294)

Cars also created problems within towns. The formerly neutral area between the sea and the town, once inhabited by amusements or gardens, has often been transformed into an expanse of bland car parking, 'an annoying barricade between the visitor and the sea'.[52] The promenade that ran along the seafront became a busy road carrying a constant stream of cars along the length of the resort. Although it might be an appealing idea to return this space to pedestrians, the reality is that the traffic in most resorts would grind to a halt without it (*see* Fig 3.15).

While the station became the emblem of the newly arrived railway, the car's primary architectural contribution to the heart of resorts has been the car park. In 1931 the country's first underground car park was built near the seafront at Hastings, with space for up to 600 cars.[53] In 1936 the annual report of the British Association for the Advancement of Science observed that Blackpool did not have enough car parks;[54] to correct this, Talbot Road multi-storey car park and bus station was designed by GW Stead and built in 1937–9, a rare example of a multi-storey car park outside London or a major industrial city before the Second World War.[55]

Conclusion

The presence of the sea and the natural form of the coastline defined the form of all emergent resorts and had profound effects on their ensuing development. The impact of visitors, arguably less immediate or dramatic, was no less profound, although its effects have been more varied and sometimes more subtle. Combined, they have created a special and highly distinctive form of settlement. The familiar town pattern of concentric rings of development applies to some extent in resorts, but the lure of the sea has stretched the shape of these towns along the coastline. The premium of a seafront location has influenced expansion and created sea-facing buildings that are frequently taller, larger and more expensive than houses a few yards away in streets leading back from the sea. Some seaside resorts, unencumbered by geographical concerns and the presence of earlier settlements, have regular plans with dense grids of streets aligned to the sea and the major seafront road. Where there was an historic settlement onto which resort functions were grafted, the familiar, haphazard layout of an older settlement survives in the centre of the town. In the outer parts of the settlement greater regularity will be obvious in new developments promoted by the arrival of railways in the mid-19th century and the car during the 20th century.

Resorts contain traces of the progress of their visitors through time. The first wealthy visitors prompted development in the central part of the town, and the emergence of substantial terraces and squares on its edges. In the 18th century the seafront still appeared in its natural, largely unspoilt, state, with the beach often leading directly to the first line of buildings. At many resorts, it may have been a focus for conflict between the interests of local industry and those of visitors, as demonstrated by the competition for the beach at Hastings. With the democratisation of the seaside during the 19th century wealthier residents and visitors preferred to move out of the centre into quieter, more exclusive areas above and behind the town, or to resorts unaffected by the arrival of holidaymakers *en masse*. In some resorts, this process led to the creation of closed estates, but in other places the means of segregation were more subtle, perhaps involving channelling visitors down particular thoroughfares, from their point of arrival to the sea. The seafront, now the unchallenged domain of the visitor, was transformed during the 19th century. Sea defences were built, suppressing the natural, ever-changing face of the seafront and imposing a new regularity on the shoreline. The promenade, the by-product of this new relationship between land and sea, at first a place for promenading, was soon transformed into an arena for new facilities demanded by growing numbers of holidaymakers.

Today, the seafront remains at the heart of the seaside holiday. Visitors emerge from the hotels and bed and breakfasts that line the seafront and the streets behind, struggle across a large road on to the promenade where they find entertainment, food and, in inclement weather, shelter. Looking out to sea, or gazing at the bodies on the beach, holidaymakers are perhaps unaware that they are standing on a massive piece of civil engineering. Seaside resorts stand at the edge of nature, facing the untamed beauty of the sea. The desire for this proximity, to be beside the sea, has created something special: only at the seaside does our dense urban environment meet, so abruptly, the uncompromising and overwhelming natural domain.

Fig 3.43 *(opposite)* Aerial photo of Ingoldmells, Lincolnshire
In 1974 the coast between Cleethorpes and Skegness had 21,000 caravans, 8 per cent of the national total. The impact of this vast number of caravans on the ground can be witnessed in Figures 7.27 and 7.28. (NMR17471/15)

61

4

The architectural styles of seaside buildings

The 20th century saw the beginnings of an interest in the architecture of the seaside resort: for example, in 1908 *The Architectural Review* posed the question 'What is our seaside architecture?'[1] Although there were many books published in the ensuing century that proclaimed the joys of seaside architecture, typically these only examined a discrete selection of seaside buildings: those designed to entertain the visitor, and usually sited on the seafront or promenade. Is this how seaside architecture should be defined? Is it, indeed, simply a collection of fairly conventional buildings embellished with decoration from the florid end of the prevailing style? Or does a broader spectrum of distinctive seaside architecture exist, beyond the spotlight of the promenade? Should the question, more accurately, seek to consider/discuss seaside *architectures*?

The term 'architecture' covers various categories of resort buildings – for example those associated with work and defence, those linked directly to tourism, and the wide range of domestic buildings. However, the first of these examples can be found equally at working ports, where the economy is not driven primarily by tourism, while defences were erected widely, to protect vulnerable stretches of coastline rather than resorts *per se*. Both categories add an architectural dimension to seaside towns and serve as curiosities for visitors, but do not in themselves define the distinctive architecture of resorts. This is to be found in the unassuming house and the multiplicity of entertainment buildings.

The vast majority of buildings in resorts were built for residents and to accommodate visitors. Although houses were required to perform both functions, and were often the venue for a range of other services, their plan forms still followed those of houses found all over England. However, those nearest the seafront, where most visitors preferred to seek accommodation, were consistently taller, with additional storeys incorporated into their design, and placed a greater emphasis on the treatment of fenestration. This exploited sea views and fresh air, providing landlords with higher financial returns, as well as catering for the desire, of both visitors and residents, to watch the social scene unfolding on the streets and seafront below.

Facilities for entertaining visitors led the way in extravagance. The first visitors to resorts were entertained in makeshift facilities, many of which were scarcely superior to outbuildings. These were soon replaced by purpose-built buildings in the prevailing style of the period: though they were often more decorative than contemporary buildings in less fun-loving towns, and seaside buildings have been regularly replaced, or renewed, as visitor numbers have grown and tastes have changed. A theme of exoticism, stemming from the Royal Pavilion at Brighton, permeates the design of seaside entertainment buildings, not only in terms of the motifs employed, but also in the taste for exuberant interiors and exteriors.

Before considering in more detail the architectural styles adopted in seaside resorts, it is necessary to trace how the buildings of these towns accreted during the 18th and 19th centuries. The story is one of increasing confidence in the seaside as a place to visit, and more crucially, for resort buildings, as suitable places in which to invest.

The vocabulary of resort expansion

The impact of the first visitors to resorts was initially limited to small-scale building, such as the refurbishment of existing buildings, the construction of a few new houses in a pre-existing street, an extension to an inn to serve as an assembly room, or the conversion of a barn into a theatre. New development, restricted at first to a town's historic centre, could only occur piecemeal, as single plots of land or the site of an old building became available for construction. Addi-

Fig 4.1
Beach Street, Deal,
Kent
In this central, Georgian part of the seafront no two houses are the same in terms of size, shape or colour, producing a kaleidoscopically chaotic face to the sea. (DP022295)

tionally, few individuals with the means to invest in early resorts had confidence that the vogue for sea bathing would last and therefore speculators seem to have been unwilling and unable to risk financial outlay in large schemes. The results of this can be seen, for example, at Beach Street in Deal, which runs along the seafront, and which has an irregular cluster of older houses near the heart of the resort, flanked by more-orderly, 19th-century terraces, built by entrepreneurs who enjoyed greater confidence in the seaside phenomenon (Fig 4.1).

After an initial phase of haphazard devel-opment within or immediately beside an existing town, most construction in resorts took place on open land, allowing builders a relatively free hand in the layout of schemes. Most new developments in the 18th century comprised terraces set out along the sea-front or on a cliff top, but some larger schemes were built around squares set fur-ther inland, effectively establishing alterna-tive centres for the social heart of the resort. For example, Cecil Square in Margate, built in 1769, contained the Assembly Rooms, 'a row of decent shops' and large houses built for fashionable families, including the Duke

Fig 4.2
Cecil Square,
Margate, Kent; 1769
onwards
The Duke of Cumberland's house still dominates the west side of the square and is distinguished from others by a pediment over its three central bays. Cecil Square was a coordinated development, but Hawley Square (see Fig 4.12), laid out a few years later, developed in a more piecemeal fashion. (AA049298)

Fig 4.3
Oxenden Square,
Herne Bay, Kent

This square was laid out in the 1830s and construction work began at one corner. However, it was soon halted and it was never completed as a polite Georgian square. Instead, the central part is a park and the sides are lined with a variety of 20th-century houses.
(DP022296)

of Cumberland (Fig 4.2).[2] The square remained a key feature of resort expansion in the 19th century. For instance, at Herne Bay the new town of St Augustine's, laid out in the early 1830s, comprised a regular grid plan with the northern part of the design incorporating a chain of three squares linked by short roads.[3] This ambitious scheme was never completed, although its footprint has survived in the modern layout of the town (Fig 4.3).

The crescent is a particular architectural form associated with towns catering for visi-

tors. Often conceived as a centrepiece in ambitious developments, most deferred to the architectural fashion for uniformity, with consistent detail employed across the façade. But where the limited controls of the speculative building system failed, treatments could be haphazard and even chaotic (Fig 4.4). A typical crescent contained a single continuous terrace of housing, but others deviated to include a centrepiece with a contrasting function. For instance, a hotel forms the central features of Hesketh Crescent in Torquay, Pelham Crescent at

Fig 4.4
Nelson Crescent,
Ramsgate, Kent; early
19th century

Nelson Crescent has a series of houses of four stories with basements, tall sash windows and canopied balconies on the first floor, but there the unity ends. No two houses are the same in their detailing or even the levels of their windows.
(DP022297)

Fig 4.5
The Den,
Teignmouth, Devon;
1825–6
This late 19th-century photograph of the Den shows the Assembly Rooms in the foreground with one of the two quadrants of the crescent behind. In the distance is Cockram's Hotel, which was demolished in 1988 and replaced by a block of flats that echoes the shape of its predecessor.
(BB82/13455B)

Hastings has a detached chapel separating two quadrants of the crescent, and Teignmouth's Den Crescent had the Assembly Rooms at its heart (Fig 4.5, *see also* 3.34). A further variation appeared at Montpelier Crescent in Brighton, where a series of large, semi-detached houses, with or without linking blocks, produced a composition similar to the Paragon at Blackheath.

A small number of resort towns, initially those on the south coast, employed a layout specifically designed to exploit the seafront location. The three-sided square (Fig 4.6), with the fourth side to the sea left undeveloped for sea views, first appears in the early 19th century, inspired by the Steyne at Brighton: the open area at the east side of the pre-resort town, around which much of the earliest, fashionable construction was arranged, including the Royal Pavilion. Two early examples even adopt the name as well: the New Steine at Brighton and the Steyne at Worthing. Further afield this form was adopted at Weston-super-Mare, where Ellenborough Park has villas on two sides, with Ellenborough Crescent at the landward end of development. Scarborough also has smaller examples, though they are too far inland to benefit from a prominent sea view. Brighton has two examples of a grandiose variation on the open-ended square, with crescents attached to the seaward ends of the development. At the west end of Brighton Palmyra Square and Adelaide

Fig 4.6
Regency Square,
Brighton, East Sussex;
1818–28
In Regency Square, one of the largest three-sided squares, Georgian terraces enclose a huge garden. The rear part of the square is bounded by a palace-fronted terrace, while the sides have more haphazard arrangements of terrace houses. (DP017951)

Crescent form the composition, while at the east end of the town this is achieved by Sussex Square and Lewes Crescent, which form the heart of Kemp Town (Figs 4.7, 4.8).

The principal change that took place in the layout of towns between the mid-18th century and the mid-19th century was a shift from small-scale, piecemeal development to large-scale, speculative schemes. Confidence in investment was an essential prerequisite for this transformation. While the seaside was a new fad in 1750, it was a well-established phenomenon a century later. Early development was haphazard as single entrepreneurs or house owners sought to improve or rebuild their properties, but by the 19th century landowners and wealthy speculators were taking the lead in the now rapid expansion of resorts.

Resort development may have changed during the 18th and 19th centuries as confidence grew, but another factor that influenced the growth of resorts was the pattern of landownership. For example, Blackpool and Southport had comparable origins in the second half of the 18th century, but by the end of the 19th century they were almost at

opposite ends of the social spectrum. Their differing evolution can, in part, be ascribed to the patterns of landownership; Southport had two dominant land-owners while Blackpool, after enclosure in 1767, was shared between 108 proprietors. Southport subsequently came under the control of a small number of wealthy citizens, but 'the whole central area of Blackpool became an ill-planned mass of small properties, boarding houses, small shops, working-class terraces, and so on, with no space for the grand public buildings, broad avenues and gardens of Southport'.[4] The pattern of ownership is still reflected in buildings today. At Weymouth, for instance, the corporation leased out seafront land to developers on long leases, leading to the erection of a series of large, unified terraces facing the sea. Where terraces in resorts are under the control of the local authority the unity of the original conception is evident through the regularity of the fenestration and the colour of the paintwork. However, where individual houses in the terraces are in separate ownership, owners have often opted for different colours and architectural detailing (Fig 4.9).

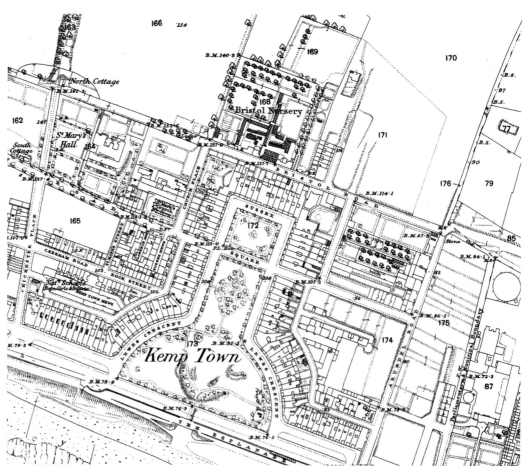

Fig 4.7
Kemp Town,
Brighton, East Sussex;
1823 onwards. Amon
Wilds and Charles
Augustus Busby
*(Reproduced from the 1877
Ordnance Survey map.)*

Fig 4.8
Lewes Crescent,
Kemp Town,
Brighton, East Sussex;
1823 onwards. Amon
Wilds and Charles
Augustus Busby
*This variation on the
theme of the three-sided
square is only found at
Brighton, where the
aristocratic visitors and
residents wanted grand
houses like their homes in
London. Thomas Read
Kemp made this 'square'
the centrepiece of his
exclusive development,
which tried to emulate
John Nash's Regent's
Park. (DP017940)*

Fig 4.9
Britannia Terrace,
Great Yarmouth;
1848–55
*This palace-fronted terrace
was built following the
construction of a sea wall
in 1847 by the local
landowner, Charles Cory.
It is an extreme example of
a terrace built as a unified
design that has fallen
victim of the tastes of
individual occupiers.
(DP022298)*

Fig 4.11 (opposite)
Meeting House Lane,
Brighton, East Sussex

*The area of the earliest
settlement in Brighton is
identifiable today as the
Laines, a group of narrow,
irregularly laid-out streets
with some surviving
timber-framed buildings.
(DP017965)*

Domestic architecture in Georgian and Victorian resorts

The first resorts began as small working towns, or as John Byng snootily described them 'fishing holes'.[5] These first resorts each had their own distinctive character, reflecting the status of the towns, the prevailing local styles and the locally available building materials. Whereas Scarborough, which had been entertaining visitors to its spa since the 1620s, had basic facilities in place by 1734, Margate was described in 1723 as 'a small fishing Town, irregularly built, and the houses very low'.[6] A map of the same year shows a town that was huddled around the edge of the sea and along three main streets running inland, with the parish church above the town (*see* Fig 2.4). It had a variety of timber-framed and flint buildings, the oldest surviving house probably being the 16th-century Tudor House on King Street. Nearer the sea in King Street there is a two-storied knapped-flint building with brick dressings, dating from the 1680s, and an early brick building survives in Lombard Street, beside the market (Fig 4.10). The other early resort, Brighton, had grown

little since the infamous French attack in 1514, and in the late 18th century still occupied the area known today as the Laines (Fig 4.11).[7] In 1761 Anthony Relhan provided a concise description of Brighton in his history of the town:

> The town at present consists of six principal streets, many lanes, and some places surrounded with houses, called by the inhabitants squares. The great plenty of flint stones on the shore, and in the cornfields near the town, enabled them to build the walls of their houses with that material, when in their most impoverished state; and their present method of ornamenting the windows and doors with the admirable brick which they burn for their own use, has a very pleasing effect.[8]

Some visitors to seaside towns were intrigued by vernacular styles, but no matter how attractive these quaint cottages appeared, the desire for the type of comfortable accommodation they enjoyed in London or at home was stronger. Residents began to build or rebuild houses to make them more appealing to the growing influx of visitors. Relhan witnessed the start of this process at Brighton:

Fig 4.10
8–9 Lombard Street,
Margate, Kent; late
17th century

*This two-storied house was
built of brick with pilasters
and arches decorating the
upper floor. Once probably
one of the most
distinguished buildings
beside the market, it has
since been dwarfed by
newer developments.
(AA050156)*

The town improves daily, as the inhabitants encouraged by the late great resort of company, seem disposed to expend the whole of what they acquire in the erecting of new buildings, or making the old ones convenient. And should the increase of these, in the next seven years, be equal to what it has been in the last, it is probable there will be but few towns in England, that will excel this in commodious buildings.[9]

In 1791 Edward Clarke noted the improvements that were beginning at Weymouth: while he felt that the town as a whole was 'a little, narrow, dirty place, ill-paved and irregularly built', he observed that 'the new street, called the Esplanade, is well situated, and facing the sea, has a handsome appearance'.[10] Not all early resorts were improving quickly enough to satisfy visitors, however. For example, William Thornber described building work that was beginning to take place at Blackpool in the 1830s, but he bemoaned the pace of development:

Great improvements were made in the appearance of the village; shops beautified and increased in number, cottages ornamented and built upon a more modern construction … . Neatness and ornament, however, was not the order of the day – the turf-stack and dunghill kept their hereditary site, from which they were not displaced without much persuasion and angry debate; as for trelliswork, verandahs, or other fancy appendages, there was a total dearth.[11]

The presence of visitors and new residents had a direct impact on every resort. They brought in new fashions and activities as well as new architectural forms, all derived ultimately from London and major spa towns. A guidebook of 1770, for example, noted that in Margate some houses had been built to emulate contemporary buildings in parts of London and Westminster.[12] By the early 19th century most new development at seaside towns resembled the most fashionable London suburbs of the period. It is easy to find parallels for south-coast terraces of the late 18th or early 19th century in Camden, Islington or Dulwich, and houses built later in the 19th century have obvious parallels with new estates being developed in west London. The constant is that seaside developers wished to emulate the latest residential fashions in the capital and replicate what visitors were used to, or aspired to, in London (Fig 4.12).

South-eastern resorts were clearly within the architectural orbit of London, but more distant resorts such as Weston-super-Mare or Teignmouth drew their visitors, their investment and their architectural inspiration from Bristol and Bath. A key part of the annual social cycle in the 18th century, Bath had a major influence on the appearance and layout of Georgian seaside towns. German author Johanna Schopenhauer saw its influence, perhaps erroneously, in the architecture of Brighton:

Rows of spacious houses for visitors, all under one continuous roof, give the impression of a grand single palace. One forms a crescent with a pleasant view towards the sea and there are several terraces, and the so-called parade for strolling, with these handsome houses on one side and the ocean on the other. It is laid out much in the pattern of Bath, only on a smaller scale.[13]

By the third quarter of the 18th century buildings of greater architectural distinction began to appear in resorts. One of the earliest was East Cliff House (1760–2), built on a platform that had previously formed part of the East Fort at Hastings (Fig 4.13).[14] The house is two storied with polygonal bays at either end of the façade and originally had elaborate interiors, though these fittings have since been removed. Margate was growing rapidly, usually by the construction of fairly conventional Georgian houses, although India House was a more interesting building, apparently influenced by contemporary houses being built on the

Fig 4.12 *(opposite)* 31–7 Hawley Square, Margate, Kent; 1770s–1780s
Margate's second square, Hawley Square, was gradually developed during the 1770s and 1780s. The tall, but rather austere, houses were built in a style and on a scale reminiscent of the expanding suburbs of London. (AA050144)

Fig 4.13 East Cliff House, Rock-a-Nore Road, Hastings, East Sussex; 1760–2
This once grand house sits on the seafront, behind the area still dominated by net lofts and fishing boats. Its creator, Edward Capell, was a Shakespeare scholar who spent his summers at Hastings. (DP018019)

Fig 4.14
India House,
12 Hawley Street,
Margate, Kent; c.1766
*India House is a very
different type of building
from the plain,
conventional houses being
constructed elsewhere in the
town. It was built by
Captain John Gould
(1722–84), a wealthy tea-
planter and it is reputed to
be a copy of his house in
Calcutta.*
(AA050186)

Fig 4.15
Marlborough House,
54 Old Steine,
Brighton, East Sussex;
1786–7, Robert Adam
*This was the grandest
house in Brighton before
the Prince Regent built the
Royal Pavilion a short
distance to the north.
Originally built in 1765,
it was remodelled in a neo-
classical style in the 1780s
for the MP William
'Single-Speech' Hamilton.*
(DP017968)

sub-continent (Fig 4.14). The most prestigious of the first generation of substantial houses was Marlborough House on the Steine at Brighton, built between 1765 and 1769 as a large Georgian townhouse, and rebuilt in a grander style by Robert Adam in 1786–7 (Fig 4.15).[15]

These were exceptional buildings. Most early housing developments took the form of long, severe terraces, usually three or four storied, sometimes with a taller *piano nobile*, and normally astylar. Early visual sources and examination of their fabric show that many of their façades have since been gradually, sometimes haphazardly, altered. For example, Fortfield Terrace at Sidmouth, which was built in the 1790s, is shown in the Long Painting of 1814 as being plain (*see* Fig 1.4), though a balcony had been added to one house.[16] Its façade was enlivened by the addition of canopied balconies in 1850, when it was also stuccoed. Balconies applied to the *piano nobile* were the predominant choice in Georgian houses, especially in the south of England, but in many south-coast resorts an alternative preference is reflected in bewildering arrays of bay and oriel windows. These can be single or multi-storied, curved or polygonal and were found in combination with balconies by the mid-19th century. Polygonal bay windows adorned East Cliff House, where they echoed the current practice of country house and villa design, but by about 1800 most houses employed semicircular or elliptical bays. Later in the 19th century the polygonal bay window became standard, often rising through the full height of the house. Although bays and balconies might adorn the exterior of buildings, their

primary function was to allow people inside the buildings to enjoy the view, the sea air and the social comings and goings below (Figs 4.16, 4.17).

Most substantial, late-18th-century terraces were astylar, but by the first half of the 19th century some new developments show greater aesthetic ambition. The earliest example of a palace-fronted terrace at the seaside appears to be the Royal Terrace at Southend (1791), with its four-bay centre-piece topped with a pediment and a pair of end pavilions, one of which forms the body of the Royal Hotel. Its inspiration was palace-fronted streets such as Portland Square in London (1776), and Milsom Street (1781–3) and Great Pulteney Street (1789) in Bath. In the early 19th century, Brighton, or at least its suburbs, led the way in the development of the prestige terrace. Kemp Town and Brunswick Town both provided large terraced houses behind the grandest palace fronts found at the seaside. Their inspiration was developments in London such as John Nash's Regent's Street and Regent's Park, or Thomas Cubitt's Eaton Square (Fig 4.18).

Palace fronts enjoyed a brief heyday during the second quarter of the 19th century. In the south-east, Brighton, St Leonards and Ramsgate had the most substantial

Fig 4.16
Fortfield Terrace, Sidmouth, Devon; begun 1790, balconies added 1850, Michael Novosielski

Novosielski was involved with the construction of this terrace for Thomas Jenkins, the lord of the manor, at the time of his death in 1795. Set on a slope a short distance from the sea, it seems to have been meant to be aloof from activity on the seafront.
(DP022299)

Fig 4.17
Buenos Ayres, Margate, Kent; 1803
Two-, three- and four-storied bay windows were added to this terrace at various dates in the 19th century.
(AA049285)

schemes, but terraces and crescents with palace fronts appeared all over the country (Fig 4.19, *see also* Fig 4.9). For example, The Crescent at Scarborough was designed in 1832 and built over the next 25 years, and in Torquay Hesketh Crescent (1848), to the east of the town, has three-bay end pavilions and a five-bay centrepiece with Corinthian pilasters, which marks the location of the hotel (*see* Fig 7.12).

By the middle of the 19th century standard house forms were appearing in resorts all over the country. These three- or four-storied terraces with polygonal bay windows can be found on, or near, the seafront in every resort of any size.[17] In effect, these are larger versions of the standard Victorian terraced house that was beginning to populate the streets of every rapidly expanding town. Away from the seafront, most houses were likely to be two or three storied and indistinguishable from those in the back streets of similar inland towns.

While the terraced house remained the dominant architectural form in seaside towns, growing numbers of villas and substantial semi-detached houses began to be built. This shift in taste marks a departure from the intimate character of life in a terrace, even a grand one, to a more private, quasi-rural existence. This clear reaction to the Picturesque was not only limited to the seaside resort: it had even begun to take place in Bath, the home of the grand palatial terrace.[18]

The first visitors to the seaside in the 18th century had been, perhaps unwittingly, unconscious pioneers of the Picturesque, forced to stay in humble, rural cottages. Fanny Burney, who visited Teignmouth in 1773, stayed in 'a small, neat, thatched & white Washed Cottage neither more nor less' that belonged to a sea captain.[19] However, though aristocratic visitors might enjoy the novelty of a brief sojourn in humble circumstances, the terrace soon supplanted the homes of the working people of the towns as the preferred place to stay. Then by the early 19th century the impact of the Picturesque movement was being felt in some seaside resorts. This is demonstrated at Sidmouth, where a series of large thatched houses with Gothic detailing were designed as cottages in form, but not size, and were clearly intended for wealthy residents and visitors (Fig 4.20).

The Sidmouth buildings are among the quaintest types of villa built at the seaside, but most adopted more conservative forms.

Stylistically, seaside villas followed current tastes as they changed during the course of the 19th century and make the standard allusions to their 'elders and betters'. For instance, it is not uncommon to see references in suburban villas to Osborne House, Queen Victoria's Isle of Wight retreat, the ultimate seaside villa (Fig 4.21). These homes were intended for the growing numbers of genteel residents, including many retired people, who wished to live by the sea, but were in search of more peace and quiet than could be achieved in a terraced street. Therefore most villas, by definition, stand within their own secluded grounds and are usually set within discrete areas of a resort, usually high above the bustle of the town and, trees permitting, with a sea view. The word 'villa' implies a certain grandeur, but contemporary builders also used it as a marketing term to boost the status of sometimes modest developments of semi-detached and detached houses.

Villas are most common in resorts that were regarded as 'quiet' or 'genteel' during the 19th century. Hence, they were not common in the south-east, but were popular further west at resorts such as Torquay, Bournemouth, Sidmouth and Ventnor. In the north-west, Blackpool was a magnet for working-class tourists and much of the housing stock reflected this clientele. However, in contrast, the area around Stanley Park grew, during the course of the late 19th century, through the addition of villas, creating a pocket of more affluent residential streets. A similar group of villas exists at Hesketh Park, at nearby Southport, where developments of this status were more the norm. At St Leonards, a number of villas, designed in classical, Gothic and other

Fig 4.18 *(opposite, top)* 1–6 Brunswick Terrace and Embassy Court, Brighton, East Sussex; after 1825 and 1934–6

Brighton's seafront has the contrast between the Regency-style and modernist Embassy Court (see Fig 4.36).
(DP017926)

Fig 4.19 *(opposite, bottom)* Victoria Terrace, The Esplanade, Weymouth, Dorset; 1855–6, Charles B Fookes

Victoria Terrace was one of the last seaside, palace-fronted façades using classical forms. It is worth contrasting the visual unity of this terrace with houses in Great Yarmouth's Britannia Terrace (see Fig 4.9).
(AA037430)

Fig 4.20 *(above)* Clifton Place cottages, seafront, Sidmouth, Devon; after 1814

These quaint houses were inspired both by Blaise Hamlet (1810–11) and the local vernacular style.
(DP022300)

Fig 4.21
Bourne Hall, Poole
Road, Bournemouth,
Dorset; *c*.1870

*This villa in a leafy
suburban setting makes an
allusion to Osborne House
through the Italianate
tower added to the side of
the house.*
(DP022301)

Victorian styles, were laid out around a park, set back behind the seafront with its earlier, more regimented, hotel and terraces (*see* Fig 5.12). In resorts, villas were associated with requisite open spaces, hence their location around parks, or on hilltops overlooking towns (Fig 4.22). A similar association existed in towns and cities away from the coast, so that, for instance, in Liverpool the select Sefton Park is surrounded by large, prestigious villas.

A derivative of the villa with a particular seaside association is the bungalow. These were originally conceived as purpose-built leisure or holiday dwellings, sometimes pre-fabricated and predominantly single storied.[20] The first bungalows in England were especially popular at the seaside and in the countryside, and were often created for people seeking a tranquil place of retirement where they could improve their physical and mental well-being. For instance, following the death of its owner, Sir Erasmus Wilson, 'Sea Lawn' at Westgate on Sea beside Margate was put up for sale in 1887, with health being one of its selling points:

> The position of this Bungalow is unique, enjoying the full sea breeze from the German Ocean, its style and internal arrangements perfect, and the Sale affords a rare chance of acquiring a most complete Seaside Residence for either occupation or investment.[21]

Percival T Harrison, who published a handbook for bungalow construction in 1909, recommended general layouts and external designs for bungalows. For a site on a rugged coast he suggested a bungalow of 'bold design, possessing strong outlines and projections'.[22] He also considered traditional bungalow characteristics that could be transferred from colonial designs: the roof should project over the gable ends and eaves to protect walls from heavy rain and to provide shade in summer. Harrison

Fig 4.22
Rest Haven, 41 Park
Crescent, Southport,
Merseyside, *c*.1870

*Large Victorian houses
built around the park, once
the homes of prosperous
families, are often no longer
economically viable as
houses. Like so many other
seaside houses they have
been subdivided or
converted to other uses.*
(AA058260)

accepted that a veranda should form an integral part of bungalow design, but it should not go around the whole of the building as this would restrict the light entering the interior.

The earliest bungalows were built at the Kent resorts of Westgate on Sea and Birchington. The concept of a local businessman who was backed by Coutts Bank, Westgate evolved as an exclusive resort, situated to the west of Margate and only one-and-a-half hours from London by train.[23] Its air of exclusivity was maintained through the use of covenants that only permitted the construction of detached houses.

The first seaside bungalow was built at Westgate between August and October 1869 and the second was erected in the following year, on a plot facing the Esplanade (both now demolished). Also in 1869, two bungalows were built at Westcliff in Birchington and it is possible that the easternmost of these bungalows survives as 'Corby Tower'. A further six bungalows designed by John Taylor were built at Birchington in the mid-1870s, including 'Fair Outlook' (1872–3). In 1881–2 four bungalows, collectively known as 'Tower Bungalows', were designed and built by John Seddon, again in Birchington (Fig 4.23).[24]

In contrast to the exclusive bungalow developments at Westgate on Sea and Birchington, a novel circular bungalow appeared as part of a development of semi-detached houses in Hythe on Kent's southern coast. 'The Whim' was built between 1874 and 1878 by a local builder for a Mr Scott, a grocer and valuer from Ashford. Scott designed the building himself with the intention of using it as a seaside retirement home. 'The Whim' is reminiscent of colonial bungalow designs where a central communal area was surrounded by bedrooms and other ancillary rooms.

Bungalows, and bungalow settlements, soon spread around the coast to become an essential feature of inter-war coastal developments. These could comprise purpose-built, pre-fabricated structures, or the *ad hoc* buildings of the plotlands or 'sea-shanty-towns' vilified by Laurie Lee (*see* p 59). One of the most colourful was Bungalow Town at Shoreham-by-Sea, where a motley collection of houseboats are among the last traces of this once thriving settlement. The first settler was reputed to have been a lone camper who erected a disused railway carriage on the beach at the end of the 19th century. In 1900 Marie Loftus, the 'Sarah Bernhardt of the Music Halls', arrived and in the following years she and her friends had bungalows built, creating a thriving artistic community.[25] The ingenious economy with which such seaside dwellings were erected is, perhaps, epitomised by the railway-carriage home. One such arrangement involved fixing parallel pairs of railway carriages onto concrete foundations, leaving a space between to be roofed and enclosed to provide further living space.[26] This created a plan similar to the Anglo-Indian, colonial bungalow with a central multi-functional space flanked by more private accommodation.

As well as forming the backbone of new plotland developments, the bungalow became the building of choice for much of

Fig 4.23
Bungalows, Spencer Road, Birchington, Kent; 1881–2, John Seddon

This development tried to appeal to artistic circles through naming estate roads after artists and scientists. The sculptor George Frampton was employed to decorate the exteriors of the coach house and domestic offices. (DP022302)

Fig 4.25 *(right)*
Clocktower, Central
Parade, Herne Bay,
Kent; 1837, Edwin
James Dangerfield
This clock tower flouts
many of the rules of
classical orders. It has
fluted Doric columns on the
ground floor, a first storey
with plain Corinthian
columns and a top storey
with debased Corinthian
pilasters, a pediment and a
polygonal 'cupola'.
(AA052830)

Fig 4.24
Baths, 11 Bath
Terrace, Blyth,
Northumberland; late
18th century
At Blyth a terraced house,
indistinguishable
architecturally from its
neighbours, still bears the
word 'BATHS' on its
porch.
(AA050655)

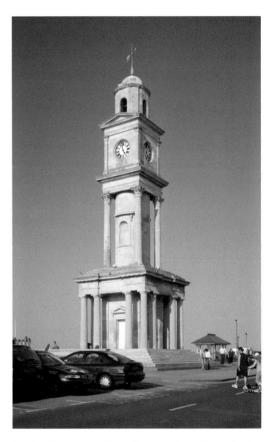

suburbia, particularly with people who were retiring to the seaside. Research in the early 1970s found that over 40 per cent of retired people at Bexhill and 70 per cent at Clacton were living in bungalows that had been built since the 1920s.[27]

A taste for the exotic

Many of the functions of public and commercial buildings in Georgian resorts were at first conducted in buildings that were difficult to distinguish from adjacent houses or inns (Fig 4.24, *see also* Fig 7.2). In 1832, warm and cold baths were available on the Steyne at Bognor, where an apparently conventional, three-storied Georgian house with a curved bay window and first-floor canopied balcony still bears the name of the Bath House.[28] By the mid-19th century, public buildings at resorts had adopted some version of the classical style: assembly rooms, theatres, libraries and baths emulated the forms used in major public buildings in London and provincial towns, though the seaside examples were rarely executed with the same aplomb as the works of skilled, metropolitan architects and masons. For example, the façade of the former Castle Inn Assembly Rooms in Brighton has Doric pilasters and is dominated by an over-size pediment, and Margate had a classical assembly room of uneducated proportions (destroyed by fire in 1882), a classical library with Adam-style interiors and even a gasworks using the Doric order. The important thing was, clearly, a show of sophistication, but this

broke down on close inspection, though the style marked these public buildings out from the rest of the town (Fig 4.25, *see also* Figs 6.1, 6.9).

In the early 19th century a single building transformed the architecture of the seaside as a whole, especially the public and commercial buildings designed primarily for visitors. The story of the Royal Pavilion at Brighton began in 1786 when George, Prince of Wales, leased a farmhouse overlooking the Steyne. In the following year Henry Holland was employed to enlarge the building, creating a large, shiny, white-tiled, but rather dour, neo-classical design incorporating the original farmhouse as one of a pair of blocks separated by a central domed structure. In 1803 William Porden designed a large domed riding school behind the pavilion, decorated externally with Indian detailing, which the Prince reputedly believed was better than his own accommodation. Therefore, John Nash was employed to extend and transform the neo-classical house into a building that combined Indian, Islamic and even Gothic detailing on the exterior with lavish, predominantly Chinese interiors (Fig 4.26).[29]

The Royal Pavilion was not the earliest building to employ oriental detailing, but it

was the first to be built in full public view and was therefore able to capture both public and architectural imaginations. In 1822 William Cobbett described it as resembling the Kremlin, but a century later its exotic charms had become commonplace: 'Its ornaments are scarcely more extravagant than those of the roundabouts at Hampstead, which they closely resemble; for singularity of form it has long ago been surpassed by the Crystal Palace and the White City; and for richness it compares unfavourably with the Granada Cinema at Tooting'.[30]

While the pavilion had some influence throughout the country, its lasting legacy was at the seaside, where architectural frivolity was more acceptable (Fig 4.27). In 1827 Amon Wilds built a pair of houses on Western Terrace in Brighton with eastern detailing, one of which survives, while the Athenaeum, which was to be built in Hove

in 1827, was a glazed, domed structure reminiscent of the riding school beside the Royal Pavilion. Brighton can also boast a house mixing Gothic and Islamic detailing in Sillwood Road.

Along with eastern-derived forms, a few tentative essays in the Gothic style also appeared during the first half of the 19th century. This may have partly been a response to the oriental forms of Brighton, but it was of course also part of a wider, national re-evaluation of this style. For instance, in Brighton itself Sillwood Place employs a Gothic style that borders on Moorish, while Wykeham Terrace employs more conventional Gothic detailing. Some resorts felt a stronger affinity with Gothic forms than others, such as Sidmouth, where a series of thatched villas with Gothic detailing was built in the early 19th century, imitating a version of the local, vernacular style. Architecturally this was a response to

Fig 4.26
Royal Pavilion, The Steyne, Brighton, East Sussex; 1815–22, John Nash
The unmistakable roofline of Brighton's Royal Pavilion ushered in new themes in seaside architecture, the exoticism of the east and a new eclecticism in architectural form.
(DP017969)

Fig 4.27
Hanbury Arms
Ballroom, former
Sassoon Mausoleum,
St George's Road,
Brighton, East Sussex;
1892

*Perhaps the most bizarre
use of oriental detailing
was when Sir Albert
Sassoon opted for a tented
Indian structure as a
fitting setting for his
mausoleum. In a dramatic
change of function, it is
now part of a public house.*
(DP017937)

projects such as John Nash's cottages at Blaise Hamlet. Ilfracombe is one resort where Gothic forms became standard in the second half of the 19th century, and many seaside towns have at least a few buildings with medieval-inspired detailing.

Piers seem to form a missing link between the oriental fad in the immediate wake of the Royal Pavilion and a resurgence of exotic forms in mainstream architecture at the end of the 19th century. The first piers were simple utilitarian landing stages with a long deck on which visitors could promenade. In the 1860s Eugenius Birch included entry kiosks in the West Pier at Brighton with detailing derived from the

pavilion. From this simple beginning, the taste for exotic detailing on piers spread throughout the country, and by the early 20th century most piers had kiosks, entrance booths or pavilions with some oriental-influenced detailing. The harsh environmental conditions that piers and other seafront buildings had to endure made iron and steel the most appropriate material, and iron also had the virtue of being able to be formed, relatively cheaply, into any shape that took a designer's fancy. Around 1900, formal buildings inspired by the oriental appeared at a number of resorts (Figs 4.28, 4.29). One of the most striking is a terrace of cottages on the seafront at Bexhill, built

Fig 4.28
Victoria Pier
(South Pier),
South Promenade,
Blackpool,
Lancashire; 1892–3,
TP Worthington;
photograph W. & Co,
*c.*1900

*Exotic forms became
essential on piers and other
entertainment buildings,
though the debt to Brighton
is more obvious than any
re-examination of eastern
forms. The vitality of the
rooflines at the end of piers
would have served to tempt
visitors to pay their
admission fee at the
turnstiles.*
(OP00487)

Fig 4.29
Buccaneer Public
House, 10 Compton
Street, Eastbourne,
East Sussex; early
20th century
Many seaside buildings are
architecturally reminiscent
of the Buccaneer Public
House in Eastbourne,
namely a fairly standard
building with a few oriental
details or an exotic
roofscape.
(DP017986)

in 1903–7 in a 'Moghul' style, apparently to celebrate Britain's greatest imperial possession. In 1911 one of these was chosen for the Maharajah of Cooch Behar to stay in while recuperating, but he died soon after his arrival.

At the beginning of the 20th century, architects enjoyed a new freedom to adorn their façades interchangeably with classical elements and a wide range of exotic motifs, and at the seaside this was most evident in entertainment buildings on or near the seafront (Fig 4.30). The façade of the Grand Theatre at Blackpool is adorned with motifs that can be derived, often only remotely, from classical architecture, but their profusion and the irreverent sense of fun in their use can be traced back to Brighton. The

Fig 4.30
Grand Theatre,
33 Church Street,
Blackpool,
Lancashire; 1894,
Frank Matcham
*Matcham combined the
exuberance brought to
seaside architecture by the
Prince Regent's house in
Brighton with fairly
standard late 19th-century
forms. To provide the
viewer with a visual clue
for the origins of this
riotous design, the architect
has incorporated finials
that look as if they were
directly borrowed from the
Royal Pavilion
(see Fig 4.26).*
(AA053253)

Winter Gardens at Morecambe is another
peculiar mixture, with mainstream red-brick
Edwardian forms and some Italianate arcad-
ing, topped with a line of pepper-pot finials
inspired by Indian temples. From theatres
and winter gardens, the taste for elaborate
applied external decoration spread to the
first cinemas, established before the First
World War. The Gem Cinema in Great
Yarmouth, built in 1908, is the earliest
surviving seaside cinema: it has a façade
resembling the *Westwerk* of a Romanesque
cathedral, but adorned with florid roundels
and Ionic pilasters, and topped with shaped,
domed roofs (*see* Fig 6.33).

The 20th century – from modernity to kitsch

By the early 20th century, eclectic, exotic
motifs had become part of the mainstream
of Edwardian architecture throughout
England. These forms that had once been
restricted to small, garden buildings had
become part of the vocabulary of large
buildings, perhaps most dramatically in
Blackpool's celebrated tower, built in 1894
in imitation of the Eiffel Tower in Paris (Fig
4.31). This was quickly followed by less
elegant and less durable towers at New
Brighton and Morecambe. While they all

Fig 4.31
Tower Buildings,
Promenade,
Blackpool,
Lancashire; 1891–4,
Maxwell and Tuke
*The ultimate symbol of
Blackpool and the British
seaside, this dramatic copy
of the Eiffel Tower (1889)
still dominates the seafront.
Although the tower is the
most obvious feature of the
complex, the building at its
base should not be
overlooked. It contained a
variety of entertainment
venues, including the
famous circus and
ballroom.*
(AA058315)

share something of the quirky frivolity ushered in at Brighton, they also serve as strong
symbols of a new theme in seaside architecture, or perhaps more correctly a strong
affirmation of a latent theme: modernity.

By the mid-19th century, guidebooks to
resorts proclaimed the modernity of their
services such as gasworks and waterworks.
The most obvious symbol of this at the
seaside was the pier, while on the seafront of
some resorts, cliff lifts and funicular railways
provided convenience and a technological
attraction for visitors. However, for the
seaside the most important technological
development around 1900 was the introduction of electricity. Visitors could see the
earliest electric railways and tram systems,
while Blackpool, with the development of its
illuminations, provided the ultimate example of how the simple street light could be
developed into an entertainment in itself.
Electricity and the combustion engine were
the power behind the fairgrounds that were
beginning to develop at many resorts, providing thrills beyond anything that earlier
gravity-powered rides could offer.[31]

The emphasis on technology, which had
been strong at the seaside before the First
World War, seemed to weaken immediately
after the horrors of the world's first techno-

Fig 4.32
Winter Gardens,
Royal Parade, Weston-
super-Mare,
Somerset; opened
1927

A stolid neo-Georgian style was employed in some public buildings during the inter-war years, before modernist forms made their dramatic appearance during the 1930s. (PC08651)

logical war, and during the inter-war years there seems to have been a renewed affection for the homely (Fig 4.32). Individual, architect-designed seaside houses built between the wars might have adopted forms from the Modern Movement, but the vast majority of mass-produced homes employed elements from vernacular traditions. For example, mock-Tudor predominated on many estates and was even adopted by the Butlins holiday camp to decorate the exterior of the chalets at Skegness (*see* Fig 7.24).

A taste for the vernacular, in combination with a liking for the exotic, may have informed the decision by some architects to adopt a style loosely based on Spanish architecture, or more accurately the Spanish mission style popular in Florida and other states of the southern USA in the early 20th century. This minor vogue can be witnessed in some public buildings and in various hacienda-type houses, but its supreme expression was San Remo Towers at Boscombe, built in 1935–8 by the American architect Hector Hamilton (Fig 4.33).

Although there was a strong vernacular

Fig 4.33
San Remo Towers,
Michelgrove Road,
Boscombe, Dorset;
1935–8, Hector
Hamilton

The accommodation was divided into five blocks set around a central courtyard, which covered an underground garage. This high-class development was created as a self-contained community with hotel-standard facilities. There were resident staff, a residents' club containing a library, a reading room, billiard rooms and games rooms for children. The ground-floor lobbies contained small shops, and on the fifth floor there was a restaurant. (DP001266)

revival in domestic architecture after the First World War, some seaside buildings began to follow a new direction. In the 1930s modernist architecture found a second home by the sea, away from its base in London and the Home Counties; new construction techniques matched perfectly with new attitudes towards fresh air and sunshine. Architectural forms that had 'more justification in the clear atmosphere of the seaside' inspired the design of numerous leisure and entertainment buildings, hotels, blocks of flats and private houses.[32] The ninth Earl De La Warr led the way at Bexhill-on-Sea. The need for a new entertainment venue had been recognised for many years and in 1933 it was decided that

the corporation would develop a seafront site.[33] The design brief specified that the building 'should be simple in design' with large windows, and that 'Modern steel-framed or ferro-concrete construction [could] be adopted'.[34] With the appointment of Thomas Tait as the assessor of the competition, it seemed inevitable that a Modern Movement design would be selected, and it was: Serge Chermayeff and Erich Mendelsohn's winning design was built during 1935 (Fig 4.34).[35]

Another seaside visionary, Herbert Carden, wanted to turn Brighton into a modern, forward-looking city, and was willing to destroy much of the resort's historic townscape to do so; he cited the modernist

Fig 4.34
De La Warr Pavilion, Bexhill-on-Sea, East Sussex; 1935, Serge Chermayeff and Erich Mendelsohn
The building, of welded steel-frame construction, contained a multi-purpose auditorium, restaurant, conference hall, library and reading room, with sun terraces and balconies to the south side.
(CC47/02381)

Embassy Court as the model building. If Carden's plans had been realised, the Royal Pavilion would have been replaced by a conference and entertainment centre, and the Laines would have disappeared.

New structural techniques that allowed expanses of glass and minimal walls were particularly suitable for the construction of a relatively new type of seaside building, the block of flats. One such building is the present Grand Hotel in Folkestone, which began life in 1903 as a block of 'gentleman's residential chambers'.[36] It had communal facilities on the ground floor and apartments on the upper floors. The Grand could easily be mistaken for a conventional hotel and it is indeed very similar to the adjacent Metropole Hotel, which, for the sake of confusion, has now been converted into flats (Fig 4.35, *see also* Fig 7.16).

By the 1930s the blocks of flats that were being built at many resorts were relatively conservative in design; modern but not modernist, with metallic windows and curved balconies applied to plain brick structures. However, more in tune with the modernist agenda was Wells Coates' twelve-storey reinforced-concrete Embassy Court, which has dominated the western end of Brighton's seafront since it was erected in 1934–6. Each of the nine types of flat included an open balcony and an enclosed sun-room that could be reached through the living room and bedrooms. The windows to the sun-room had sliding, folding windows to create an open-air room, and there was also a sun terrace on the roof (Fig 4.36).[37] Embassy Court was a bold counterpoint to the adjacent Regency terraces, but its visual impact seems modest compared with that of Kenneth Dalgliesh and Roger K Pullen's Marine Court, which overshadows Burton's 19th-century resort at St Leonards (Fig 4.37).

Modernism arrived at a number of other resorts through the construction of a large

Fig 4.35
Grand Hotel, the Leas, Folkestone, Kent; 1903, built by local builder Daniel Baker
This huge block of flats, now a hotel, is located on the Leas, the most fashionable part of town. The gentleman guests originally occupied the rooms around the outside of the building, while their servants were in the accommodation around an inside courtyard, across the corridor from their masters. (DP022303)

Fig 4.36
Embassy Court,
King's Road,
Brighton, East Sussex;
1934–6, Wells Coates
Embassy Court took
seaside accommodation
upwards, in marked
contrast to the horizontal
form of traditional terrace
developments. It
incorporated features such
as sun lounges and large,
sliding and folding
windows that accorded
with prevailing views about
healthy living. These flats
were designed for an up-
market 'modern' clientele.
Therefore, the basement
included a car park and
lock-up garages, and the
interiors included works of
art, textiles and furniture
by leading designers.
(DP017945)

Fig 4.37
Marine Court, The Marina, St Leonards-on-Sea, East Sussex; 1938, Kenneth Dalgliesh and Roger K Pullen

Inspired by the ocean liner the Queen Mary, this 14-storey building contained an underground car park, ground-floor shops, a two-storey restaurant, a fourth-floor tea lounge and a tenant's promenade deck on the thirteenth floor. All the flats on the seaward side above the second-floor level were provided with balconies overlooking the sea.
(DP018000)

MIDLAND HOTEL, MORECAMBE.

93

Fig 4.38
Midland Hotel, Marine Road Central, Morecambe, Lancashire; 1932–3, Oliver Hill

Built for the LMS Railway, this is one of the first modernist buildings erected at the seaside. It replaced a Victorian hotel that had been built by the railway company for passengers travelling by ship from Morecambe.
(PC10615)

Fig 4.39
Lido, Saltdean, East
Sussex; 1938, RWH
Jones

Saltdean is one of only
three seaside lidos that are
still open in England.
Open-air pools were once a
major and striking feature
of the seafront of many of
the largest resorts. The hotel
of the same date was built
on the hillside above.
(DP017982)

concrete block with a strong central semi-circular projection reminiscent of the stair turret of the nearby De La Warr Pavilion (Fig 4.39).

Other types of seafront buildings designed to entertain and amuse visitors might seem to offer architects the greatest scope for innovation, yet with the exception of the De La Warr Pavilion and two other schemes, they are notable by their absence. The honourable exceptions are at Folkestone and Blackpool: on the seafront at Folkestone, David Pleydell-Bouverie built a circular fun-fair building, shops, a shelter, restaurant and boating lake, and at Blackpool the Pleasure Beach was redeveloped over a number of years by the architect Joseph Emberton (Fig 4.40, *see also* Fig 6.27).[40] The intention was to re-organise the site and enforce a co-ordinated architectural treatment. The largest addition was the casino, which contained a range of air-conditioned facilities such as a restaurant, a bar and a cafeteria. To this small group of seafront entertainment buildings can be added the Odeons and other cinemas, the largest example being the former Odeon at Blackpool (*see* Fig 6.43).

The most widespread type of modernist building at the seaside was the house. At many resorts there are single examples amid rows of undistinguished, historicist suburbia, but in some towns there is evidence of a more adventurous speculator prepared to invest in two or three modernist houses on a plot they were developing. Wells Coates, Marcel Breuer and Harry Weedon of Odeon cinema fame all built individual houses by the sea, but the most radical modern housing scheme was at Frinton, where Oliver Hill was appointed in 1934 as the leading architect of a scheme to build 1,200 houses (Fig 4.41).[41] A handful were built in a rigorous modern idiom, but in other houses the impact was toned down by the application of pitched, green-tiled roofs. However, most of the estate was not developed until after the Second World War, when a more conservative architectural mood prevailed.

The War damaged the fabric of resorts, but it had a more subtle and more damaging effect on seaside architecture. In the 1930s, many major modernist buildings were built at resorts and there was a vigorous culture of radical architecture at the seaside. The war interrupted the momentum and, although people flocked back to the seaside once peace returned, there were few, if any, significant architectural essays until the

hotel. The most celebrated of these is the Midland Hotel at Morecambe, by Oliver Hill, commissioned by the London Midland and Scottish Railway.[38] Built in 1932–3 using concrete and rendered brick around a steel frame, its form is asymmetrical and curved, with a long convex façade facing the sea. As in Embassy Court, progressive art and design were incorporated into the architecture, including seahorse sculptures on the exterior, and a carved stone relief by Eric Gill (Fig 4.38).

Saltdean, a short distance to the east of Brighton, is fortunate to have two signature Art Deco buildings, the Ocean Hotel and the Saltdean Lido. Both were designed by RWH Jones and opened in July 1938.[39] The hotel's 426 bedrooms were contained in a main building and six detached blocks, which could be closed during the off season. The lido's pool lies in front of a long, curved

Fig 4.40
Fun House, Pleasure
Beach, South Shore
Promenade,
Blackpool,
Lancashire; 1934,
Joseph Emberton
*Built on the site of the
demolished Water Chute
lake, Emberton's Fun
House contained numerous
attractions created by the
roller coaster designer
Charles Paige. The
building was destroyed by
fire in 1991.
(CC47/01518)*

Fig 4.41
6 Cliff Way and
former site office,
Frinton-on-Sea,
Essex; 1934, Oliver
Hill
*The striking circular office
building in the background
with its flat roof and a
band of windows around
the first floor marks the
start, geographically and
chronologically, of this
ambitious scheme. The
adjacent house is one of the
few completed in the
original style of the scheme.
(DP022304)*

establishment of the Tate Gallery at St Ives in 1993. This does not imply an absence of construction at resorts between the 1950s and the 1980s, but simply that the majority of new buildings were scarcely at the cutting edge of architectural thinking. Perhaps it is significant that no large, new towns were created on or near the coast, and it was inland new towns, as well as the hearts of major industrial cities and London, that took priority when money was being allocated by local and national government.

Most large-scale post-war seaside architecture took the form of substantial tower blocks or buildings that could best be described as utilitarian: high-rise blocks that were planned to house residents as well as the growing numbers of retired people heading for the seaside (Fig 4.42). While new development may have broken the skyline of some resorts, particularly at Brighton, many new blocks of flats were built at the edge of resorts and helped to counter the problems caused by suburban sprawl along coastlines (*see* Fig 3.21). Although the vogue for large blocks had

diminished by the 1970s, the debate about their role at the seaside has recently been rekindled by proposals in 2005 to build new blocks at Brighton; the prospect of a series of fractured towers by Frank Gehry was met with a mixture of bewilderment, anger and enthusiasm.

Seaside blocks of flats seem to follow national trends in tower-block design, but these blocks cannot be confused with the congregations of flats found in inner cities. Bizarrely they have some qualities in common with the seaside houses used as lodgings during the Georgian period, in that they were larger and occupied by people of a higher status than equivalent buildings in inland towns. There is also a greater emphasis on balconies and windows, as affluent residents want to maximise the value of staying at the seaside.

Many modern facilities at resorts were created in utilitarian boxes, effectively small, industrial units that provided blank canvases on to which any decoration could be applied. By exploiting themes including pirates, dinosaurs or ancient Rome and Egypt, seafront entertainments target visitors in search of excitement and seeking to get away from everyday life (Fig 4.43). Some amusement arcades try to evoke the glamour of Las Vegas by associating themselves through their name, such as the Las Vegas at Leysdown on Sea, the Golden Palms in Torquay, or the Golden Sands at Seaton Carew. Others apply a veneer, often electrified, to their buildings to recreate the bright lights of the Strip.[42]

As well as amusement buildings, in recent years many leisure centres and aquariums have been built on seafronts. Bathhouses were prominent on seafronts in the 19th century, but these have disappeared at almost every resort. The lido, which became popular in the 20th century between the wars, has also almost disappeared (*see* Chapter 5). These attractions have now been superseded by indoor swimming pools and leisure centres executed in more or less unattractive, modern styles. Although they could be located anywhere in the towns, if they are to attract large numbers of visitors they are built on seafront sites, sometimes on the site of one of their predecessors. Of the large aquariums in England, today 15 are at seaside resorts. Brighton's Sea Life Centre still occupies the site of its Victorian forerunner, but most are housed in a range of unappealing, modern buildings in seafront locations (Fig 4.44).

Fig 4.42
Albany Flats, Manor Road, East Cliff, Bournemouth; 1962–4, Ivor Shaw
This 17-storied block of flats with prominent balconies and sun lounges provides the residents with sea views. Its complex shape was probably devised to maximise the number of flats that could catch a glimpse of the sea.
(DP001252)

Fig 4.43
Coral Island,
Promenade,
Blackpool, Lancashire
On the seafront, modern buildings include a strong strand of kitsch and fantasy. The excitement of pirates with the obvious symbolism of hidden treasure is meant to entice visitors into this amusement arcade. (AA053085)

Fig 4.44
Aquarium, Weston-super-Mare, Somerset
At a number of resorts large, modern structures have been built on the seafront to house aquariums. (AA049330)

Although the core of every seaside resort is dominated by 18th- and 19th-century buildings, no seafront has been immune from recent intrusions. In resorts there is a need to balance the nostalgia of past holidays with exciting new facilities. As long as the seaside remains at the heart of popular culture, striking a suitable balance will be a challenging test for planners and architects alike.

Conclusion

When visitors first arrive at the seaside they are struck not by the form of resorts, but by the exotic, anarchic quality of the seafront, with its colourful, eye-catching buildings decorated with bright lights. Beneath modern, superficial embellishments, there is often another, hidden layer of historic decorative motifs: the glitz of an earlier era.

So what are our seaside architectures? Lively seafront buildings may be the most obvious expression of the holiday atmosphere of seaside towns, but underpinning the story of resorts are more humble structures. The majority are houses, broadly similar in form to their equivalents in any other town, but at the seaside the carnival quality of the place, the wish for a sea view and the economic impact of visitors have left their mark on domestic architecture. Many resorts have also had a working life centred on the harbour, and its buildings have entered the culture of the seaside holiday, entertaining inquisitive tourists seeking glimpses of a different and curious way of life.

The other factor is, of course, function: seaside resorts look different because their buildings perform different roles. The presence of visitors required facilities that were not to be found in towns without a significant holiday trade. In the next two chapters, health and entertainment facilities will be examined, in terms of their architecture, and also in terms of the ways in which they contributed to the overall development of the seaside. In a further chapter, the accommodation needed to house the influx of visitors will be considered in greater detail. At the heart of this chapter, once again, will be the house: without its contribution the seaside would not have flourished and we would not possess the seaside towns we know and love.

5

The health of visitors

As we have seen, seaside towns have a special character derived from their peculiar geography and the flamboyant and, at times, anarchic appearance of their architecture. However, much of this distinctive character is a result of the activities that took place in resorts, which can be grouped under the broad headings of health, entertainment and accommodation. The *raison d'être* for the first resorts was a desire for improved health, which, it was thought, could be obtained in and about the sea. As a consequence, wealthy visitors resorting to the coast required entertainment and comfortable places to stay. To an extent, these needs and activities also occurred in inland spa towns, while entertainment and visitor accommodation were required in London and large county towns, but at the seaside the concentrations were greater. Where an inland town might have a theatre and, eventually, one or two picture houses, busy resorts could have several of each, often established on a larger scale. However, in terms of activities and facilities to improve health, seaside towns were unrivalled, even by spas.

In the 18th century, there was a belief that a wide range of diseases and conditions could be cured or improved by drinking seawater, bathing in the sea, or simply by spending time at the seaside. This gave rise to the first seaside health structures: the bathing machine, with its associated waiting rooms, and seafront bathhouses. As resorts grew in sophistication, health treatments increasingly began to be practised within comfortable surroundings that offered space for other leisure activities. During the 19th century, the emphasis shifted towards a broader recognition that time at the seaside was good for you, and, of course, preferable to the poor physical conditions of growing industrial towns. Initially this was based on notions that the sea air was fresh and bracing, but by the end of the 19th century the curative value of the sun was increasingly interesting doctors as a treatment for conditions such as tuberculosis. Buildings evolved to match new ideas about medical treat-

ments and the seafront bathhouse was supplanted by the hydropathic hotel, the hospital, the sanatorium and the convalescent home. During the 20th century the seaside was still seen as a beneficial environment for sick children and convalescing patients, but for the majority the emphasis shifted from curing disease to increasing one's feeling of well-being. A sun tan came to imply healthiness as well as wealth, and warmth and sunshine were considered healthier and more desirable than bracing North-Sea breezes. Ultimately, this change in consciousness led, in the late 20th century, to growing numbers of people fleeing southwards to the Mediterranean in a new era of mass international tourism. However, at the time sun worship was evolving in the early 20th century, the first seeds of caution were being sown by researchers who identified links between exposure to the sun and growing instances of skin cancer.

Facilities for sea bathing

A desire for improved health and a belief in the curative qualities of the seaside prompted people with disposable time and income to head to the coast, creating England's first seaside resorts. Historical sources provide occasional references suggesting that this trend began in the 17th century, and by the early 18th century the number of references to sea bathing was increasing. So why did seawater become such a focus of attention and belief? Numerous contemporary scientific writers seem to have had their own theories to explain the medicinal value of the sea. For instance, in 1735 Peter Shaw believed that it was heavier than other waters and therefore exerted greater pressure on the body and thus stimulated greater circulation. This pressure, he said, also forced the salt water through the pores of the skin resulting in the blood being mixed and diluted with the health-giving water.[1] Dr Richard Russell in 1750 believed that the sea was enriched with particles supplied by 'Submarine Plants, Salts, Fishes, Minerals,

&c' and that bathing in and drinking sea-water could provide cures.[2]

Early sea bathing by men was often conducted in the nude, while women wore voluminous shifts. Bathing beaches, bathing machines and bathhouses were all subjected to segregation, with separate facilities for male and female bathers, and there was also discrimination between social classes and between the able-bodied and disabled. For example, by 1768 the beach at Brighton had been segregated, with the eastern section allotted to ladies, but prominent local doctor John Awsiter wanted further restrictions on the grounds of class, suggesting that 'no man servant or inhabitant, be permitted to bathe on that side of town during the season'.[3] Segregation could also be achieved temporally, for example at Blackpool where a bell was rung to indicate when male bathers should retire from the sea to allow female bathers to enter.[4] At Torquay, the female bathing beach, Beacon Cove, was shielded from prying eyes with a fence and bushes, and was policed by a council-employed guard.[5] This strict segregation of beaches continued through the 19th century, but was in decline by about 1900.

Bathing machines

The bathing experience was dominated, from the 1730s until the early 20th century, by the bathing machine. In 1735, for example, ladies in Scarborough were described as having 'Guides, Rooms and Conveniences' for the purpose of sea bathing.[6] John Setterington's view of Scarborough of the same year includes a four-wheeled vehicle drawn up close to the shore from which a bather is shown emerging. This is presumably what was meant by a bathing 'convenience' (Fig 5.1). Fourteen years earlier, in August 1721, Nicholas Blundell escorted an acquaintance 'to Leverpoole & Procured him a Place to lodg at & a Conveniency for Baithing in the Sea'.[7] Perhaps this reference to 'a Conveniency' is an earlier example of a primitive form of bathing machine.

Zechariah Brazier was said to have been the first sea bathing guide to have taken a bather into the sea at Margate in a 'simple machine, a cart'.[8] Brazier was born in 1729 and so could have been taking bathers into the sea before Benjamin Beale's fully developed bathing machine appeared at Margate, an event usually ascribed to 1753. Beale was a Quaker who is said to have added what became known as the modesty hood to the rear of a bathing machine. This was a hinged, concertina canvas canopy that could be lowered and raised by the driver of the machine. It enabled the modest or disfigured bather to enter the sea unobserved and could also provide some protection from wind and waves (Fig 5.2).

Beale's hood design was soon adopted at other seaside resorts. A request was made for half of the bathing machines at Brighton to be fitted with 'skreens', similar to those

Fig 5.1
View of the antient Town, Castle, Harbour, and Spaw of Scarborough; 1735, John Setterington
The lone bathing convenience featured in John Setterington's famous view of Scarborough does not appear to be the favoured method of entering the sea at this time. It was more customary for male bathers to jump into the sea from boats, locally known as 'cobbles'.
(By Permission of the British Library [Maps K.Top.44.47.b.])

used at Margate. On this occasion, the reason was not just for modesty's sake, but also for safety: John Awsiter recognised that the sea was too dangerous to bathe in at times of high wind and suggested that bathing machines could be positioned in the sea to act as a breakwater and a wind-break.[9]

A famous description of the use of a bathing machine appears in Tobias Smollett's *The Expedition of Henry Clinker*, published in 1771.[10] In tone it is more instructive than descriptive, and as late as 1793 a guide to Margate needed to include a lengthy explanation of how these machines functioned:

> That sea bathing may be attainable with the strictest decency, there are near forty machines employed in a season: ... they consist of a carriage similar to that of a coach, but more simple, much stouter and considerably higher, that it may resist the waves in blowing weather; the wheels are high and strong, and made dishing, but stand at right angles with the axles; in the front is a platform, from which you have admittance into the machine, which forms a neat dressing room, 6½ feet long, 5 wide, and 6½ high, with a bench on either side for the bathers to undress upon, the sides and top are framed and covered with painted canvass; at the back opens a door, and, by means of a flight of steps attached to the machine, the bathers descend into the water, concealed from public view by a large umbrella of canvas stretched on hoops, which is let down by the driver, by means of a rope which comes to the front of the machine, until it touches the water, and forms a bath 10 feet long and 6 wide. There is a horse to each machine, and the proprietors employ very careful drivers, under whose guidance the machines are drawn out to the depth the bather may require: it is a pleasing sight to behold between thirty and forty of these curious machines in a morning hovering on the surface of the water, as they appear to do, and continually revolving in their course either returning with their cleansed guest, or going out with a freight of, perhaps, jolly citizens preparing to wash off the dust and care of a six months attendance to their counting houses. – happy mortals![11]

Bathing from bathing machines was a time-consuming and labour-intensive activity, particularly when the amount of time spent in the sea was usually only a few 'dips'

at a time. At Scarborough in the 1780s each lady bather was attended by two guides, and gentlemen by one guide, if required. A 'lad' looked after the horse, which was used to pull the machines into the water, unhitched for the period of bathing and then re-hitched to pull the machine back to shore once bathing had been completed. It cost one shilling to use the bathing machine and a further payment was required for each guide used.[12]

Though they all performed the same function, the form of bathing machines varied significantly during the 18th and 19th centuries. They could be a horse-drawn or man-drawn, two- or four-wheeled, with or without a modesty hood or fixed side screens. Capstans and steam-powered winding engines were also used to draw bathing machines back onto dry land. Wheel size and width depended upon the material covering the beach and the angle of its slope. Most machines were rectangular but some were square and octagonal, including one at Weymouth reserved for George III. Some were canvas-covered over a wooden frame, but most had wooden sides and pitched, pyramidal or curved wooden roofs. Sliding or louvred openings in the sides or in the roof provided light and ventilation. One type of bathing machine had a safety crate called 'The Bath' attached to the seaward end of the machine so that bathers could dip within an enclosed area without fear of being washed away. Above the crate were hoops to support an awning that would effectively act as a modesty hood.

Although bathing etiquette and the modesty hood suggest that bathing was a private affair, some bathing machines were used to take more than one bather at a time into the sea. For example, as early as the 1750s, at

Fig 5.2
A View of Margate Peer and Harbour; after 1736, James Theobald *James Theobald's drawing and description of a bathing machine at Margate was inserted into a copy of the 1736 edition of the Reverend John Lewis'* The History and Antiquities, Ecclesiastical and Civil, of the Isle of Tenet. *It shows the kind of fully developed bathing machine that has been credited to Benjamin Beale. (DP017642 Courtesy of the Society of Antiquaries of London)*

Weymouth, vehicles might carry up to eight people into the water at once:

> The bay of the sea that lies east of Weymouth has a very clayey bottom, uncomfortable for persons who might wish to take cold baths. Wagons have therefore been constructed carrying huts made of boards, capable of carrying seven or eight people, who are driven out into the water, where they can enter the sea by means of steps and get out again, without being crowded or seen from the shore.[13]

Similarly, in 1829 the 'Terms of Bathing' at Ramsgate included a fee for 'Two or more ladies, guide included', while Capp's Family Machine could be found at the beach in Gorleston-on-Sea near Great Yarmouth at the end of the 19th century.[14]

A number of popular resorts had rails laid on the beaches to aid entrance into the sea. As early as 1784 a sophisticated machine with a crate and hood could be found at Lowestoft: 'Seabathing is also done here from a little hut, mounted on a track which takes it into the sea, and attached by a cable to the beach. Outside the hut, a platform is lowered. It is covered with canvas in the form of a tent, under which you bathe.'[15] Walter David Fagg, the manager of the Folkestone Bathing Establishment Company, introduced one of the most extraordinary bathing contraptions at the end of the 19th century. His New and Improved Safety Carriage, patented in 1888, was advertised in the 1894–5 *Guide To Folkestone*:

> Fagg's Patent Bathing Carriage comprises a number of cabins on an iron frame fitted with wheels, running on a tram line. The floor is horizontal and remains so at all states of the tide. The carriage is drawn up and let down by a wire rope, and can be worked by hand, gas or other power. The cabins open on either side into a corridor. At the sea end is a safety crate in which non-swimmers can bathe in safety. Diving boards are arranged at the sides and end of the crate from which a 'header' can be taken into deep water, a thing unsafe from an ordinary machine. ... The carriage travels smoothly on the rails, and it is easily adjusted to the rise and fall of the tide.[16]

The decline in the use of bathing machines corresponded with a liberalisation of attitudes towards bathing at the end of the 19th century, resulting in bathing from the beach becoming the norm for both sexes. Alternative changing facilities were provided, including small tents and the ubiquitous beach hut, which evolved from static bathing machines drawn up beyond the level of the high-water mark. In 1906 a bathing-machine operator in Hastings replaced some of his machines with Continental-style, canvas bathing cabins, which he claimed to be the first in England, while at Thorpeness 'Dhoolie bathing cabins', portable canvas cabins, took the place of the 'old-fashioned, unwieldy bathing machines of other days'.[17] In 1920 the local authority at Broadstairs replaced the 'old-fashioned' bathing machines with tents and huts, and in 1935 added permanent changing facilities and a sun deck to the beach.[18] Bathing machines continued to be used as changing rooms until the outbreak of the Second World War, but with the threat of invasion beaches were cleared. At Margate, disused bathing machines were even used as road blocks and elsewhere redundant machines were put to use in allotments and farms as sheds and hen houses.[19]

Bathing rooms

At some resorts bathing machines could not cope with the numbers of bathers and it became necessary to provide a waiting room. Bathing rooms had been established at Margate in the 1750s, to the south-west of the harbour, and in 1763 they were described in the first guidebook:

> The bathing Rooms are not large but convenient. Here the company often wait their turns of bathing. The guides attend, sea water is drank, the ladies' dresses are taken notice of, and all business of the like kind is managed. There are three of these rooms, which employ 11 machines till near the time of high water, which, at the ebb of the tide, sometimes runs two or three hundred yards into the bay.[20]

Bathers entered the bathing rooms from the High Street and chalked their name on a blackboard. Once a bathing machine became available, they descended an external staircase on the seaward side to a waiting machine, where they would undress and enter the sea. The bathing rooms were also social venues where subscribers could read the latest newspapers, drink coffee or seawater and look out to sea while they waited. In the evenings parties could gather and enjoy

Fig 5.3
Margate, Kent; *c.1812*
This engraving shows the recently rebuilt bathing rooms, including Philpot's Warm Sea Water Baths. Their low profile enabled the buildings on the eastern side of the High Street to retain their sea views.
(DP022308)

piano recitals and other musical entertainments.[21]

In 1808 a major storm destroyed many of the buildings on Margate seafront and new bathing rooms had to be built (Fig 5.3).[22] By 1816 there were eight along the High Street, from which over forty bathing machines operated.[23] By this time the bathing rooms had evolved into bathhouses offering warm and cold baths, shower baths, douche baths and shampooing. Although these buildings have been demolished, they have left their imprint on the street. The west side of the lower end of the High Street still has a series of single-storied shops that echo in scale the small bathing rooms that were there 200 years ago (Fig 5.4). Their low height was apparently due to legal covenants preventing the construction of taller buildings that would obstruct the views from properties on the east side of the street.

Margate was not the only resort to provide bathing rooms, though in the 18th century they do seem to have been confined to the south-east. In around 1795, improvements were made at Ramsgate 'for the accommodation of the company, while waiting for their machines'.[24] *The Bathing Place, Ramsgate*, an engraving published in 1782, reveals that the basic accommodation comprised a few weatherboarded huts situated at the base of the cliff to the north of the harbour. From here, bathers passed beyond the sea wall to the beach, where they could board bathing machines via gangplanks. At Hastings, the waiting room in 1797 was baldly described as 'a small box, called the bathing-room, for the use of the company while waiting for the machines'.[25]

Bathing stations and platforms

After bathing machines had declined in popularity, bathing stations were provided at some beaches. Sited above the high-water mark, these simple structures consisted of rows of cubicles in which bathers could change and store their clothing. One such

Fig 5.4
High Street, Margate, Kent
Margate High Street no longer runs beside the shore, as land reclamation has created Marine Drive. Modern buildings on the new line of the seafront rise higher than the single-storey shops on the western (left) side of the High Street, obstructing the views to the sea that the buildings on the eastern (right) side once enjoyed.
(BB67/08933)

bathing station was opened at Herne Bay, at the base of the East Cliff, in 1912 (Fig 5.5).[26] It comprised a row of fixed cabins on the promenade, divided into colour-coordinated male, female and family sections. Bathers would enter the water via narrow, horizontal gangplanks which extended out over the beach towards the sea. Similarly, at Broadstairs, in 1935, the Urban District Council erected a two-tier station at the base of the cliff. The design, of reinforced concrete, incorporated 66 bathing cubicles and 32 chalets, and the flat roof acted as a promenade and sun deck.[27]

Bathing platforms, a type of pier specifically for sea bathing, proved popular at resorts in southern Europe during the 19th century. However, they were relatively rare in England and were not as sophisticated as their Continental counterparts. They were essentially bathing stations in the water, with lines of changing rooms erected over the sea, either perpendicular or parallel to the shore. For instance, Thomas Pettman leased part of the foreshore in the Cliftonville area of Margate and established a bathing platform near Newgate Gap.[28] The mile-long Pettman Bathing Platform lasted for 75 years, until the outbreak of the Second World War.[29]

Fig 5.5
Bathing station,
East Cliff, Herne Bay,
Kent; 1912,
Mr Palmer
As well as incorporating colour-coordinated cabins for males, females and families, the East Cliff bathing station included caretaker's accommodation, a ticket office and toilets. The water chute provided an exhilarating way to enter the sea.
(From Official Guide to Herne Bay, *1936 DP022309)*

Bathhouses and hydropathic hotels

Bathing in the sea was not ideal for all people and was not deemed appropriate for all medical conditions. One notable casualty was the former admiral and governor of Jamaica Sir Charles Knowles, who died after suffering a paralytic stroke attributed to his bathing in the sea at Weymouth in 1777.[30] The bathhouse provided a solution, allowing more delicate visitors to partake in sea-water bathing, and, as no seaside resort in England could boast a hot-water spring, hot-water bathing could only be undertaken in bathhouses. They developed into multi-functional health and leisure complexes where subscribers could enjoy reading newspapers and drinking coffee, as well as bathing. Such establishments also helped to extend the season into the colder months of the year. By around 1810 nearly half of all seaside resorts could boast at least one bathhouse, and in 1836 Brighton had several:

> The principal bathe [*sic*] in Brighton are Mahomet's Turkish and Indian medicated vapour and shampooing baths, situated at the corner of the Junction Parade: Harrison's baths, nearly adjoining; Lamprell's swimming baths, at the bottom of East-street; Hobden's Artillery bathe, facing the Battery; Wood's warm and cold sea-water baths, near East-street; William's, at the bottom of the Old Steyne; the New Steyne baths; and Smith's Brunswick baths, in Western-street.[31]

The first reference to a seaside bathhouse dates from 1736, when an advertisement appeared in a Kent newspaper:

> Whereas Bathing in Sea-Water has for several Years, and by great numbers of People, been found to be of great Service in many Chronical Cases, but for want of a convenient and private Bathing Place, many of both Sexes have not cared to expose themselves to the open Air; This is to inform all Persons, that Thomas Barber, Carpenter, at Margate in the Isle of Thanett, hath lately made a very convenient Bath, into which the Sea Water runs through a Canal about 15 Foot long. You descend into the Bath from a private Room adjoining to it. NB There are in the same House convenient Lodgings to be Lett.[32]

The advertisement suggests that Barber's bath was for cold-water bathing only and

Fig 5.6
Hot brine bath,
Shanklin Chine,
Shanklin, Isle of
Wight; *c*.1845
The marble brine bath
was constructed in
c.1845 and removed
from the former
Fisherman's Cottage
bathing establishment in
1970. The integral steps
and ramped wooden
handrails aided entry
for the invalid bather
into the pre-heated sea
water.
(DP005391)

therefore served as a bath for those who did not want to expose themselves to the elements or the gaze of non-bathers. It was such a success that he soon constructed a second larger bath that could be filled with seawater regardless of the state of the tide.[33] The size of the bath is unclear, but in later references and in the case of the rare surviving example at Shanklin on the Isle of Wight, they were often for one person and were approximately the size of a modern bath (Fig 5.6).

By 1768, Dr John Awsiter was advocating that bathhouses could be used by invalids all year round and he included a blueprint for a bathhouse:

A building whose area is thirty feet, and twelve feet high, will admit of four rooms, with a bath in each, a lobby for servants to wait in, with a space behind them the whole length of the building, for the copper, the fuel, and cold bath, which must be kept supplied with fresh sea-water pumped out of the sea at half tide. One end of this room may be made also a sweating room, by a proper serpentine disposal of the copper flue.[34]

A year later Awsiter built the first bathhouse in Brighton in the area known as The Pool, at the southern end of the Steine, close to the established sea-bathing section of beach (Fig 5.7).[35] By 1803 the building was

Fig 5.7
1803 engraving,
The Baths at Brighton;
1769, Robert Golden
Built in 1769, Dr John
Awsiter's baths were the
first of their kind to be
erected in Brighton.
The baths later became
Wood's and finally
Creak's Baths.
(Courtesy of Sue
Berry)

Fig 5.8
Creak's Royal Baths,
Pool Valley, Brighton,
East Sussex
*The enlarged Creak's
Royal Baths was
demolished in the 1860s
and the site incorporated
into the Brill's Baths
complex.*
*(The Royal Pavilion
and Museums, Brighton
& Hove).*

Fig 5.9
Ingram's Warm Baths,
Southend-on-Sea,
Essex; 1804
*Ingram's Warm Baths,
shown here in c.1865,
were originally
established in 1804 on
the lower slopes of the
hill between the pier and
The Shrubbery. They
were demolished in 1879
to make room for a new
pier approach and toll
building, and new baths
were built further up the
hill.*
*(Reproduced by courtesy
of Essex Record Office)*

rectangular in plan and had a neo-classical façade that included a pediment and dentils (Fig 5.8). It contained two cold baths, four hot baths and a shower bath.[36]

The form of bathhouses varied from simple, makeshift or adapted buildings to complex, purpose-built structures constructed as part of grand resort development schemes. Ingram's Baths at Southend-on-Sea appeared to be little more than weatherboarded huts containing baths and heating apparatus, and the Brine Baths on the shore at Shanklin was an adapted fisherman's cottage (Figs 5.9, 5.10, 5.11). In contrast, the baths at St Leonards were an essential element within James Burton's new seaside town development and complemented the grand seafront hotel, terraces, assembly rooms and library (Fig 5.12).

Through their architectural style some baths consciously tried to associate their appearance with cultures thought to be linked with good health. The neo-classical style, the predominant style for public buildings in the late 18th and 19th centuries, evoked Greek and Roman bathing and medical traditions, an association sometimes made explicit through representations of ancient physicians, gods, symbols and inscriptions such as the *Hygea Devota* on Awsiter's baths in Brighton. In Greek and Roman mythology, Hygea was the goddess of healing, health and welfare, the daughter of Asclepius, the god of medicine and healing. A Greek Revival bathhouse was built in Ilfracombe in 1836 (Fig 5.13), and the Royal Baths at Weymouth, built in 1842, had engaged Doric columns to its St Mary Street elevation and Ionic details on its St Thomas Street elevation. The pointed arches, polychromatic materials and Solomonic columns used by George Gilbert Scott at Brill's extended baths in Brighton

Fig 5.10
Fisherman's Cottage
original bathing
house, Shanklin
Chine, Shanklin,
Isle of Wight; *c.*1817,
W Colenutt
Originally constructed
as a cottage, this
building was taken over
by James Sampson in
1845 and opened as a
bathhouse. Seawater
was piped into a large
tank, heated in a copper
boiler, and was then
fed into marble baths
(see Fig 5.6).
(BEC Howarth-Loomes
BB82/12142)

Fig 5.11
Fisherman's Cottage
original bathing
house, Shanklin
Chine, Shanklin, Isle
of Wight, *c.*1817,
W Colenutt
The former bathhouse is
now the Fisherman's
Cottage public house.
(DP005399)

Fig 5.12
St Leonards on the
Sea, East Sussex;
c.1834, from a
lithograph after
John Foulon

*This view shows the new
resort's combined
bathing establishment
and library of 1829 to
the seaward side of the
hotel. The low profile of
the baths was deliberate
so as not to obscure
views from the hotel.
(Hastings Museum and
Art Gallery)*

Fig 5.13
The Bath House,
Runnacleave Road,
Ilfracombe, Devon;
1836

*The Bath House was on
the landward side of the
tunnel to the Tunnels
Beach and tidal pools.
The main entrance was
through a portico,
leading to hot and cold
baths. (BB49/00021)*

Fig 5.14
Brill's Baths, East Street, Brighton, East Sussex, *c*.1866–9, George Gilbert Scott
Brill's Baths evolved during the 19th century until it occupied a large L-shaped island between Pool Valley and Grand Junction Road. Shortly before demolition began in 1929, the baths contained a large, circular sea-water swimming bath, a rectangular ladies' swimming bath, a cold plunge bath, and salt- and fresh-water shower baths.
(BB83/04428)

(*c*.1866–9, demolished 1929), gave the buildings a Middle Eastern flavour, but the strongest example of eastern exoticism in a resort bathhouse was the Clifton Baths of 1837 at Gravesend (Figs 5.14, 5.15).

The plans of seaside bathhouses shared a number of features. Male and female patrons were separated from each other soon after entering the building, or after leaving communal waiting rooms, meaning that many of the bathing facilities had to be duplicated. Three main plan types catered

for this social convention: one separated the sexes on either side of a ground-floor hall, the second used different floor levels for males and females, while the third type comprised a central block of shared facilities flanked by separate male and female bathing wings. An example of the first type is Fox's Baths on Knightstone Island, Weston-super-Mare, built in 1832 by Dr Edward Long Fox, a Quaker physician who was an advocate of sea-bathing for the treatment of mental and physical

Fig 5.15
The Old Baths, Clifton Marine Parade, Gravesend, Kent; 1837
The Clifton Baths, later known as the Old Baths, were constructed to the east of baths built in 1797. The monumental exotic style contrasted with the vernacular weatherboarding of the earlier building. Gravesend had been a river-bathing resort from the late 18th century and increased in popularity with the introduction of steamboat excursions in the 19th century. Both buildings survived until about 1910.
(BB67/02461)

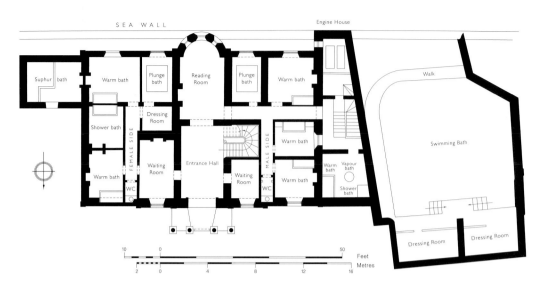

Fig 5.16
Fox's Baths,
Knightstone Island,
Weston-super-Mare,
Somerset; 1832, plan
of ground floor in
1860

*Knightstone Island was
the focus of the town as
a health resort following
the establishment of the
first baths there in
1820. Dr Edward Long
Fox acquired the site in
1830 and developed it
further to provide fresh
and salt water baths,
hot and cold vapour
baths, shower baths and
various medicated
baths. Bathing was
separated by sex, and in
addition invalids could
use the baths exclusively
on Sundays after 6p.m.*

illnesses (Fig 5.16).[37] In this building, a central hall separated the sexes, the male waiting rooms and baths being situated on the western side, the female facilities on the eastern side. Sake Dean Mahomet's purpose-built baths at Brighton, which he ran from 1821 to 1841, are an example of the second type: male bathers remained on the ground floor after entry, while female bathers were directed to the floor above.[38] Both levels had bathing rooms accessed from a central corridor and south-facing waiting rooms with balconies on three sides of the building.[39] The third type is illustrated by Ramsgate's Isabella Baths, which comprised a central saloon block flanked by separate bathing facilities on either side.[40] In bathhouses that did not have duplicate facilities, a sense of

propriety was retained by segregating the sexes (and invalids) according to the time of day, with most time usually devoted to male use.

Seaside bathhouses of the 18th and 19th centuries, like the pump rooms of inland spas, provided not only a variety of bathing facilities, but also rooms in which to relax and socialise. The Royal Kent Baths on the west cliff at Ramsgate had a saloon that contained daily newspapers and allowed views of the French coast.[41] The Clifton Baths at Margate, which were excavated from the chalk cliff north-east of the harbour, were fort-like in form and included a room that contained newspapers, an organ and, by 1851, a billiard table (Figs 5.17, 5.18).[42] Torquay's Baths Saloons (later the Marine

Fig 5.17
The New Baths
Margate, Kent; *c.*1829
engraving

*The New Baths, or
Clifton Baths, were
begun in 1824 and
completed by 1831.
The picturesque location
of the baths added to the
appeal of the bathing
and leisure facilities
available, and
contrasted to the earlier
sea-bathing culture that
had been centred on the
relatively sheltered bay.
(DP022310)*

Fig 5.18
Lido Beacon,
Ethelbert Terrace,
Margate, Kent
The site of the Clifton Baths was redeveloped in the late 1920s, to provide an outdoor swimming pool that opened in summer 1927 and was renamed the Lido in 1938. One of the original Clifton Baths chimneys was transformed into a beacon for the Lido, and still survives as a monument to two generations of bathing facilities.
(AA046224)

Fig 5.19
Remains of Baths
Saloons, Living
Coasts, Beacon Cove,
Torquay, Devon;
opened 1857
*The blocked arches are
the remains of the
swimming pool
constructed beneath the
Torquay Baths Saloons.
The pool had ceased to
function as early as
1869. It is now the site
of the Living Coasts
coastal and marine life
zoo, which opened in
July 2003.*
(DP001337)

Spa), designed in the 1850s as a combined health and leisure complex, was the social hub of the resort. It had a large, multifunctional hall and reading rooms over a swimming pool that had steps down to the sea (Fig 5.19).[43] Following treatment in the Medical Department, patients could retire to the ornately decorated cooling lounge, a Victorian equivalent of the Roman frigidarium.[44] It was not only large established resorts that had bathing facilities; smaller, more remote coastal settlements also provided baths combined with other facilities. For instance, Allonby on the Solway Firth had its own combined seawater baths and assembly room, built in 1835 (Fig 5.20).

Bathhouses in the early 19th century usually contained a number of small, often individual baths, but pools large enough for communal swimming also began to appear at some seaside bathhouses. Lamprell's Royal Brighton Baths (1823) contained a circular pool 53 feet (16m) in diameter and varying in depth from 3 feet to 5 feet 6 inches (1–1.5m). It held 100,000 gallons (450,000l) of water supplied by a steam engine and a horse engine that pumped 7,000 gallons (32,000l) of water per hour.[45] The swimming pool's domed ceiling was capped with a circular lantern. The architectural inspiration for this building seems to have been William Porden's riding school and stables built beside the Royal Pavilion.

Swimming-pool provision at 19th-century bathing establishments had to improve to match the quality of the municipal pools that were beginning to appear in towns across the country. For example, Folkestone's Bathing Establishment opened in 1869, but within ten years its swimming pool was deemed to be too small and a larger pool was built to the front of the building.[46] The Bathing Establishment closed in 1958, though the swimming pool remained in use until 1966.[47] New baths were also built at Teignmouth in 1883 at a cost of £2,500 and, unlike the previous baths, included a swimming pool as well as hot and cold baths.[48]

A strange variation on the bathhouse was the floating bath, which provided a relatively safe sea-bathing experience by creating a bathing pool on the sea. The hull of the vessel acted as a barrier to the waves and contained bathers in an enclosed environment. The decks housed the changing facilities. At Weymouth the King's Floating Baths were for the use of the Royal Family and may have been constructed following George III's criticism that the quayside baths did not contain enough sea salt in the water![49] The interior of the vessel was divided into two, one half containing the King's Bath and dressing room, the other half containing two separate baths and dressing rooms, presumably for other members of the royal family or aristocratic guests (Fig 5.21). Floating baths catering for a less regal clientele could also be found at Southend, moored off the beach to the west side of the pier (Fig 5.22).

Seawater bathing facilities were not restricted to purpose-built bathhouses. Enclosures were sometimes constructed on beaches to form pools that trapped seawater at high tide and provided an enclosed bathing place free from waves and currents. For example, Ilfracombe's Tunnel Beaches were made accessible after Welsh miners cut a tunnel through the cliff in 1823, and later

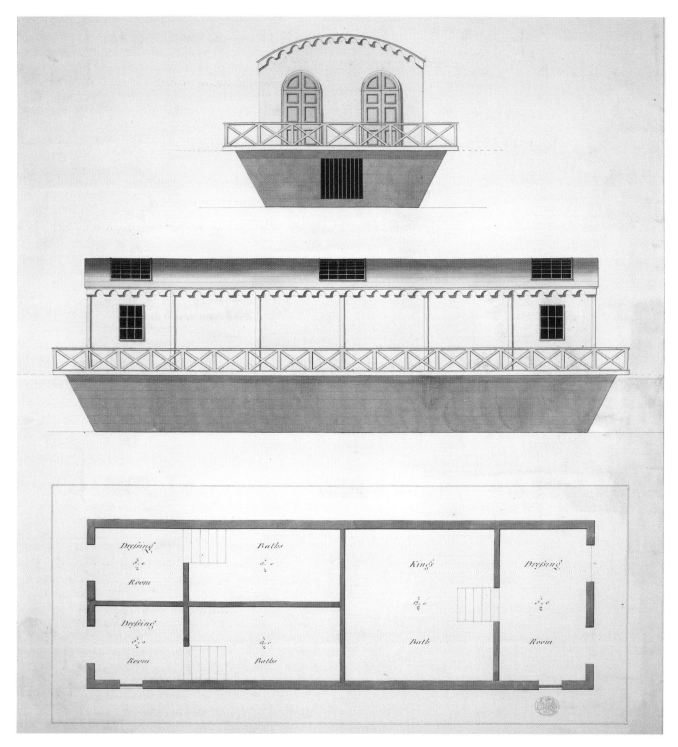

Fig 5.20 (opposite, below)
Allonby House, The Square, Allonby, Cumbria; 1835
Built as a combined seawater baths and assembly room, and costing £1,800, which was raised in £5 shares, this has a monumental classical façade that sets its apart from other buildings in this small coastal settlement. Known for its broad, firm sands, Allonby's reputation as a seaside resort had begun to decline by the end of the 19th century, and the baths and assembly rooms were converted into a private dwelling. (DP022311)

Fig 5.21
Front and side elevations and plans of the King's Floating Baths at Weymouth, Dorset; drawn by John William Hiort, c.1765–1800
King George III's Floating Baths comprised a hull bath divided into three by partitions and top-lit by a shared roof light. The Floating Baths could provide a greater bathing area and privacy than any bathing machine. (By Permission of the British Library [K.Top.12.h.])

Fig 5.22
Floating Baths,
Southend-on-Sea,
Essex
*Dated 1891, this
photograph shows a pair
of floating baths, owned
by the bathhouse and
bathing machine
proprietors Ingram and
Absolom. They were
moored off the beach to
the west of Southend
Pier, and bathers
entered the vessels via
external stairs, changed
in the changing rooms
surrounding the baths,
then descended into the
open hulls to bathe.
(Reproduced by courtesy
of Essex Record Office)*

in the 19th century male and female tidal pools were constructed.

Hotels and inns often installed hot and cold baths and even swimming pools to increase their appeal, and visitors staying in rented accommodation could also indulge in seawater baths in their holiday homes. In an 1894–5 guidebook, Walter David Fagg, the manager of the Folkestone Bathing Establishment Company, advertised that hot and cold seawater could be delivered to any part of the town.[50] At Blackpool, a company was formed in 1877 with the purpose of supplying seawater directly to houses via street mains;[51] the flat in Joseph Emberton's Blackpool Pleasure Beach Casino still contains a bath with three taps for hot, cold and seawater.

For the more discerning visitor hydropathic hotels were established to provide a wide range of water treatments for residents and other paying customers. This kind of establishment was generally for a higher class of visitor and provided virtually all the facilities of a resort in one exclusive location, a retreat from the increasingly boisterous seafront. Hydropathic hotels first developed in England in the 1840s following the success of the Grafenberg establishment of Vincent Priessnitz (1799–1851) in Silesia, and by the end of the 1890s there were 75 hydros around the country (*see* Fig 7.15).[52]

One such hydropathic hotel was Mont Dore Hotel at Bournemouth, built away from the seafront to the landward side of the gardens that flanked the course of the Bourne. It consisted of a 120-bed hotel with a separate baths building, set in acres of grounds planted with the resort's characteristic pine trees (Fig 5.23).[53] Some of the

treatments were based on those practised at Mont Dore in the Auvergne, from where spring water was imported for bathing and drinking. As well as sea- and spring-water baths, the treatments included Turkish baths, and pine inhalation and vapour baths. The hotel accommodation included an indoor tennis court, skating rink, winter gardens, reading room, smoking room, basement billiard room and a first-floor ballroom.[54]

The seaside environment and health treatments

Seawater was seen as an almost magical substance by some early medical writers and an entire leisure industry was founded on its curative properties. However, as Samuel Jones' poem about Whitby in 1718 had intimated (*see* p 11), sea bathing was not the only reason why a trip to the seaside could be beneficial to health, and the seaside environment increasingly became associated with good health. Nicholas Blundell noted on two occasions in 1710 that he had travelled to the seaside near his Crosby home to 'take the Aire', and in 1791 John Byng, fifth Viscount Torrington, recorded that Saltfleetby was 'an excellent station' for its sea air.[55] Thomas Reid, writing in 1795, was convinced that the air at the seaside was far more beneficial to health than that over land and believed that there was no healthier spot in the whole of England than the Isle of Thanet.[56]

A key element of the seaside environment was believed to be ozone, which was defined as 'a modification of oxygen, occasioned by repeated, electrical discharges, and characterised by a peculiar penetrating odour'.[57] Its disinfectant quality was considered beneficial to health, and locations where ozone was present were allegedly free from certain diseases. Ozone was seen in the 19th century as a seaside phenomenon, whereas the air in cities was thought not to contain ozone unless it was subjected to a thunder storm. As ozone could apparently be generated by passing electrical currents through oxygen, attempts were made to recreate it at inland bathing establishments where it was claimed that a single hour's treatment would equate to a two-week seaside holiday.

The sun also came to be seen as an important factor in improving health, and the science of heliotherapy and its artificial counterpart, phototherapy, grew in popularity in the late 19th and early 20th centuries. Although the ancient civilisations of the

Mediterranean may have used the sun for therapeutic purposes, it was not until the late 18th century that it was employed for specific treatments in Europe.[58] In the 1770s ulcers and tumours were treated with sunlight, but it took until 1859 for Jean-Martin Charcot to demonstrate that the sun had a therapeutic effect that was not dependent on its heat, and in 1893 Dr Niels Finsen began experiments that would lead to the creation of phototherapy.[59] By the 1890s scientists had discovered that heliotherapy could help children with rickets and the victims of tuberculosis.[60] It was also used in some cases of rheumatism, renal disease and syphilis.[61]

Climate was used as an advertising feature in most English seaside resort guidebooks from the end of the 18th century into the 20th century. The geographical situation of a resort was noted for its health-giving properties and was used to promote one resort over another. Commentators on climate also contrasted different climatic zones within resorts, which would be more or less suitable for different types of visitor. For instance, Brighton's air east of the Steine was 'eminently dry, sharp and bracing',

while the air west of the Steine was 'somewhat damper, but milder'.[62] Dr Barker's *The Climate Of Worthing* devoted chapters to temperature, humidity, pressure, ozone, electricity of the atmosphere, local vegetation, drainage, soil, purity of the air and how this particular climate and place could cure disease.[63] An 1867 guide to Bournemouth devoted a chapter to the 'Sanitary Character' of the resort, insisting that the information given was not a case of 'puffing' but was genuine medical opinion.[64] The pine trees were always an important feature in any description of Bournemouth's charms: 'The balsamic emanations of these Pines, possess curative properties of an invaluable nature to persons suffering from pulmonary diseases or weak and debilitated constitutions.'[65]

Although much of the science of climate of the 18th and 19th centuries may arouse more amusement than admiration, its impact was profound. By the end of the 18th century the first seaside hospital had been established and during the next two hundred years various types of formal, medical institutions were established.

Fig 5.23
Former Mont Dore Hotel, Bourne Road, Bournemouth, Dorset; 1881–5, Alfred Bedborough
One of the grandest hydropathic hotels, and described as 'by far the finest building in Bournemouth', the Mont Dore Hotel was built in 1881–5 to the designs of Alfred Bedborough in the fashionable Franco-Italianate style employed in contemporary hotels. The wealth of facilities provided at the hotel made it a resort within a resort.
(DP001306)

Institutional health care at the seaside

In the 18th century health-improving activities at the seaside were concentrated around bathhouses and the seafront, and medical treatment was seen as part of the busy routine enjoyed by wealthy visitors to resorts. However, by the end of the 18th century the first medical institutions in a modern sense had begun to appear at the seaside. The earliest was established by the far-sighted Quaker physician John Coakley Lettsom, who believed that seawater bathing and sea air were appropriate treatments for the kind of scrofula he witnessed among the poor of London.[66] He convened a meeting of like-minded gentlemen at the London Coffee House on 2 July 1791 to establish 'The Margate Infirmary, for the Relief of the Poor whose Diseases require Sea-Bathing'.[67] Margate was chosen because of the 'extreme salubrity of that part of the Coast, and the ready and cheap Conveyance hither'. The building, initially for 30 patients, was designed to deliver the type of treatments

Fig 5.24
The General Sea Bathing Infirmary, near Margate, Kent; 1793–6, Reverend John Pridden
Pridden's original building was modest in size compared with the later institution. The remains of the original building can be found in the east wing of the present quadrangle, behind the remodelled south entrance.
(BB94/19942)

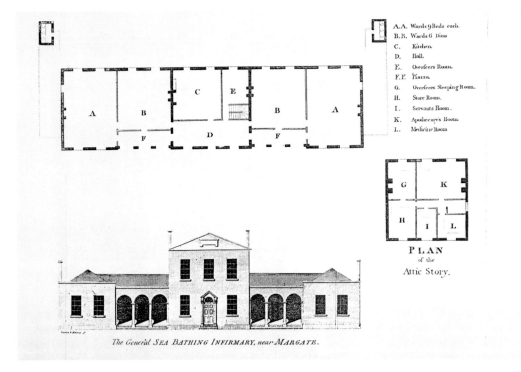

Fig 5.25
Royal Sea Bathing Hospital, Canterbury Road, Margate, Kent; 1793–6, 1816, c.1820, c.1853, 1857–8, 1882, Reverend John Pridden, James Knowles Junior
This view gives some impression of the growth of the hospital from its modest origins. The columns of the portico are reputed to come from Holland House at Kingsgate.
(BB91/21379)

Fig 5.26
Former Royal
Northern Sea Bathing
Infirmary, Foreshore
Road, Scarborough,
North Yorkshire;
1858–60, William
Baldwin Stewart
*Scarborough was one of
the first resorts to follow
Margate's example, and
a new sea-bathing
infirmary was
constructed facing the
South Bay beach in
1858–60.*
(DP006183)

Fig 5.27
Roof-top Promenade,
Royal Sea Bathing
Hospital, Canterbury
Road, Margate, Kent
*A 400-foot-long
(122m-long), single-
storey building was built
in 1882 by James
Knowles Junior to the
west of the hospital.
The new extension
included wards, an
indoor swimming pool
and a chapel. The flat
roof was balustraded,
and formed a long
promenade for exercising
and exposure to the sea
air and direct sunlight.
(BB91/21367)*

being advocated by Lettsom. It consisted of open colonnades in front of wards on either side of a two-storey staff and administration block (Figs 5.24, 5.25).[68] The sea-bathing treatment was conducted using the infirmary's own bathing machine, and by 1853 various baths had been installed in the hospital.[69] Patients were initially admitted during the bathing season, which ran from May to the end of October or early November and it was not until the installation of indoor seawater baths in 1858 that patients could be treated during the winter.[70] A large, heated seawater baths block, designed by James Knowles Jr, was added to the site in 1883 but Lettsom's seawater bathing treatment effectively ended before the outbreak of the First World War when the swimming bath was converted into a ward in 1910.[71] The regime and architecture of the Margate Infirmary proved inspirational and led to the construction of sea-bathing hospitals at English resorts, including Scarborough, Brighton, Felixstowe and Southport (Fig 5.26).

Although seawater cures ended, fresh-air treatment continued at the hospital during the 20th century. Knowles added a new ward which included a roof-top promenade, while balconies were incorporated into wards of the Wilson wing (Fig 5.27). However, during the 1960s and 1970s alterations were made to the wards which ended Lettsom's notion of 'solaria'. Balconies and wards were enclosed and heating installed so that patients were no longer exposed to the elements.[72]

Lettsom's ideas on fresh air and sunshine anticipated the work of scientists by almost a century. Research by Arthur Downs and TP Blunt in 1877, and Robert Koch in 1890,

Fig 5.28
Royal National
Hospital for
Consumption and
Diseases of the Chest,
Ventnor, Isle of
Wight; 1868–99
*This hospital was built
with detached patients'
blocks flanking the
chapel, dining and
administration
buildings. Most
bedrooms and sitting
rooms had south-facing
canted bay windows,
and all were fronted by
verandas.*
(AA93/06234)

demonstrated that sunlight was lethal to the tuberculosis bacillus and this led to the design of sanatoriums, which made maximum use of natural sunlight as well as fresh air.[73] The high-altitude, atmospheric treatments of Continental Europe could not be replicated in England, although sanatoriums were established in upland areas such as the Lake District, Mendip and Dartmoor. In 1903 Arthur Ransome addressed the question of the best location for sanatoriums:

It is obvious that pure air is indispensable, and therefore that we must avoid proximity to large towns, or to factories giving forth soot, dust, or deleterious gases. The best places are those in which there is an abundance of ozone in the air, and where the prevailing breezes sweep over the sea, or over moorland, or, better still, where these two conditions are associated, and fresh pure air comes from all quarters of the compass.[74]

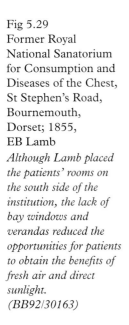

Fig 5.29
Former Royal
National Sanatorium
for Consumption and
Diseases of the Chest,
St Stephen's Road,
Bournemouth,
Dorset; 1855,
EB Lamb
*Although Lamb placed
the patients' rooms on
the south side of the
institution, the lack of
bay windows and
verandas reduced the
opportunities for patients
to obtain the benefits of
fresh air and direct
sunlight.*
(BB92/30163)

A variety of purpose-built private, voluntary and local-authority sanatoriums were created to provide patients with facilities to rest, to be exposed to fresh air and sunlight, to exercise and to eat well. Typical features included balconies, verandas, large numbers of windows, communal dining rooms and recreation rooms, a place of worship and wooded gardens. The ward buildings were generally oriented to face south and south-east, and therefore not necessarily to the seafront. Larger establishments had single- or multi-storey ward blocks, either attached to or separate from each other and the service buildings. The wards could be arranged in straight lines or have the end wards or wings canted to embrace morning sunshine and fresh air (Fig 5.28).[75] To maximise the circulation of fresh air and exposure to sunlight, administration and service blocks normally occupied the northern side of the site. One of the earliest, large-scale, purpose-built seaside sanatoriums was the Royal National Sanatorium for Consumption and Diseases of the Chest, built in Bournemouth in 1855 to designs by EB Lamb. It was built on the hillside to the north of the Bourne and faced south across the valley. The original building consisted of two storeys with a wide corridor on the north side providing access to the patients' rooms in the southern part of the building (Fig 5.29).[76] The same general principles of location and form endured in sanatoriums until the discovery of streptomycin.

Tuberculosis sanatoriums often incorporated innovative features to exploit their seaside location. A site at Gimingham near Mundesley on the north-east Norfolk coast was identified by Dr Burton-Fanning at the end of the 19th century as an ideal setting for a private, open-air, tuberculosis sanatorium. It was sheltered from northerly winds, but was favoured with bracing south-westerly winds, mild winters and high winter sunshine levels.[77] The main building, designed by Burton-Fanning in 1899, contained south-facing patients' bedrooms, and although there were no balconies leading off the bedrooms there was a full-length, glass-covered veranda fronting the ground-floor communal rooms (Fig 5.30). A feature of the institution was the use of Boulton & Paul Revolving Wind Shelters, which could be turned to face the sun or protect patients from strong, prevailing winds (Fig 5.31). Revolving shelters were also a feature at Kelling Sanatorium near the

Fig 5.30
Main Block, Former Mundesley Sanatorium, Gimingham, Norfolk; 1899, Dr FW Burton-Fanning
When this private sanatorium opened, there was accommodation for twelve patients, each with their own bedroom and sitting room. This proved financially unsustainable and so the sitting rooms were converted into bedrooms. (BB92/07266)

Fig 5.31
Revolving Wind Shelters, Former Mundesley Sanatorium, Gimingham, Norfolk
Believed to have been invented by Burton-Fanning, these revolving shelters were partially open-fronted timber sheds with pitched corrugated-iron roofs. They provided shelter for consumptive patients who were required to be exposed to the outdoor climate. (BB92/07249)

Fig 5.32
London and Brighton
Female Convalescent
Home, Royal
Crescent Mews,
Marine Parade,
Brighton, East Sussex
*Established in 1870,
this convalescent home
provided a seaside
retreat for 'respectable
women of the working
classes, over 15 and
under 65, convalescing
after illness'. Patients
were permitted to stay
for between two and four
weeks.*
(BB90/09300)

During the 19th century seaside resorts became popular locations for convalescent homes for patients recuperating from operations or injuries sustained elsewhere. Convalescent homes were established in England from the mid-19th century, and especially after 1870. Prior to this, patients had generally been sent home to recuperate, a practice that was not always conducive to the restoration of good health. Like sanatoriums, the favoured locations for convalescent homes were in the countryside and at the seaside, where the quality of the air was superior to that in towns and cities. Florence Nightingale wrote that:

> It is scarcely necessary to say that convalescent establishments should be placed in healthy, cheerful positions, varying in local climate according to the class of cases for which they are intended. The best climates can easily be determined by the usual practice adopted by physicians with private convalescents. Certain irritable chest cases do best in the moist relaxing sea-side climates of the S.W. of England. Diseases requiring a medium character of climate are usually sent to the southern districts, and to the Isle of Wight. If bracing sea-side climates are required, the S.E., E. and N.E. coasts and part of the N.W. coast are generally chosen.[78]

Some establishments combined convalescence with hydropathic treatments. Therefore these included purpose-built bathing facilities or were erected close to the sea. Many homes were built with particular groups of patients in mind, such as children, working men, and mothers with newborn babies. Some had associations with inland general and cottage hospitals, or organisations representing specific industries, unions or friendly societies. Accommodation varied greatly. Existing buildings such as houses and hotels were acquired and converted, while large, purpose-built homes were erected on big plots of land either on the seafront or in secluded areas a short distance inland (Fig 5.32). A general consideration was that the homes were designed to avoid a form and style that would remind patients of institutions; some homes were therefore designed to resemble large houses or hotels, although many still accommodated patients in dormitories rather than in separate bedrooms. As much as possible of the visitors' time was supposed to be spent away from their beds, so there was an

north Norfolk coast (opened 1903), which Burton-Fanning also helped to establish, and at the Royal National Hospital for Consumption, Ventnor. At Gimingham the Central Block, which was built about 1923, included the 'Mundesley' pattern window, which was invented by SV Pearson in 1921. The window could be fully opened by lowering the sashes and shutters below the window-sill. The sanatorium also provided accommodation in a detached bungalow and chalets for patients with special needs.

The discovery of streptomycin in 1943, and its successful use in the treatment of tuberculosis in the following year, revolutionised the treatment of the disease. Further antibiotics were produced during the 1950s and 1960s and, as a result, seaside establishments that specialised in climatic tubercular treatments declined in importance.

Fig 5.33
Drawing Room, John
Howard Convalescent
Home, Roedean
Road, Kemp Town,
Brighton, East Sussex;
1932
*The drawing room at
the John Howard
Convalescent Home in
Brighton had all the
comforts of a large
private dwelling or
modest hotel.*
(BB90/09343)

emphasis on day facilities, including communal lounges, libraries, reading rooms, writing rooms, billiard rooms and children's play rooms (Fig 5.33).

The Pease family, industrialists from Darlington, founded a convalescent home for its employees in Saltburn in 1867, using two houses in Garnett Street, then five years later, the firm opened a purpose-built home at the resort (Fig 5.34). The building was designed by Thomas Oliver of Newcastle, who took his inspiration from the renowned Imperial Asylum at Vincennes near Paris, established by Napoleon III.[79] Oliver was also responsible for the Prudhoe Memorial Convalescent Home in Whitley Bay, which was built in 1867–9 to serve the Newcastle Infirmary and replaced a home that had been established at Marsden near South Shields in 1862.[80] In contrast to the home at

Fig 5.34
Club & Institute
Union Holiday and
Convalescent Centre,
Marine Parade,
Saltburn-by-the-Sea,
Cleveland; 1872,
Thomas Oliver
*Built at a cost of
£12,000 by the
industrialist Pease
family as a convalescent
home for its employees,
the building was
purchased by the Club
& Institute Union in
1909. It is now their
only holiday and
convalescent centre.*
(DP006393)

Saltburn, which it resembled stylistically, the Prudhoe Memorial Convalescent Home faced east towards the sea, 'conveniently placed for sea-bathing purposes'.[81] The bathing facilities in the home included salt-water as well as fresh-water baths.[82]

Another provider of convalescent accommodation was the Railway Convalescent Homes organisation, established in 1899. In the previous year the philanthropic newspaper proprietor John Passmore Edwards had offered to pay for the building of a convalescent home for railwaymen on a site at Herne Bay, adjacent to the Friendly Societies' Convalescent Home, which he had also funded.[83] The architect Alfred Saxon Snell was commissioned to design both homes, and he produced schemes for three-storied buildings that would initially accommodate 50 patients in dormitories.[84] The Passmore Edwards Convalescent Home for Railwaymen opened in 1901, and six years later an extension for 50 more patients was built (Fig 5.35).[85] However, the home could not cope with demand and so a second Railway Convalescent Home was opened, this time in the north of England: Leasowe Castle on the Wirral peninsula dates from the late 16th century, and was converted from a hotel into a convalescent home in 1911.[86] While other Railway Convalescent Homes were established around the coun-

try, including some at the seaside (Dawlish, Rothesay, Par, Margate and Llandudno), the first home, at Herne Bay, was the only purpose-built one. Falling demand and rising costs led to the closure of some homes from 1961 onwards, to pay for renovation and modernisation at others.[87] The home at Herne Bay was not sold, but was leased as a residential care home for the elderly.[88] The Old Abbey at Llandudno closed in 2005, leaving Bridge House at Dawlish as the last remaining Railway Convalescent Home.

The Miners' Welfare Fund's preferred method for providing convalescent accommodation was the conversion of existing houses. During the 1920s provision was made for the miners of several mining districts, but only two homes were purpose-built when no suitable properties could be found for adaptation. The Lancashire and Cheshire Miners' Convalescent Home in Blackpool contained a range of facilities, including a smoking room, a reading room, a billiards room, a winter garden, a concert hall, retiring rooms and a cinema.[89] It was set in seven and a half acres of grounds and could accommodate 132 men. The second purpose-built convalescent home was built for Derbyshire miners on a four-acre site at Ingoldmells, near Skegness, and could accommodate 124 male and 34 female patients (Figs 5.36, 5.37). The home is

Fig 5.35
Former Passmore Edwards Convalescent Home For Railwaymen; Culver Road, Betlinge, Herne Bay, Kent; 1899–1901, A Saxon Snell
Externally faced in Canterbury red brick with Bath-stone dressings and hanging tiles, Snell's convalescent home for railwaymen was built in a rural rather than a seafront setting at the resort. Due to its popularity, it soon had to be extended. (BB90/09350)

GROUND FLOOR PLAN

SCALE OF FEET

Fig 5.36
Derbyshire Miners'
Convalescent Home,
Winthorpe Avenue,
Ingoldmells,
Lincolnshire; 1927,
FH Bromhead
*The Derbyshire Miners'
Convalescent Home was
designed in a neo-
Georgian style by
FH Bromhead of the
firm of Percy B Houfton
and Company of
Chesterfield. It cost
around £45,000 to
construct and was
completed in 1927.
(DP022312)*

Fig 5.37
*The ground-floor plan
of the Derbyshire
Miners' Convalescent
Home, which featured
in* The Builder *on
6 July 1928, shows the
double courtyard plan .
(BB94/19950)*

Fig 5.38
Sun lounge, Royal Victoria Hotel, The Marina, St Leonards on Sea, East Sussex; 1828–9, James Burton, 1903 (CC51/00480)

Fig 5.39
Sun lounge, Royal Victoria Hotel, The Marina, St Leonards on Sea, East Sussex; 1828–9, James Burton, 1903 (CC51/00479)
Sun lounges became a feature of many seafront hotels in the inter-war years. The ground-floor walls were pierced and extensions built out towards the line of the pavement.

two-storied, with two quadrangles accessible from the surrounding corridors and the central dining hall. These courtyards act as sheltered sun-traps where patients can rest and exercise. Both floors contain bedrooms and the ground floor has communal recreation rooms at the front of the building. These include reading and writing rooms with adjacent open-air rooms, sheltered from the coastal winds by larger billiard and recreation rooms on their eastern sides.[90]

Provision was also made for children to receive the benefits of the sea air. The Sea Bathing Infirmary at Margate had introduced a programme of schooling for its child patients in 1874, but it was not until the early 20th century that purpose-built schools for children with a variety of ailments were opened at or near the seaside. In Britain by 1910 there were just 7 open-air schools, but, by the mid-1930s, after a vigorous campaign promoting their virtues, there were 153, capable of accommodating 16,000 children.[91] Their regimes included plentiful fresh air and sunlight, a balanced diet, rest, cleanliness from regular bathing, physical training and medical treatment, as well as educational classes. For example, the Suntrap Residential Open Air School on Hayling Island was taken over on 1 October 1930 by Tottenham Education Authority, who rebuilt and enlarged it at a cost of around £30,000. The school was designed to accommodate 60 boys and 60 girls, aged from 5 to 16 years old, whose stay lasted from six weeks to six months. They were suffering from acute or prolonged illnesses, malnutrition and respiratory diseases such as bronchial catarrh and asthma. Most of the accommodation was arranged around a large quadrangle. On the north and south sides there were parallel dormitory blocks for the girls and boys respectively, with verandas on the south side with sliding blinds. On the east side there were classrooms and a playroom, while on the west side were the dining room, kitchen, baths, lavatories and stores. To the south of this complex were the isolation block and the staff hostel and administration block. All parts of the complex were linked by corridors or covered walkways.

Modernism, health and the lido

One of the themes of the Modern Movement was to employ features designed to introduce more sun and fresh air into buildings (*see* Fig 4.36). These included balconies, terraces and roof-top gardens, and the use of structural steel and reinforced concrete enabled the creation of larger openings. Folding and sliding windows opened up rooms to the outdoors, while new forms of glass, such as vita-glass, were incorporated into sun lounges so that users could benefit from ultra-violet sunlight. Private houses, leisure buildings and sanatoriums adopted these features, both to create brighter interiors and to improve sea views. Residential flats – such as Embassy Court, Brighton and Marine Court, St Leonards – incorporated sun rooms, balconies and roof gardens, and the Midland Hotel, Morecambe and the Northumberland Hotel, Margate included roof-top solaria (*see* Figs 4.36, 4.37, 4.38). Hotels of the 19th century were adapted to embrace the vogue for sun and fresh air: for example, a sun lounge with folding, sliding windows was added to the south front of Burton's 1828–9 Royal Victoria Hotel at St Leonards. The modernity of the form was tempered by the inclusion of topiary and conservatory furniture, and the curved fenestration at the junction of wall and ceiling echoed the form of the lead roofs over the bay windows added to the original façade (Figs 5.38, 5.39). Bathing establishments such as Bournemouth's Pier Approach Baths and Torquay's Marine Spa also possessed solaria during the 1930s, the latter's being described as a 'vita glass sun lounge'.[92] Visitors to Skegness' Sun Castle solarium, built in 1932, could relax and sun themselves under a vita-glass roof and additional ultra-violet lamps.[93]

Open-air swimming pools, later commonly known as lidos, can be viewed as the ultimate architectural expression of early 20th-century attitudes towards health and leisure. These complexes, built throughout the country, combined freshwater or sea-water bathing, sunbathing and fresh air in an enclosed space that was affordable to most

people. The popularity of these pursuits led to the construction of open-air pools at most seaside resorts from 1915 onwards, financed by the local authority and usually designed by local-authority engineers and architects.[94] Although their lifespan was shorter than the pleasure piers that came before them, they also became defining features of resorts, with images of open-air pools and bathers appearing in brochures and on posters, conveying a message of health, fun and Continental sophistication (Fig 5.40). This imagery continued to be

Fig 5.40
Plymouth, British Railways (WR) poster; 1950s, Harry Riley
This British Railways poster features Plymouth's Tinside Lido, in what resembles a Mediterranean landscape.
(National Railway Museum/Science & Society Picture Library)

Fig 5.41
Morecambe and
Heysham, LMS
Railway poster;
between 1923 and
1947, Frank Sherwin
*The centrepiece of this
advertising poster is
Morecambe's Super
Swimming Stadium,
here described as the
New Luxury Swimming
Pool. Illuminated by the
high summer sun, the
pool is suspiciously
devoid of the masses of
trippers that it usually
attracted.*
(National Railway
Museum/Science &
Society Picture Library)

THE NEW LUXURY SWIMMING POOL

MORECAMBE and HEYSHAM

BRITAIN'S MOST MODERN AND PROGRESSIVE RESORT

EXPRESS SERVICES and CHEAP TICKETS by L M S

OFFICIAL HOLIDAY GUIDE FROM ADVERTISING MANAGER, TOWN HALL, MORECAMBE.

used to seduce holidaymakers after the Second World War, but no new outdoor swimming pools on the scale of those of the inter-war years were constructed at England's seaside resorts after 1939.

The importance of an open-air pool to a resort was reflected in the scale of some of the developments. In 1923 Blackpool Corporation spent £75,000 on a pool measuring 376 feet by 172 feet (114.6 × 52.4 m), which could accommodate 1,500 bathers and 8,000 spectators.[95] Morecambe's Super Swimming Stadium, as the name suggested, was much more than an outdoor swimming pool (Fig 5.41). Described as being built in the 'modern style, and harmonising delightfully with the lines of the New Midland Hotel', it was constructed on reclaimed land adjacent to the harbour in 1936 and was the most expensive lido in the country, costing £130,000.[96] The pool measured 396 feet by 110 feet (120.7m × 33.5 m) and included within it a championship swimming course, a water-polo area and diving stage, and, at the shallow side, an 'artificial beach for sunbathing'.[97] Spectators were accommodated on a three-deck promenade and two grandstands that could seat around 2,000. At either end of the pool were colonnades that each had room for 500 deck chairs. Despite repairs, the pool was prone to flooding and leaking, and in 1975–6 it was closed and demolished.[98]

Changing attitudes towards open-air swimming and sunbathing, together with maintenance costs, led to the decline, closure and destruction of many lidos at England's seaside resorts. Those lidos that have survived, such as at Penzance (1935, reopened 1994), Plymouth (1935, re-opened 2003) and Saltdean (1938, re-opened 1998), have attained a new level of architectural and historical significance since their restoration (Fig 5.42; *see* Fig 4.39).

The seaside and health today

The English seaside environment is no longer recognised as a means of curing or relieving disease, and health considerations no longer form a significant factor in prompting visits to English resorts. However, the seaside climate is still considered invigorating and the beach and the sea remain the key environments for those who wish to relax, play or indulge in sports. The sun tan, which

first became fashionable in the 1920s, came to be perceived as a status symbol and an indicator of good health and, despite doctors beginning to recognise the risk of skin cancer in the early 20th century, millions of people each year still toast their bodies beneath the hot sun on beaches in Britain and in hotter climes.[99]

Health tourism in England is now centred on spa hotels that offer treatments based on cosmetic rather than medical benefits, and it has little or no relationship with the natural environment in which it is provided. However, health tourism at the seaside is still popular around the Black Sea, the Middle East and Japan. In France thalassotherapy – which includes a range of treatments using seawater, seaweed, algae, sand and mud – is an extension of ideas first

explored in England almost 300 years ago. The first thalassotherapy centre was founded in Roscoff in 1899, but of approximately forty establishments that exist around the coasts of France, over half were opened between 1985 and 1991;[100] in 1999 over 200,000 people visited French thalassotherapy centres.

The return to the origins of the seaside health resort, where the individual ventures to the coast in search of treatments for specific ailments, has not occurred (yet) in England. Seaside tourism is now largely entertainment driven and the most striking feature that separates resorts from ordinary towns is no longer the bathhouses and bathing machines, but the entertainment facilities that dominate the seafronts of most seaside towns.

Fig 5.42
Jubilee Pool, Battery Road, Penzance; 1935, Captain Frank Latham
The national penchant for outdoor swimming pools between the World Wars was expressed most confidently at seaside resorts. Designed by the Borough Engineer, Captain Frank Latham, the Jubilee Pool's striking triangular form distinguishes it from other lido designs. (AA031412)

6

Entertaining the visitor

The Georgian visitor headed for seaside towns in search of improved health, but while staying they expected a social scene with entertainments approximating to those they enjoyed in London and in spa towns. Before the end of the 18th century, at least one doctor was expressing his concern about this duality, fearing that the good work achieved by sea bathing was being undone by patients indulging in excessive amusements.[1] At the heart of Georgian resort life was the 'Company', which gathered daily at the formal entertainment institutions of the town. As discussed in Chapter 4, in the initial development of resorts relatively small sums were invested on makeshift facilities, but, as with housing, when confidence in the permanence of the seaside and its profitability grew, more significant investments led to the creation of larger, purpose-built facilities.

The Georgians established much of the pattern for seaside entertainment, including many of the informal pastimes of the modern seaside holiday, but of the formal institutions of the 18th century only theatres have remained popular until the present day. In the 19th century changing tastes and the growing numbers of visitors prompted profound changes to the entertainment available at the seaside. The sociability of the 'Company', and their intimate facilities were superseded by mass entertainments, often based on new technology. The earliest manifestation of this was in piers, but the winter gardens and other large entertainment complexes, the cliff railways and cliff lifts, aquariums and cinema were all dependent on new technology. In addition, from the end of the 19th century electricity had a marked impact on the entertainments that were on offer.

The types of entertainment available to the seaside holidaymaker today are not fundamentally different to those enjoyed a century earlier, but as tastes have changed, so have the detailed functions of many seaside entertainment buildings. Despite the destruction of many piers, aquariums and other types of entertainment buildings, those that have survived, like the resorts themselves, demonstrate an ability to adapt to the changing tastes of visitors.

Georgian entertainment at the seaside

At the heart of the Georgian day at the seaside was a series of gatherings and events in the formal institutions of the resort, usually organised and regulated by the Master of Ceremonies. The day began with bathing: for example, Lady Mary Coke, who visited Margate on at least three occasions in the 1780s, often bathed at 6a.m. or 7a.m.[2] Of course, not all visitors bathed and many seem to have stayed in bed or walked early in the morning. Once bathing had taken place, visitors to seaside resorts returned to their lodgings for a hearty breakfast. Between breakfast and dinner they socialised in inns and taverns, and, if a subscription was paid, in coffee houses, circulating libraries and assembly rooms. After dinner visitors went to the theatre or returned to take part in a new round of social events in the libraries and assembly rooms.

Employing a Master of Ceremonies to regulate the daily activities of the 'Company' was a practice derived from spas. The most famous was Richard 'Beau' Nash (1674–1761) of Bath, whose role was described as follows:

> His office included the introduction of all new arrivals to those who were already there, the arrangement of the minuet dancers according to their turn, and seeing that proper order was kept and that all the rules were duly observed; in short, he was the director and head of the whole society, and was called the titular King of Bath.[3]

As the uncrowned 'King of Bath' he changed the atmosphere of the spa and created a strict code of etiquette and behaviour, including regulating smoking and drinking.[4] The Master of Ceremonies also inspected lodging houses and fixed a tariff for every room, but at the heart of his work was the regulation of behaviour at formal events such as assemblies.[5] For example, Mr T Rodber, who was the Master of Ceremonies at Weymouth from 1784 until at least 1815, included among his rules the times of dances, a dress code, and 'That Gentlemen will be pleased to leave their Swords at the Door'.[6] To avoid accusations of cheating, a Master of Ceremonies was also involved in regulating card games: Charles Le Bas at Margate sold packs of cards and levied a fee from people wishing to play on 'lottery tables'.[7]

The circulating library

> Would you the page of History Peruse?
> Or Prose, or Poetry, or Novels chuse?
> The Circulating Libraries will send
> An ample choice of Books to ev'ry friend.[8]

Circulating libraries were at the social heart of resorts during the day, offering places for people to congregate and indulge in some 'light Summer gossip'.[9] They appeared at resorts as soon as the first visitors arrived. At Scarborough in 1734 there was 'the Book-sellers Shop, where Gentlemen and Ladies subscribe five Shillings, for which they have the use of any Books during the Season, and take them home to their Lodgings. ... They likewise take in all the News-Papers.'[10] Circulating libraries evolved from book sellers, coffee houses, inns or stationers and continued to serve as multi-functional entities, as lending books does not seem to have provided sufficient income (Fig 6.1). The writer Johanna Schopenhauer was clearly smitten with the joys of the circulating library:

> What bliss then to take refuge in those lending libraries. There one always meets company, exchanges a few politenesses with acquaintances, staring at strangers who stare back at one. And then there are many novels, newspapers, journals and pamphlets, most elegantly presented, which can be browsed through or taken home. And that is not all. Apart from these spiritual treasures, one also finds in these premises other more worldly ones. There are collections of all those many trifles, made of precious metals and stones which seem indispensable to the world of fashion, also all manner of articles needed for writing or drawing, from a simple sheet of paper to the most luxurious writing case or portfolio.[11]

As visitors spent weeks living in lodgings, they needed to hire items for the house and in some resorts the library provided these. For example, Powell's Library in Hastings in about 1820 offered a range of musical instruments, including pianofortes, as well as sofas, plate, linen and cutlery for hire (Fig 6.2). Libraries also served as an entertainment and administrative centre: Wallis' library at Sidmouth sold lottery tickets, and on the façade of a circulating library in Milsom Street in Bath a painted sign proclaims that it was the 'State Lottery Office'.[12] Libraries could also be made viable by combining them with other major features of a resort, such as at St Leonards, where the Royal Victoria Library, reading room, baths and hotel were all part of one complex (Fig 6.3, *see also* Fig 5.12).

Fig 6.1
Interior of Bettison's Library, Hawley Square, Margate, Kent; 1786, Mr Crofts
Jane Austen, in her unfinished novel Sanditon, *said that: 'The library, of course, afforded everything: all the useless things in the world that could not be done without'. In this early 19th-century view ladies and gentlemen promenade in the library. In the shop area behind there are small, glass display cases around the walls.*
(Margate Library Local History Collection, Kent Libraries and Archives)

Fig 6.2
Ambassador Restaurant, former Powell's Library, East Parade, Hastings, East Sussex
This house and restaurant was Powell's Library in the early 19th century. It originally had a bow-fronted shop front with a sign indicating that the library was on the ground floor and billiard tables were placed on the floor above.
(DP018007)

Fig 6.3
Royal Victoria
Library, The Marina,
St Leonards, East
Sussex; *c.*1828,
James Burton

Fig 6.3
Royal Victoria
Library, The Marina,
St Leonards, East
Sussex; *c.*1828,
James Burton
*A library was a key part of
Burton's scheme for a new
resort. This small but
elegant classical building
was built beside the baths
in front of the Royal
Victoria Hotel.
(Reproduced by permission
of East Sussex Library and
Information Service)*

Fig 6.4
Former Library,
Esplanade,
Weymouth, Dorset;
late 18th century
*This was the first purpose-
built library in the resort.
It was built on the seafront
and was originally
freestanding, though the
adjacent terraces were built
against it a few years after
its construction.
(AA037420)*

Fig 6.5 *(opposite)*
Former Library,
3 Regent Street,
Teignmouth, Devon;
1815, William Edward
Rolfe
*Internally the two-storied
front section of the building
is open to the first-floor
ceiling and surrounded by
a gallery, but at the rear,
which is single storied,
there is a large skylight
with plaster decoration
around it. This
arrangement appears to be
original, indicating that
this may have been the site
of the billiard room.
(AA046140)*

A library could be housed in any building: often it was to be found in a terraced
house indistinguishable from adjacent
houses that may have contained shops on
their ground floors. For instance, a book
plate inside a copy of Commin's *Improved
Weymouth Guide* in the Weymouth Public
Library, published in 1836, shows that it was

located in a terraced house in Charlotte Row
behind a large shopfront with Ionic
columns.[13]

Purpose-built libraries survive in a few
resorts, such as Weymouth and Teignmouth.
In the mid-1780s the main library in Weymouth was on the Esplanade, between Charlotte Row and York Buildings. The building
was divided into two parts by a courtyard:
the front block contained a library on the
ground floor, with a card room above, while
the apartments at the rear consisted of a
drawing room, a dining room, a parlour,
bedrooms and offices (Fig 6.4).[14] At Teignmouth the library also served as an accommodation bureau and a theatre-booking
agency, and contained a billiard room (Fig
6.5).[15]

These surviving buildings were not the
grandest examples of circulating libraries at
seaside resorts, however. In 1786 Margate's
librarian, Joseph Hall, moved into a new
purpose-built library, on Hawley Square (Fig
6.6, *see also* Fig 6.1),[16] described as being
built 'in an elegant and magnificent stile'.[17] It
was 42 feet square (164m²) and was divided
transversely by a row of Corinthian columns,
separating the library from the shop.[18] Over
the centre of the shop a dome with a diameter of 18 feet (5.5m) was topped by an
8-foot-high (2.5m high) octagonal lantern,
and Adam-style plasterwork decoration was
extended to the bookcases around the
library.[19] Samuel Silver, who took over Hall's
former library in the Assembly Room,
moved into a new building on Cecil Square
in March 1783.[20] Like its rival a few doors
away in Hawley Square, it contained a shop

Fig 6.6
Engraving of exterior
of Bettison's Library,
Hawley Square,
Margate, Kent; 1786,
Mr Crofts
This library was a
prominent feature at one
corner of Hawley Square,
near the social heart of the
resort. The dome lit the
shop at the front of the
building.
(Margate Library Local
History Collection, Kent
Libraries and Archives)

selling plate, Tunbridge cabinet-ware and stationery.[21] In 1809 it was described as consisting of two elegant rooms with an arch between them, and in 1811 a new music and reading room was built overlooking the garden.[22]

Circulating libraries were a key part of the Georgian resort, but they did not disappear with the advent of mass tourism. While the Public Library Act 1850 allowed the creation of free public libraries, it was not until the late 19th century that funding libraries through the rates became general.[23] However, changes in the publishing industry had prompted the decline of the circulating library by the end of the 19th century, but the last of the national chains of libraries only ceased lending in the 1960s.

Assembly rooms

And oft with rapture mem'ry shall recall,
The evening banquet and the op'ning ball;
Where splendour, taste, and elegance
   combin'd;
Transcendant beauty in perfection shin'd;[24]

Resorts provided at least one venue where visitors could socialise, gamble and drink tea during the day. In the evening the same building would serve as a venue for assemblies, balls and concerts. Unsurprisingly, the earliest seaside assembly room was at Scarborough:

This is a noble, spacious building, sixty two
Foot long, thirty wide, and sixteen high …
Here are Balls every Evening, when the
Room is illuminated like a Court Assembly
… on one side of the Room is a Musick-
Gallery, and at the lower end are kept a Pharô
Bank, a Hazard-Table and Fair Chance; and
in the side Rooms, Tables for such of the
Company, as are inclined to play at Cards:
below Stairs you have Billiard Tables.[25]

Scarborough had an assembly room because of its spa, but in other resorts the process of development was more gradual. As the number of visitors grew, enterprising innkeepers offered a room as a rudimentary facility (Figs 6.7, 6.8). For example, by 1763 an assembly room was provided in Margate at the New Inn on the Parade, and in 1772

Fig 6.7
Former Assembly
Room, Old Rooms
Inn, Cove Row,
Weymouth; 1770s
By the early 1770s a new
assembly room had been
built at the rear of a 16th-
century building on the
south side of the harbour at
Weymouth, near Ralph
Allen's house. This simple,
two-storied brick building
survives as the Old Rooms
Inn. It had ceased to be an
assembly room by 1785 due
to the success of the new
assembly room in the Royal
Hotel in Gloucester Row.
(DP022313)

Thomas Hovenden held his first assembly at the Swan Inn in Hastings in 'a suitable room, with a gallery for music'.[26]

The new, purpose-built assembly room at Margate, built beside Fox's Tavern in Cecil Square in 1769, marked a major increase in the status of entertainment facilities, and presumably also in their cost.[27] On the ground floor, beneath the loggia, were Hall's first circulating library, a toyshop and a coffee room. There was also a billiard room, but it is unclear whether it was on the ground or first floor. The assembly room was on the first floor and over it there was a 'Flight of Bed-chambers neatly furnished, for the Accommodation of such Persons as are not provided with other Lodgings at their first coming'.[28] The main hall measured 87 feet (26.5m) long and 43 feet (13m) wide, apparently making it one of the largest in the country, and there were adjacent rooms for taking tea and for playing cards (Fig 6.9).

During the 19th century some assembly rooms were built independently of inns or hotels, suggesting that they had become sufficiently profitable to be viable as separate institutions. The Public Rooms, built in Teignmouth in 1796, were described as 'a neat brick building, containing apartments for tea, coffee, assembly, and billiards'.[29] However, the growing resort needed a larger building and therefore a new assembly room was erected in 1826 using money provided by 40 shareholders.[30] The building contained a ballroom on the first floor, which was large enough for 100 couples to 'dance at ease' (see Fig 4.5).[31]

The end of the Georgian era marked the end of the heyday for assembly-room construction, though they continued as important venues through the 19th century (Fig 6.10). At Teignmouth, for example, the vogue for assemblies declined in the 1850s and the building was converted into a club in around 1870.[32] The assembly rooms at

Fig 6.8
Façade of First Base Day Centre, Montpelier Place, Brighton, East Sussex; c.1776, John Crunden
The façade of this day centre began life as part of the Castle Tavern's assembly room. Assemblies had taken place there since 1754 but this new, prestigious façade suggests a growth in the business of the inn. The assembly room was attached to a smaller three-storied building. Beyond it was the main body of hotel, a five-bay-wide, three-storied building.
(DP017962)

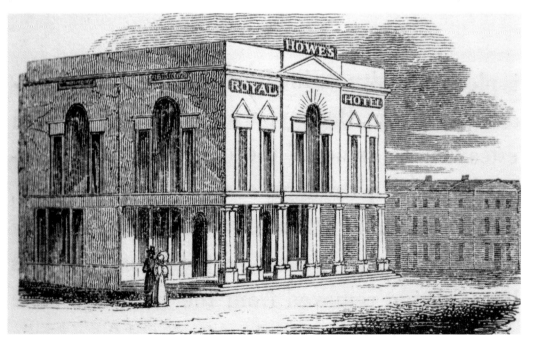

Fig 6.9
Engraving from Kidd 1831, Royal Hotel and Assembly Rooms, Cecil Square, Margate, Kent; 1769, William Hillyer
The main feature of the exterior of this building was 'a large piazza', a deep colonnade, facing the square. Small windows, set within the frieze beneath the parapet, may have lit the overnight lodgings that new arrivals could occupy. Behind the assembly room was the four-storied building that housed the accommodation of the hotel.
(Courtesy of the Society of Antiquaries of London)

Fig 6.10
Former Assembly
Rooms, South Beach
Parade, Great
Yarmouth, Norfolk;
1863, HH Collins
The assembly room
occupied the central block
and originally rose through
both storeys. There were
small additional rooms
attached to the main hall,
probably providing tea
rooms and card rooms.
The building was partly
burnt out in 1870 and
became a Masonic lodge.
(DP022314)

Fig 6.11
Engraving from Kidd
1831, Theatre Royal,
Addington Street,
Margate, Kent; 1787
This unprepossessing
exterior contained a small
but elegant theatre, which
served visitors from the
1780s until it was rebuilt in
the 1870s. Although it has
survived, this theatre was
closed for long periods in
the 19th century, an
indication of the fragility of
the theatrical business, even
at a busy seaside resort.
(Courtesy of the Society of
Antiquaries of London)

Margate were destroyed by fire in 1882 and a theatre was built on the site.[33] However, some new assembly rooms were built in the 19th century, including two at Bognor Regis, constructed in 1837 and in 1886. Both have survived, the later one having been converted into a cinema.

Theatrical entertainment

> Tho' no Marine Pavilion it can boast,
> Nor Royal Guests have visited the Coast.
> And soon Thalia's pleasures shall be shar'd,
> A decent Theatre is now prepar'd.[34]

The third major entertainment institution of the Georgian seaside resort was the theatre, but unlike the circulating library and the assembly rooms it was able to adapt and expand during the 19th century. In 1730 a company of actors from Canterbury performed during the summer at Margate, and as there was no purpose-built theatre they probably performed in an adapted building. By 1761 a converted barn was being used as a theatre and in 1771 a new theatre was created in a stable at the rear of the Fountain Inn.[35] Scarborough had a venue for plays by 1734, and by the 1760s Brighton had a makeshift theatre in a barn on the north-west corner of Castle Square.[36] Blackpool had a similarly rudimentary facility by 1789: 'Beauty displays itself in the dance, and the place is dignified with a Theatre; if that will bear the name which, during nine months in the year is only the threshing-floor of a barn … . Rows of benches are placed one behind another, and honoured with the names of *pit* and *gallery*'.[37]

The first purpose-built theatres began to appear at seaside resorts in the late 18th century. Legislation constrained theatrical performances but they were tolerated, and seaside resorts were one of the few places where actors could find regular, albeit seasonal, employment.[38] In 1788 an Act of Parliament allowed local magistrates to grant licences not exceeding 60 days, leading to a growth in the number of small theatres,[39] although the first purpose-built theatres had already appeared at the seaside. The first performance at what was later known as the Theatre Royal in Weymouth was on 8 July 1771.[40] In 1799 George Saville Carey described the theatre as being 'on a contracted scale, built in the shape of a wig-box, and not much wider'.[41] In 1831 a young actress Fanny Kemble recounted how: 'I got ready my things for the theatre, and when I got there I was amused and amazed at its absurdly small proportions; it is a perfect doll's playhouse, and until I saw that my father really could stand upon the stage, I thought that I should fill it entirely by myself.'[42] Externally it had a three-storied façade to the Esplanade with large shop windows on the ground floor flanking the central entrance, with a second entrance at the south side of the façade.[43] This theatre had a capacity of around 300–400, housed in a U-shaped auditorium with a gallery and boxes running around it, and a pit in the middle, below the level of the stage and boxes.[44]

New Georgian theatres at the seaside were usually rather plain externally, but their interiors were often described as being smaller versions of major contemporary London theatres, such as Drury Lane or Covent Garden (Figs 6.11, 6.12). A guidebook published in 1816 described Margate's Theatre Royal:

> It is an unornamented brick structure, totally divested of exterior decoration, its inside is fitted up in a handsome though chaste style, something after the plan of Covent-Garden; and is possessed of a complete wardrobe, as well as some excellent scenery, painted in a bold and masterly manner by Hodgins.[45]

Theatrical investment was a risky business, especially as theatres were highly vulnerable to changing fashions and conflagrations, and many only lasted for brief periods. For example, a theatre was built in Hastings in 1825, but by 1833 it had been converted into a chapel,[46] and in 1826 TS Saville built a theatre in Ramsgate, only for it to burn down in 1829.[47]

Theatre was to remain popular throughout the 19th and 20th centuries; as well as 'conventional' drama, music hall appeared from the 1840s. The Theatres Registry Act 1843 stipulated that proprietors could either run a theatre without refreshments in the auditorium, or become music halls where drinks could be served but plays could not be staged.[48] The entertainment once enjoyed in bars emerged into purpose-built halls added to pubs, while at resorts it moved into theatres on the seafront and on piers. By the end of the 19th century music-hall shows were being staged in large, elaborate theatres capable of holding audiences numbering hundreds, a far cry from their backroom origins (Fig 6.13). Music hall was seen by many as being low-brow, even vulgar, though by 1912 its broad appeal was recognised by the granting of the first Royal Variety performance.[49] Some resorts – such as Blackpool, Southport and Eastbourne – also provided opera houses, and operatic arias were also performed on stages on the seafront, in bandstands and on variety bills in music halls.

Circus also became popular during the 19th century. The second theatre at Teignmouth, a circular building for theatrical productions and circuses, was built in 1821, though by 1825 it had been converted into a coal store.[50] If a dedicated circus was not available, shows could be performed in

Fig 6.12
Theatre Royal,
Addington Street,
Margate, Kent; 1874
JT Robinson
The unimproved, brick, side wall of the present theatre provides clear evidence of the character of the original building. The façade and the interior were rebuilt in 1874 by JT Robinson, who was also responsible for the remodelling of London's Old Vic in 1871. (AA052662)

Fig 6.13
Former Palace of
Varieties, Pelham
Place, Hastings, East
Sussex; 1897–9,
Ernest Runtz

*Music hall emerged from
the back rooms of pubs to
be housed in some of the
grandest buildings on the
seafront. The mixture of
classical forms with some
lively detailing is typical of
major entertainment
buildings erected c.1900 all
around the coast. This
building later became a
cinema, a bingo hall and
an amusement arcade.
(DP018010)*

Fig 6.14 *(opposite)*
Blackpool Circus,
Tower Buildings,
Promenade,
Blackpool,
Lancashire; 1891–4,
Maxwell and Tuke

*The Circus, set within the
legs of the Tower, was built
to house 3,000 people. Its
arena is 42 feet (13m) in
diameter, apparently the
optimum size to help
bareback horse riders stay
on horses while performing
tricks.
(AA048176)*

theatres, although many circuses also transported their own wooden building around
with them and, of course, tents were also
employed.[51] These could be huge; for example, 'Lord' George Sanger's tent measured
185 feet (56m) in diameter. By 1856 his circus could already boast a range of circus
artistes, over 60 horses, a troupe of Indian
'savages', a band and wild animals, including
lions.[52]

In 1871 Charles Hengler opened his
'Cirque' in Argyll Street in London, which

included a ring that could be flooded, and
this became the model for the two surviving
circuses at seaside resorts: Blackpool Tower
Circus (1894) and Great Yarmouth Hippodrome (1903).[53] The Blackpool circus,
which is capable of holding 3,000 people,
has a ring 42 feet (13m) in diameter, which
was lowered by hydraulic power and filled
with water for aquatic performances (Fig
6.14).[54] Shows at the Hippodrome at Great
Yarmouth also include a conventional circus
and an aquatic display after the floor sinks

Fig 6.15
The Hippodrome,
St George's Road,
Great Yarmouth,
Norfolk; 1903,
RS Cockrill

This circus stands on a street immediately behind the seafront, with the aptly named 'Circus Circus' amusement arcade in front of it. Originally this site was open and holidaymakers on the seafront could have seen its elaborate façade, which is decorated with terracotta tiling and a variety of Art Nouveau detailing. (DP022315)

into the huge water tank beneath the ring (Fig 6.15).

Alongside formal theatrical entertainment, there has always been a variety of itinerant entertainers such as jugglers, magicians, fire eaters and opera singers at the seaside. Black-faced performers and black American performers both arrived in London in the 1830s, and 'Ethiopian' performers had appeared at the seaside by the 1840s.[55] Minstrels remained popular through the 19th century, but their supremacy was challenged by the arrival of pierrot troupes after 1891.[56] German bands were also popular in the bandstands that adorned every seafront and park but, unsurprisingly, they disappeared abruptly at the time of the First World War. Although these types of acts were all at home on the seafront and on the beach, they also formed the backbone of the fare enjoyed in variety theatres and music halls (Fig 6.16).

Glove-puppet shows had appeared in England by the 14th century and by the 1660s these were probably the 'Punch and Judy' shows that are still recognisable today.[57] The earliest-known reference to puppets in a coastal town is from 1710, when a puppet show was held in the Tolbooth at Whitby.[58] By the mid-19th century the Punch and Judy show was a familiar entertainment at the seaside and in the summer the London Punchmen went into the country carrying or wheeling the frames of their booths in front of them (Fig 6.17).[59]

The abiding joys of the seaside

For the social elite who visited resorts in the 18th century, the formal entertainment institutions in which the 'Company' met occupied a large part of the day. However, visitors could also indulge in many simpler pleasures that are still enjoyed by modern seaside holidaymakers. By the 19th century, these activities were focused on the resort's greatest asset, its beach.

Fig 6.16
Postcard of Seafront
around 1900,
Scarborough, North
Yorkshire

In the foreground, two minstrels on a makeshift wooden and canvas stage entertain visitors sitting on deckchairs. In the background, dozens of bathing machines in and out of the sea are joined by a few people paddling in the sea. The business of the beach is reminiscent of a modern summer's day, though the heavy clothing looks out of place to a modern spectator. (DP022316)

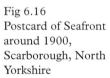

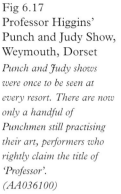

Fig 6.17
Professor Higgins'
Punch and Judy Show,
Weymouth, Dorset
*Punch and Judy shows
were once to be seen at
every resort. There are now
only a handful of
Punchmen still practising
their art, performers who
rightly claim the title of
'Professor'.*
(AA036100)

Fig 6.18 *(below, left)*
Detail of page 11
from Leighton 1847
*This cartoon shows the
hazards of a donkey ride.
Although donkey rides
today are confined to short
trips along the sands, early
accounts frequently refer to
trips into the country or
along cliffs.*
(Courtesy of Bryn Mawr
College Library,
Pennsylvania)

Fig 6.19 *(below)*
Sand Sculpture,
Weymouth, Dorset
*Visitors to Weymouth can
enjoy the latest works by
Mark Anderson. This
sculpture contrasts with the
limited architectural
ambition of most family
castle-builders. Sand
sculptures have been on
display at Weymouth since
the 1920s.* (DP022317)

Riding donkeys on the beach was a popular fad from the beginning of the 19th century (an 1819 guidebook dated the start of the pastime to around 1805); a writer in 1820 described the dual purpose of donkeys, providing fun by day and carrying smuggled goods at night (Fig 6.18):

ASSES HERE TO LET!
For all purposes right!
To bear angels by day,
And Spirits by night![60]

If riding donkeys proved too energetic, a holidaymaker could hire a chair and enjoy the view. Deckchairs, in the modern sense, may not have been invented until the late 19th century, but chairs were available to hire on the sands of Ramsgate as early as 1829.[61] Visitors also indulged in building sandcastles, and collecting seaweed and shells. Probably the earliest reference to 'sandcastle' construction comes from Giraldus Cambrensis in the late 12th century, describing how during his childhood he built churches and monasteries while his older brothers built towns and palaces in the sand (Fig 6.19).[62] In another account, Mr and Mrs Mount in 1759 walked on the beach one evening where they 'Gathered Sea Weed

ETS | AS THE DAY HAS BEEN ONE OF DISASTERS, THEY
THE | INDULGE A LITTLE IN THE DELIGHTFUL SPORT
IES | OF DONKEY RIDING — EXPECTING A LITTLE RURAL
ENJOYMENT ON A GIPSY PARTY —

Fig 6.20
The Rotunda
Museum,
Scarborough, North
Yorkshire; 1828;
RH Sharpe, extended
1861

The architect designed a
tall rotunda decorated with
pilasters and topped with a
dome. Two wings were
added in 1861 once
sufficient funds were
available. The building's
running costs were met by
annual subscriptions and
contributions from visitors.
(DP006190)

and past an hour or two in such Amuse-ments'.[63] An interest in natural history peaked in the mid-19th century, when thou-sands of holidaymakers sought examples of plants and wildlife for their collections, unaware that their apparently harmless pas-time would denude beaches of much of their flora and fauna. Some visitors also had an interest in fossils, and by the early 19th cen-tury Lyme Regis had established an industry based on fossil-collecting that has continued to the present day.[64]

The beach was also a venue for sporting events and a place from which to watch events taking place at sea. For example, races were held on the sands at Scarborough as early as 1734, and horse racing became a major feature of many resorts.[65] On 2 August 1773 the writer Fanny Burney went to see the races at Teignmouth: 'The sport began with an Ass Race. There were 16 – some of them really ran extremely well – others were indeed truly ridiculous: but all of them diverting. Next followed a Pig Race.'[66] These

races were part of two days of festivities, including a cricket match and wrestling bouts, and the entertainment culminated in a major rowing match between the women of Teignmouth and Shaldon.[67]

The working women of Teignmouth probably never intended to be part of the entertainment for visitors, but the working life of resorts was, and still is, a constant source of amusement for people on holiday. While staying at Deal in July 1815 Thomas Lott visited a local corn mill, where he saw the 'two large stones which grind the Corn and are very dangerous to go near'.[68] Charles Powell, while on holiday in September 1823, went to look at the steamer in Ramsgate har-bour and visited a lighthouse where he was intrigued by the oil lamps and the reflector.[69]

Holidaymakers also spent time at the types of historic buildings that still attract millions of people. In 1815 Thomas Lott enjoyed a youthful visit to Deal Castle: 'I for-got to mention that before we went to the play we went to deal castle a very nice Large one with excellent rooms and furniture. I brought a wafer from there and also ground my knife on a Stone there. Pulled the alarm Bell. We went on the Battlements and climbed up the Ladders to the towers etc'.[70] Charles Powell in 1823 was interested in more recent coastal fortifications, visiting Martello towers on the Kent Coast.[71] Other types of buildings also attracted visitors, including nearby country houses, cathedrals and, in the case of holidaymaker Charles Powell in 1823, the new prison at Maidstone.[72] The idea of having 'a cheap holiday in other people's misery' was also indulged in by Daniel Benham, who visited the Sea Bathing Infirmary at Margate in 1829 (*see* Figs 5.24, 5.25, 5.27).[73]

Museums and art galleries provided visitors with some 'rational recreation': the Rotunda Museum, built for the Scarborough Philosophical Society in 1828, was extended in 1861 (Figs 6.20, 6.21);[74] a guide to Bridlington published in 1846 boasted that 'a splendid Museum, the property of A Strickland, Esq, was added a few years ago'; while in Hastings a Literary and Scientific Institution, established in 1831, included a good library and a museum of natural history.[75]

As well as enjoying attractions on land, holidaymakers could take boat trips, launched from the beach or the harbour. These are still popular today, and during the 20th century some visitors were able to enjoy flights around resorts. At Blackpool flights around the tower were available, while at Weston-super-Mare visitors could enjoy short hops in planes and helicopters.[76] Tethered balloon flights had appeared at resorts by the early 19th century, and today at Bournemouth it is still possible to ascend beneath a large gas balloon.[77]

Victorian and Edwardian entertainment

The advent of mass holidaymaking transformed the type of entertainment available at resorts. The exclusive social scene and the finery of the Georgian visitor were gradually replaced by the worker's day trip and the rolled-up trousers of Victorian fathers. Bathing was supplanted by swimming, though bathing machines survived throughout the period. The Yacht Club and the Golf Club became the bastions of exclusivity in many resorts after the demise of the assembly rooms and circulating libraries.

Fig 6.21
Central Library and Art Gallery Blackpool, Lancashire; 1909–10, Cullen, Lockhead and Brown
This grand library was built using £15,000 provided by Andrew Carnegie, while the adjacent art gallery was endowed by JRG and CC Grundy. Located in the heart of the resort, these institutions provide an interesting counterpoint to the nearby seafront.
(AA052998)

Industrial Britain created mass seaside holidays and took the lead in creating and codifying modern sports. At the seaside, visitors may not have been in search of any activity that was too strenuous, but the 19th century saw the addition of swimming pools, tennis courts, bowling greens, full-length golf courses and versions of short golf, which only became 'crazy' in the 20th century.

The ultimate technical innovation of the 19th century had a marked impact on seaside towns: electricity ushered in new forms of transport, lighting and at the start of the 20th century the cinema. However, technology's impact was also felt more indirectly through the ability to build large structures more quickly and cheaply than in previous centuries. Therefore, in the second half of the 19th century investment in large complexes containing a range of indoor and outdoor entertainments supplemented the creation of single discrete types of entertainment.

Technological thrills at the seaside

Technology began to provide new ways to entertain visitors. From the Chain Pier at Brighton to the Pepsi Max Big One at Blackpool visitors have enjoyed increasingly thrilling, and stomach-churning, experiences. Novelty types of transport, and some more serious forms, were pioneered at the seaside and the aquarium found its natural home during the second half of the 19th century.

Piers

The last major addition to the Georgian resort's entertainment facilities was the pier. Initially built to allow ships to land visitors at resorts, it was only in the later 19th century that it acquired the range of entertainments with which it is now associated. In 1814 a pier at Ryde was built for promenading as well as for the arrival of visitors, and in 1823 the Chain Pier at Brighton opened. One author's son described it as 'that strange-looking bridge', but the father felt it was 'one of the most agreeable walks in the town', where 'we can enjoy the pure sea breezes, without the danger or difficulty of going out in an open boat' (Fig 6.22).[78]

The Chain Pier, unlike its successors, had a suspension structure carrying the deck, hence the reference to the bridge, and although it had an unusual appearance it survived storms until 1896. Most piers were built on piles, and the key figure in the development of this technology was the civil engineer Eugenius Birch (1818–84), who erected 14 piers.[79] In his first pier at Margate (1853–6), he pioneered the use of Alexander Mitchell's patent screw-pile, which involved screwing cast-iron columns into the sea bed. This then became the standard technique in 19th-century pier construction.

While piers continued to serve as landing

Fig 6.22
Chain Pier, Brighton, East Sussex; 1823, Captain Brown
The Chain Pier was built by Captain Brown, a naval officer who had built a pier at Leith two years before. Most piers were built by driving piles into the sea bed, but his choice of the suspension form created an aesthetically pleasing design that proved to be surprisingly durable. (DP022318)

Fig 6.23
Pier, Lower
Promenade, Saltburn-
by-the-Sea, Cleveland;
1867–9, John
Anderson
*To the modern viewer
Saltburn's pier seems
puzzlingly bare, but the
original function of piers
was to provide a
fashionable promenade and
a place for steamers to land
and collect visitors. Our
modern vision of the pier,
encrusted with a range of
kiosks, stalls and rides, is a
late 19th-century
invention.*
(DP006402)

stages and promenades, many developers soon realised that they could house a wide range of visitor attractions. These included kiosks for the sale of a variety of essential items such as sweets, chips and kiss-me-quick hats and amusements ranging from simple Mutoscopes (or 'What-the-Butler-Saw' machines) to whole, albeit small, fun-fairs. Some piers were built with, or enlarged to include, theatres, where some of the country's best-loved entertainers performed 'at the end of the pier'. The simple platform structure, which can still be seen in piers such as Clevedon and Saltburn-by-the-Sea, soon became encrusted with numerous structures with complex, exotic roof lines, the type of pier now familiar to seaside visitors (Fig 6.23, *see also* Figs 2.12, 4.28).

Fig 6.24 *(below)*
West Cliff Railway
Lift, Bournemouth,
Dorset; opened 1908
*By the 1870s engineers had
developed the ingenious
counterweight system to
allow lift cars to transport
visitors up steep cliffs.
Ostensibly a convenience,
they still provide visitors
with a novelty ride between
their accommodation and
the seafront.*
(DP001300)

Fig 6.25 *(right)*
Cliff Lift, Shanklin,
Isle of Wight; 1892
*The vertical lift may be
more practical than the cliff
railway, but it lacks its
thrill and the aesthetic
appeal.*
(BB82/13476B)

Transport

Since the early 19th century transport has been part of the entertainment for holiday-makers. Arduous stagecoach or sailing-boat journeys could not have been pleasurable, but the steamer and the railway, although often uncomfortable, provided an opening thrill to a holiday. The same bittersweet quality may still be experienced by travellers waiting patiently for their flights to the sun.

Within resorts, novelty forms of transport have been popular for 200 years. Children still enjoy donkey rides, romantic couples smooch in horse-drawn carriages and whole families take to the sea in pedalos or board miniature land trains. However, the seaside resort was also a location for pioneering forms of transport, vertically, horizontally and, in the case of funicular railways, diago-nally. It was not just through a desire to be modern, but also to overcome two geograph-ical 'problems' faced by some resorts: how to ascend high cliffs and how to travel along seafronts.

To overcome the difficulty of ascending cliffs, two devices were introduced: the cliff lift and the cliff, or funicular, railway (Figs 6.24, 6.25). In 1869 a hoist is mentioned at Saltburn 'for raising and lowering people thus avoiding the toilsome ascent by road'.[80] By 1876 the first cliff railway had opened at Scarborough. The South Cliff Railway employed two counter-balanced carriages on parallel tracks. When the weight of the top carriage was increased, by pumping water into a tank beneath the carriage, it descended, pulling up the lower carriage on the adjacent track, which had emptied its tank. This system was superseded by the use of a counterweight and electric motors, elim-inating the need to have a second counter-balancing carriage. The main alternative to funicular railways was vertical lifts, which appeared at resorts from the end of the 19th century. However, in the spirit of innovation and adventure Southend opted in 1901 for a moving walkway, a forerunner of the modern escalator. Designed by the American engi-neer Jesse W. Reno, this did not survive long and was replaced by a cliff railway.[81]

Trams, trains and now land trains have been used to transport visitors along seafronts. Most trams were removed from English towns, but Blackpool is now cele-brated because, through a mixture of good luck and judgement, its tram system has survived. Resort seafronts were also locations for more unconventional railways, especially at Brighton: on 4 August 1883 the first electric railway providing a regular service in Britain was opened there by the local inventor Magnus Volk.[82] It was extended in the following year to run from the aquarium beside the pier to the Banjo Groyne in front of Paston Place, and was again lengthened in 1901 (Fig 6.26).

Volk wanted to extend his railway to Rottingdean but, faced with insurmountable geographical difficulties, he had to find a different solution. He needed cars that could go through water at high tide and came up with the 'Pioneer' or the 'daddy-long-legs'. This has best been described as a cross between 'an open-top tramcar, a pleasure yacht and a seaside pier'.[83] Its elliptical deck stood on four tall steel legs, which each ended in a small truck with four wheels and scrapers to sweep seaweed aside. On the deck, the large saloon was domestic in character, and included a carpet, plants and curtains on the seaward side, while on the deck above there was a lounge covered by awnings in summer. It opened in 1896 and, although it survived the storm that destroyed the nearby Chain Pier, it was not financially viable and had closed by 1901. Weird and wonderful it may have been, practical it was not, yet it had at least one successor: at high tide Burgh Island is cut off from mainland Devon and therefore guests to the exclusive hotel can only reach it by the sea tractor, which carries them on a platform raised above the waves.

Fairgrounds

One aspect of seaside entertainment where new technology had an immediate and dramatic impact was in fairgrounds. Their origins can be seen as an extension of the pleasure grounds of Georgian resorts, and from the 1870s Raikes Hall at Blackpool offered a more modern version of the same type of pleasure garden. Fairgrounds also evolved from annual fairs held in major towns, which gradually changed from primarily commercial events to amusement fairs.[84] However, the immediate root for Blackpool Pleasure Beach and subsequent amusement complexes was in the amusement parks that developed along the beach at Coney Island in New York. By 1890 it was a crowded, noisy, 24-hour playground with freak shows, stalls and fairground rides lit by thousands of electric lights.[85]

Blackpool Pleasure Beach evolved from 1896 on a stretch of coastline occupied by a 'gypsy' encampment, but despite an eviction order in 1910 the last 'gypsy' did not leave until 1926.[86] In 1904 'Sir Hiram Maxim's Captive Flying Machine' became the first permanent structure on the site, and during the next three decades a variety of rides were added, including in 1906 a scenic railway, the Big Dipper in 1923 and the Grand National, Britain's only twin-track roller-coaster, in 1935.[87] Other resorts such as Great Yarmouth, Margate, Morecambe and Southport provided smaller though significant amusement parks, but the only rivals to

Fig 6.26
Volk's Railway, Seafront, Brighton East Sussex; opened 1883, Magnus Volk
Blackpool's trams are celebrated as important survivals, but Volk's Railway paved the way for larger trams and electric railways. The line closed during the Second World War, but it reopened in 1948.
(DP017974)

the Pleasure Beach at Blackpool are now found at inland parks (Fig 6.27).[88]

Amusement parks included a huge range of stalls, entertainment booths and rides. Carousels had appeared at fairs by the 17th century, and were futher enhanced by the application of steam power from the 1860s onwards.[89] The Ferris Wheel was designed by George W Ferris for the 1893 Chicago Fair and captured the imagination, despite being dismantled after a few months.[90] A 'Gigantic Wheel' was erected in 1896 at Blackpool at a cost of £50,000, but it was not a great success (Fig 6.28).[91] The first water chute appeared in 1893 at the Earl's Court Exhibition, and log flumes and a range of water splash rides are still popular in amusement parks.[92] Swings of various types had been regular features of fairs and were included in the park at Southend in 1894.[93] The dodgem track was invented in the USA

in 1921 and Billy Butlin saw the potential of this entertainment and imported the first Dodgems into England in 1928.[94]

The first rollercoasters consisted of cars on wooden tracks that relied on gravity, with human, animal or steam power to return the car to its starting point. In 1884 La Marcus Adna Thompson opened the first, small rollercoaster at Coney Island, only 450 feet (137m) long and 50 feet (15m) high, but the idea soon spread through America and into Europe:[95] the first of Thompson's Patent Switchback Railways opened at Skegness in 1885, and in 1887 he opened an office in London.[96] At Folkestone, a major feature of the late Victorian seafront was a long, straight, 40-foot-high (12m-high) switchback that opened in 1891 and was dismantled in 1919–20.[97] These first switchbacks were superseded in Britain by 1910 when larger figure-of-eight rides appeared:

Fig 6.27 (opposite) Blackpool Pleasure Beach, Lancashire

An aerial photograph is the best way to appreciate the complexity of the layout of this site. Each new, larger and more exciting ride is overlaid and inserted into increasingly crowded spaces. Unlike similar large theme parks in the USA, Blackpool has retained its earlier rides when new attractions have been added.
(NMR17760/20)

Fig 6.28 Ferris Wheel, Blackpool, Lancashire; 1896

Blackpool's wheel was apparently slow, jerky and uncomfortable, but it remained in use until 1928, when it was dismantled. One of the cars has been incorporated into the nearby Abingdon Street market as a small office.
(AA84/00148)

Fig 6.29
The Scenic Railway,
Dreamland, Margate,
Kent; 1919–20, John
Henry Iles
This is the oldest surviving
scenic railway in England,
though it was restored
following fires in 1949 and
1957.
(DP022319)

Fig 6.30
Pepsi Max Big One at
Pleasure Beach,
Blackpool,
Lancashire; operating
since 1994, Arrow
Dynamics
The rollercoaster developed
in terms of the technology
employed and the thrills it
could offer. Steel structures
and new ways of holding
the cars on to the ride
meant that taller, steeper
rides and faster speeds
became possible. In
England, the ultimate
rollercoaster is the Pepsi
Max Big One with speeds
of over 80mph and an
initial, blood-curdling drop
of over 200 feet.
(DP022320)

Southend Kursaal had the Harton Scenic
Railway of 1910, which survived until the
park closed in 1973, and at Margate the
Scenic Railway of 1919–20 has survived, and
became a Listed Building in 2002 (Figs
6.29, 6.30).[98]

Aquariums

In 1850 scientific research was published
that paved the way for self-contained, self-
sustaining, salt-water aquariums, and in
1853 the world's first public marine aquarium opened in Regent's Park.[99] By the 1870s
the first aquariums had opened at seaside
resorts; in 1871 a book on aquariums
included a description of the newly built
Brighton Aquarium.[100] This was a long,
roughly triangular building with the tanks
arranged around a corridor 220 feet long
and 23 feet wide (67m by 7m), including
one tank that was 103 feet long and 40 feet
wide (31m by 12m). A central row of
coloured stone columns with capitals
adorned with shells, fish and sea birds supported the vaulted roof. A second, narrower
corridor was used to display twenty small
tanks, and there was also a conservatory,
which contained a rockwork waterfall incorporating small tanks and ferns. The building
was rebuilt in 1927–9 and is still in use today
as an aquarium, though the internal arrangements have been transformed (Fig 6.31).[101]

An aquarium was built in Southport in
1874, followed by others at Blackpool and
Tynemouth in 1875, and Great Yarmouth in
1876 (Fig 6.32).[102] The last of these was
originally designed around a large, galleried
hall with 18 tanks up to 50 feet (15m) long
around the central space.[103] Its plan made it
relatively easy to convert when the aquarium
went out of business, and there are still some
remains of the tanks in what is now a cinema. A large but short-lived aquarium was

Fig 6.31
Aquarium, Madeira Drive, Brighton 1869–72, Eugenius Birch, extended 1874–6, exterior rebuilt 1927–9 by Borough Engineer David Edwards

Aquariums are commonplace today, but until the mid-19th century no one understood how to create a balanced environment for seawater fish. In the late 19th century they were established at major resorts, but declined in popularity during the 20th century. However, a new generation of modern aquariums has been built at a number of major resorts (see Fig 4.44).
(DP017972)

Fig 6.32
Former Aquarium, Marine Parade, Great Yarmouth, Norfolk; 1876, Messrs Bottle and Olley

This substantial aquarium on the seafront, built at a cost of around £10,000, was one of the first built in the wake of Brighton's success. Its main façade is perpendicular to the sea and therefore was designed to be seen by visitors along the promenade.
(AA050681)

Fig 6.33
Former Gem Cinema,
Great Yarmouth,
Norfolk; opened on
4 July 1908, Arthur S
Hewitt

*At the beginning of the
20th century Great
Yarmouth expanded its
entertainment facilities by
the addition of a number of
cinemas, the Winter
Gardens and the
Hippodrome. Remarkably,
most of these facilities have
survived and are still in use
for some type of
entertainment.*
(DP022321)

also built at Scarborough in 1877, in an Indian style with caves and grottos complementing the fish tanks, where swimmers staged exhibitions in the summer.[104]

Electricity and the first cinemas

Before the invention of cinema, seaside visitors could enjoy visual spectacles thanks to the camera obscura and the magic lantern. Camera obscuras have been used as seaside entertainment since the early 19th century: for example, one is mentioned on the Steyne at Brighton in 1807, and there was another on the Chain Pier at Brighton by the late 1820s.[105] Magic-lantern shows could be staged in any suitable space that could be darkened, but there were some permanent venues, such as at Cromer, where there is a hall that contains a purpose-built projection box above the entrance. Photography was also an important art form at seaside resorts, where it served as an entertainment and as a way of documenting the holiday through family portraits and picture postcards. At the end of the 19th century the Mutoscope,

including the infamous 'What-the-Butler-Saw' machines, offered a way of bringing pictures to life, but it was the motion picture that was the major leap forward.

The first seaside film show seems to have taken place on 25 March 1896 at the Pandora Gallery in Brighton, within weeks of the first films being shown in London.[106] Some of the recently restored Mitchell and Kenyon films from the start of the 20th century had been filmed and shown at seaside resorts to the people captured in them. These were not expected to be shown in purpose-built facilities, but in any hall that could be darkened. The first purpose-built cinemas probably appeared between 1904 and 1906, but the Cinematograph Act 1909, which addressed the safety of cinemas, enabled an explosion in cinema construction;[107] by the outbreak of the First World War hundreds had been built.

Early cinemas are well represented in seaside towns. Great Yarmouth boasts three early, surviving cinemas, Margate has two and Scarborough had four near the seafront in 1914.[108] The earliest survivor seems to be the Gem Cinema on the seafront at Great Yarmouth, which opened in 1908, though it was originally intended to be the venue for a wild-animal show.[109] It consisted of a large open hall (140 feet long by 42 feet wide; 43m by 13m) behind the elaborate façade, the simple formula employed in other early cinemas (Fig 6.33). The Gem's façade resembled the west front of a cathedral, but the façades of other early cinemas were dominated by large classical forms, arches or arcades. Harwich's Electric Palace of 1911 is a plain box with an elaborate façade dominated by a large pediment, and the centre of the façade of the 1913 cinema at Paignton has a curved bay window flanked by tall pilasters supporting a pediment.[110] The façades of Margate's two early cinemas are both dominated by large, rusticated arches (Fig 6.34).

Electricity powered the projection equipment, but it also decorated the façade of the first cinema. The façade of the Gem at Great Yarmouth was lit by 1,500 light bulbs, a modest reflection of Coney Island's Luna Park, which in 1903 had 500,000 light bulbs.[111] In Britain, Blackpool was the supreme exponent of electricity to enliven the architecture of the resort and to attract visitors. The first, electric, seafront lighting took place in 1879, though the illuminations we recognise today began in 1912.[112] They have continued until the present day, with

the exception of two wartime eras and 1923–4, when they were replaced by an unsuccessful carnival (Fig 6.35).[113]

Winter gardens, kursaals and pavilions

Winter gardens evolved as a distinct building type, although at some resorts the name simply denoted a popular entertainment com-

plex that might, or might not, contain a few exotic plants. Equally, a pavilion or a 'People's Palace' might offer a range of facilities indistinguishable from a winter garden, and in the early 20th century the kursaal emerged at some resorts. Irrespective of their names, these attractions all share common origins in the 18th-century pleasure gardens of Vauxhall and Ranelagh in London, which were emulated in gardens established at Margate in the 18th century and Blackpool in the 19th century. They also share a recognition of the limitations of the British climate; if a resort wished to attract visitors outside the warmest summer months, under-cover facilities were essential.

Winter gardens were a category of glasshouse used by gardeners, and by the 1820s these had evolved into huge structures as confidence in the technology grew.[114] In 1827 a large circular glasshouse was built at Bretton Hall (Yorkshire), and this appears to have been an inspiration for two major schemes at Brighton. Henry Phillips designed an oriental garden near his home, which included the Athenaeum, a large glass conservatory housing palm trees and a literary institute including a library, museum, reading room and school of science.[115] Work began in 1827 only to be abandoned due to a lack of funds, but the idea was revived in 1833 when the Antheum, 'that superb and gigantic structure', was built at the west end of Hove.[116] A glazed, domed structure

Fig 6.34
Former Cinema, The Parade, Margate, Kent; opened on 26 June 1911
This cinema, on the seafront opposite the pier, appears on Ordnance Survey maps of the early 20th century. Arches often dominate the centres of cinema façades as if they are symbolic of portals to an Aladdin's cave of visual pleasures. Here they are combined with musical instruments, an odd symbol to choose in an era of silent films. Was it, like the Gem, built for another purpose, but converted into a cinema?
(AA050229)

Fig 6.35
Illuminations, Blackpool, Lancashire
JB Priestley, in his English Journey *in the 1930s, described Blackpool as the 'great roaring spangled beast' with its breath-taking illuminations and nostalgia-inducing trams. In 1930 the first tableaux were introduced, and by 1937 two million visitors were being attracted to Blackpool in September and October.*
(AA058238)

Fig 6.36
Winter Gardens,
South Beach Parade,
Great Yarmouth;
1878–81 at Torquay,
re-erected 1903
(PC09231)

*This major addition to the
seafront provided an
essential venue for visitors
when the English climate
intervened in the holiday.
Its elegant interior made it
a fitting subject for a
postcard.*

WINTER GARDENS INTERIOR, GT. YARMOUTH.

Fig 6.37
Winter Gardens,
South Beach Parade,
Great Yarmouth
(DP022338)

reminiscent of the Dome beside the Royal Pavilion, the Antheum was intended to be an early winter garden as well as a museum and lecture rooms. Flaws in its design were recognised during construction, but not rectified, so that after the scaffolding was removed, the building collapsed!

This early setback may have deterred innovators at resorts, but the success of the Crystal Palace in London revived interest. Great Yarmouth's Winter Gardens benefitted from one of the virtues of prefabricated structures – their potential for relocation: originally erected in 1878–81 at Torquay, the building was dismantled in 1903 and reconstructed in Norfolk (Figs 6.36, 6.37).[117] Although buildings were erected in seaside resorts that imitated, albeit loosely, the form of the Crystal Palace, only one attempted to reproduce its principal function: Folkestone's Art Treasures Exhibition of 1886 displayed a large array of *objets d'art* in an electrically lit hall reminiscent of the 1851 exhibition.[118]

The first phase of winter garden developments began in the 1870s with large examples in north-west resorts, as well as at Bournemouth, Torquay and Tynemouth.[119] The Southport Winter Garden was one of the earliest and largest: built in 1874 by Maxwell and Tuke, who would later build the Blackpool Tower complex, its concert

pavilion could hold 2,000 people.[120] Blackpool's Winter Gardens opened in 1878 as a direct response to the new complex at Southport and as an indoor alternative to the attractions of Raikes Hall Pleasure Gardens.[121] It offered covered promenades lined with plants as well as a concert hall and a roller-skating rink (Fig 6.38). Morecambe also had a winter garden, the earliest part of which began life as the People's Palace in 1878, with the more ornate, oriental-style façade added in 1896.

In the early 20th century a second phase of winter-garden construction took place, at least in name. The Winter Gardens at Margate, opened in 1911, contained a large concert hall, an amphitheatre, cloakrooms, offices and refreshment rooms.[122] At Weston-super-Mare the Winter Gardens had been planned as early as the 1880s, but the building was only constructed between 1924 and 1927.[123] Although the site includes an Italian garden, a sunken rose garden and a lily pond with pergolas, it is effectively just another indoor entertainment venue for the resort.[124] Bognor after the First World War clearly felt the need for a winter garden, but with an eye on the potential cost and the timescale opted to re-assemble part of an aircraft assembly shed, which opened to the public in 1922.[125]

Many of the larger and more expensive hotels created smaller winter gardens or

Fig 6.38
Winter Gardens, Church Street, Blackpool, Lancashire; opened 1878, Thomas Mitchell
The Winter Gardens was enlarged in 1889 and 1896 by the addition of an opera house and the Empress Ballroom. In 1929–30 the entrance façade was faced in white ceramic tiles, to create a more unified exterior.
(OP00478)

Fig 6.39
Cliftonville Hotel,
Ethelbert Crescent,
Margate, Kent

A palm court or a winter garden was a luxury feature added to many grand hotels in the late 19th or early 20th centuries. Rattan furniture and exotic plants strive to capture something of the atmosphere of a colonial plantation, which many of the guests would have experienced at first hand. (BL 22784)

palm courts in which their exclusive guests could relax (Fig 6.39). For example, by 1900 Bexhill's Metropole Hotel had a large 'winter garden', while long sun lounges were added to the façades of hotels such as the Grand Hotel in Brighton and the Royal Victoria at St Leonards (*see* Figs 5.38, 5.39). Access to quiet, warm lounges were not restricted to the wealthy residents of hotels. The Lancashire and Cheshire Miners' Convalescent Home in Blackpool (1925–7) included a winter garden among the facilities for the recuperating miners.

Around 1900 a new name for multi-functional entertainment complexes appeared. Although the word 'kursaal' was derived from the German for a 'cure hall', the term was used in England for buildings with no specific health facilities. Bexhill's kursaal opened in 1896 and, although it was a venue where early films were shown, its glazed,

steel form resembled a winter garden.[126] The kursaal at Southend opened in 1901 and in its heyday it provided an amusement park as well as a circus, a theatre, a ballroom, dining hall, oriental arcade and a menagerie (Fig 6.40).[127] Bognor's kursaal, which opened in 1910, included a theatre, a roller-skating rink, a tea-room and an entertainment hall called Pierrotland.[128]

In addition to kursaals and winter gardens, other buildings with various vague but alluring names provided a range of entertainments. At Margate, the Hall by the Sea had been built in 1863 as the booking hall for the London, Chatham and Dover Railway, but not used.[129] 'Lord' George Sanger, the circus proprietor, took it over in 1874 as a restaurant and ballroom and it was rebuilt in 1898 with a room capable of seating an audience of 1,400 for music-hall concerts.[130] The new complex also included an indoor menagerie

Fig 6.40
The Kursaal, Eastern
Esplanade, Southend-
on-Sea, Essex; opened
in 1901
*The Kursaal was built on
the site of the Marine Park
Recreation Ground. As
well as providing a range of
undercover facilities, the
extensive park behind was
occupied by a large
pleasure ground with rides
including rollercoasters and
swings.*
(DP022322)

Fig 6.41
Hall by the Sea,
Marine Terrace,
Margate, Kent; 1898
*The Hall by the Sea
replaced the ticket-hall
building that had been
Sanger's headquarters since
the 1870s. This
entertainment complex
offered restaurants, bars,
and an auditorium which
could stage such diverse
activities as dancing and
boxing. It was demolished
following a fire in 1931
and replaced by the present
Dreamland cinema.
(BB97/00001)*

with cages holding lions, tigers, leopards and bears, and a large, roller-skating rink was added (Fig 6.41).[131] Multi-purpose entertainment complexes were proving popular with England's near neighbours as well, such as at Rhyl, where the Queen's Palace, built in 1902, contained a large ballroom, a theatre, a winter garden, a zoo, waxworks, shops, a 'native' village and an imitation of Venice, complete with canals. In its extravagant combination of facilities this was an anticipation of the pleasures to be found in one late-20th-century Las Vegas casino.[132]

Blackpool Tower complex, like another Las Vegas casino, included a reduced version of the Eiffel Tower. The tallest structure on earth when it was built, it was an obvious icon to copy in an entertainment complex, but it was the daring step that helped Blackpool to attain the pre-eminence as an entertainment centre it still enjoys today. Blackpool Tower, which opened in 1894, was far more than just a tower. Included in the complex was an aquarium, a menagerie, a monkey house, an aviary, a seal pond, a bear cage, the circus, the ballroom, a billiard saloon, restaurant and roof gardens (*see* Fig 4.31).[133] Blackpool had three multi-functional complexes: the Winter Gardens, the Tower and the Alhambra. The Alhambra opened in 1899 with a 2,000-seat circus,

a ballroom for 3,000 people and a 3,000-seat theatre.[134] However, the scheme was too ambitious and the company went bankrupt during 1902. The Blackpool Tower Company bought it in 1903 and reopened it as the Palace in 1904.[135]

All these large, multi-functional buildings were created to provide indoor facilities and entertainment for inclement summer days and during the winter months. Today, the same challenges are met by a range of private

Fig 6.42
Dreamland, Marine
Terrace, Margate,
Kent; 1935, designed
by Iles, Leathart and
Granger

*Until the construction of
Arlington House in the
mid-1960s, the cinema at
the front of Dreamland
dominated the shoreline of
Margate, a consciously
modern intrusion into an
originally Georgian
seafront.*
(AA050161)

and municipally controlled facilities. Some resorts provide leisure centres, which extended the facilities previously offered by simple swimming pools and lidos. There are also large cinema complexes, amusement parks and large conference centres that attract major business events and political conferences, as well as providing facilities for ordinary holidaymakers.

Resort entertainments in the 20th century

The pleasures of the pier, promenade, fairground, theatre, music hall and cinema initially retained their popularity in the 20th century, but their tone and character changed. Variety shows and music hall were succeeded by the comedy and entertainment shows of the 1950s and 1960s, but today these no longer attract large numbers of visitors over several months of the year.

The character of cinema shows has also changed. A cinema audience at the start of the 20th century may have watched films of themselves or a silent comedian, the thrill of the entertainment being in the medium as well as the message, but modern viewers expect to be transported to other worlds through huge screens with vast stereo systems. The small picture house of the early 20th century was superseded in the inter-war years by much larger, city-centre cinemas, the most famous being the Odeons that appeared around the coast and in every substantial English town. These have in turn often been closed in favour of large multiplexes on the edge of town (Figs 6.42, 6.43).

While the character of venues and their programmes changed, there was also a decline in the number of theatrical and cinematic venues. In the 1930s Blackpool had 4 theatres, 5 pierrot halls, 19 cinemas, the Circus, the Marina Ice Rink and the Indian Theatre. If each could accommodate two houses per evening, about 70,000 holiday makers could be entertained.[136] However, in 1936 one author was already proclaiming that 'the traditional form of seaside entertainment has outlasted its appeal', and that minstrels, pierrots and 'the local rendering of Liszt are dead'.[137] He foresaw their demise at the hands of film and broadcasting, though it was the forthcoming war that seems to have provided an insurmountable obstacle to their continuation. Theatres began to close and the music hall went into decline. Cinemas reached the peak of their popularity in the

Fig 6.44
Hippodrome, Middle
Street, Brighton, East
Sussex
*The popularity of bingo
was once seen as
undermining the cinematic
and theatrical heritage of
many towns. However,
without conversion into
bingo halls many of the
early theatres and cinemas
that could not be adapted
to audience demands and
new technology would have
closed and probably
disappeared.*
(DP017977)

1930s when resorts like Brighton and Bournemouth could each boast 16; however, since the war many of these have become bingo halls, discotheques or amusement complexes, where they have not been demolished (Fig 6.44).[138]

During the 20th century a growing freedom was experienced on the beach. Swimming costumes contracted from suits that covered the whole body to the tiniest bikinis that only just allow the wearers to retain a semblance of propriety. These changes reflect both changing attitudes to exposing the body to the sun and air, and an acknowledgement of the greater sexual freedoms possible on holiday. Although the 'holiday romance' might be thought of as a modern phenomenon, sexual freedom, or at least a high level of titillation, has been a recurring theme at the seaside since the 18th century. As early as 1732, Scarborough was described in a poem as 'blisful Town, of Health and Mirth', and the titillation associated with bathing in the sea was already apparent:

> Now loosly dress'd the lovely Train appears,
> And for the Sea, each charming Maid
>   prepares,
> See kindly clinging, the wet Garment shows,
> And ev'ry Fold some newer Charms disclose;
> While, void of Ornament and borrow'd
>   Grace,
> Thro' ev'ry Limb, we native Beauty trace.[139]

The ethos of the body beautiful was an important strand in the seaside holiday in the 20th century and now no resort is complete without a tanning studio offering 'sunsational' treatments to give visitors the tan that the British climate might deny them. The same philosophy also had an impact on resort facilities that were created for both health purposes and pleasure. Swimming and diving became popular activities, prompting huge investments in outdoor pools between the wars. Although the initial motivation for their construction may have been to promote health, the vast majority of users were there for fun. From 1945 Morecambe's Super Swimming Stadium (*see* Fig 5.41) hosted the 'Bathing Beauty Queen' contest, an event which, from 1956, became known as 'Miss Great Britain'.[140] The contest survived longer than the Stadium, continuing in Morecambe until 1989.

Since the Beach Boys popularised the Californian dream in the 1960s, surfing has become a major pursuit in resorts where sufficient surf is available. However, surfing was mentioned in England from the second half of the 18th century, and was recorded in Devon in 1904. Its popularity rose during the 1920s and 1930s, and its healthy, youthful image was soon exploited in railway posters. Newquay became the most popular surfing resort and its hotels used surfing as part of their advertising promotions. In 1939

Fig 6.43 (*opposite*)
Former Odeon
Cinema, 5 Dickson
Road, Blackpool,
Lancashire; 1938–9,
Robert Bullivant of
Harry Weedon
architects
*Odeon cinemas were built
in the 1930s in most major
towns in England. The
largest, seating more than
3,000 people, was built at
Blackpool. It has a steel
frame clad in brick and
decorated with white,
green and black faience.*
(AA053269)

the Atlantic Hotel listed 'surfing' after 'tennis', and The Bay Hotel enthused that 'Visitors can bathe from their own rooms, on our excellent sandy beach which extends for a mile immediately in front of the Hotel, Surf-Bathing being very popular'.[141] Today, Newquay is the acknowledged capital of British surfing and its streets contain numerous surf shops and a new, purpose-built surfing facility, with a café, shop and changing facilities has opened (Fig 6.45).

At the beginning of the 21st century, most entertainment is still concentrated on the beach and along the seafront. Old photographs show beaches crowded with dozens of small traders, depressed-looking horses tethered to bathing machines and a myriad of hats and umbrellas. The only long-term survivors on today's beaches are donkey rides, Punch and Judy shows and some small fairground rides. Fast food stalls, gypsy booths and some photographers' kiosks endure on the esplanade, where they are often joined now by tourist-information offices, crazy-golf courses and ice-cream sellers. In the central areas, the ground floors of many houses that once provided visitors with lodgings have been converted into cheap souvenir shops, bars, fish and chip

shops, and amusement arcades, while the upper floors are often unoccupied or just used for storage (see Fig 8.1). Larger amusement arcades are housed in more substantial blocks, decorated with frivolous fascias designed to capture the imagination, and money, of passing visitors.

While hedonism has often been the motivation for visiting the seaside, resorts have continued to cater for people seeking a quieter stay. Many provide museums and art galleries visited by holidaymakers on a rainy day or when more cerebral pleasure is required. For example, Falmouth is now the home of the National Maritime Museum Cornwall, and many resorts have more local attractions telling the story of colourful smugglers and heroic lifeboat men. St Ives' light, landscape and quaint streets, attracted artists as diverse as Barbara Hepworth, Bernard Leach and Ben Nicholson, leading to the conversion of many working buildings into studios, and cementing the town's position as the pre-eminent art colony in England.[142] Today it still has some fine private galleries, and it was chosen as the site for a branch of the Tate Gallery (Fig 6.46). Art galleries and museums are recognised today as a potential driver for regeneration. For

Fig 6.45
Bilbo Surf Shop,
6 Station Forecourt,
Cliff Road, Newquay,
Cornwall

Newquay attracts huge numbers of surfers each year, and so throughout the town there are shops and cafés catering for the needs of these visitors.
(AA052645)

Fig 6.46
Tate Gallery,
Porthmeor Beach,
St Ives; opened June
1993, Eldred Evans
and David Shalev

*The gallery building echoes
the form of the gas holder
that it replaced, but uses
materials and colours that
evoke its seaside location.
Since it opened it has
attracted over two million
visitors.
(AA052729)*

instance, Margate is using small arts and crafts businesses and a proposed Turner Contemporary gallery to try to regenerate the historic area near the harbour.

Conclusion

The entertainment facilities of resorts are one of the most obvious indicators of how resorts have evolved in the past 300 years. In the Georgian era visitors were few in number and formed part of a fairly homogenous group, the 'Company' that would gather daily in the library, assembly rooms and theatre. These wealthy people spent weeks at a time at a resort and therefore all were probably acquainted with one another, even before they arrived.

In the 19th century the exclusivity of the earlier period was breached by improvements in transport, increased wealth, and the time to enjoy it. The 'Company' was replaced by tens of thousands of visitors who would descend on the seaside on bank holidays and other summer weekends. Facilities suitable for the 'Company' were too small for these newcomers and would have been beyond their means and outside their tastes. Sociability was gradually supplanted by technological thrills ranging from piers, allowing people to walk on water, to switchbacks, hurtling screaming visitors along rickety tracks.

Entertainment facilities are one of the major differences between seaside resorts and similar-sized inland towns. Many towns in England have a cinema, a swimming pool and perhaps a theatre, but because seaside towns have large numbers of seasonal visitors the number of attractions and the size of facilities can be disproportionately large. Resorts also have a range of entertainments that would be unsustainable without visitors.

In the 18th century health was at the heart of the seaside experience, but by the 20th century entertainment had assumed this central role. Local authorities and major private investors in seaside resorts recognise that the quality, and quantity, of their entertainment facilities will be a key factor in their town continuing as a popular holiday destination.

7

Staying at the seaside

Although today's seaside visitors associate holiday accommodation with the ubiquitous bed and breakfast, the holiday camp or the often-faded Victorian and Edwardian seafront hotels, the first 150 years of seaside accommodation was dominated by the unassuming house. Its success in meeting the needs of growing numbers of visitors has, more than any other type of building, contributed to the townscape of resorts. The house also underpinned the economic development of resorts in the 18th and 19th centuries by providing homes for the rapidly growing residential population, while accommodating visitors during the summer.

In the 18th century, when the first visitors arrived at the seaside seeking accommodation, the inns they discovered were usually relatively small and uncomfortable and were only suitable for brief stays. As the health-seeking genteel visitor needed somewhere to stay for weeks at a time, the only option was often to stay in a private house. As a consequence, by the end of the 18th century many houses were built with extra rooms for summer visitors. This type of seaside accommodation, based on lodgings and the hiring of apartments, remained the staple for much of the 19th century, only to decline in popularity in the early 20th century. Many of the houses built for this purpose were then amalgamated to form hotels and guest houses, or became the bed and breakfasts that occupy the central streets of modern resorts today.

The house as seaside accommodation

In the 18th and 19th centuries most visitors to the seaside lodged in a rented house. Wealthy visitors could rent an entire house, but less-affluent holidaymakers stayed on one floor or in one or more rooms. Visitors wanted accommodation within their budget that offered comfort and cleanliness in a convenient location near the heart of a resort. A small number of tourists found rooms in buildings described as boarding houses, but analysis of diaries and directories reveals that there was little apart from the catering arrangements to choose between these and lodging houses.

In Brighton there appears to have been a distinction between lodging houses, houses let as a whole, and lodgings, which were simply rooms available within a house.[1] New houses were initially used as lodging houses while buildings in the older streets were relegated to being 'lodgings'. In *Nicholas Nickleby*, Dickens noted a similar decline in the status of buildings in London: 'Although a few members of the graver professions live about Golden Square, it is not exactly in anybody's way to or from anywhere. It is one of the squares that have been; a quarter of the town that has gone down in the world, and taken to letting lodgings.'[2] Powell's directories of Hastings published in the 1810s and 1820s provide the names and sometimes the occupation of the lodging house's owner.[3] In most streets the rooms available to rent were enumerated, but a small number of properties were labelled as lodging houses. In this Hastings example, the distinction between lodgings and lodging houses was being observed, but this does not seem to have applied in most resorts at most dates. An advertisement for a lodging house that appeared in *The Times* on 24 May 1806 read:

> Margate. – The WHOLE, or PART of a HOUSE to be LET, elegantly furnished, situated in the pleasantest part of High-street, with a double entrance, and commanding an extensive and beautiful view of the sea. It contains 2 kitchens, 2 parlours and 2 drawing rooms; 3 bedrooms on the second floor, and 3 on the attic. Apply to Mr Beck, Sadler, Oxford Street, near Portman-street.

Guidebooks and directories from the 19th century in most resorts usually list lodgings and lodging houses in an interchangeable way. Depending on demand, a house could be let either in its entirety or a room at a time, or occupied conventionally as a private residence.

The rise of seaside lodgings

When the first visitors arrived at a seaside town they had to stay wherever they could. For example, a visitor to Brighton in 1736 recorded that 'as the lodgings are low, they are cheap; we have two parlours, two bed chambers, pantry, &c. for five shillings a week'.[4] At Worthing the first visitors lodged in a farmhouse, while visitors to Margate in 1763 stayed in 'small but neat' houses.[5] In Jane Austen's unfinished novel *Sanditon* she described this humble type of accommodation: 'The original village contained little more than cottages; but the spirit of the day had been caught, as Mr Parker observed with delight to Charlotte, and two or three of the best of them were smartened up with a white curtain and "Lodgings to let"'.[6]

It is difficult now to envisage these elegantly attired visitors living in such humble abodes, and the acerbic diarist John Byng, writing in 1782, was puzzled that the wealthy put up with such poor accommodation: 'That the infirm, and the upstart, should resort to these fishing holes, may perhaps be accounted for; but that the healthy owners of parks, good houses and good beds, should quit them for confinement, dirt, and misery, appears to me to be downright madness!'[7]

Rising demand was gradually satisfied during the 18th century as growing numbers of lodging houses appeared. These were not a distinct building type, but were standard houses that could be adapted to meet the changing demands of visitors. For example, in 1765 a guidebook to Margate recorded how:

> The lodgings, tho' small, are neat and tolerably commodious, considering they are now applied to the reception of Strangers, for which purpose they were never originally intended. Some good houses have been built within a few years, and others are building: The old ones daily receive all the improvements they are capable of.[8]

A guidebook to Hastings published in 1797 noted that 'The Lodgings here are numerous and good, several new houses having, within these three or four years, been built for the purpose of letting; and more are in contemplation'.[9] An early 19th-century document in West Teignmouth stated that 'some of the inhabitants, on account of its being much frequented as a watering place, having lately built houses which are let for lodgings a few months in the summer only'.[10] In 1792, one John Hudson placed an advertisement in which he described how he prepared his house in Blackpool for visitors:

> JOHN HUDSON at the Centre House, returns his grateful Thanks to his Friends for the Favours they have been pleased to confer on him, and hopes they will continue the same, as nothing will be wanted in his Power to render the Accommodations agreeable. He has this Season fitted up his House, in the genteelest Manner, for the Reception of the first Families. Private Parlours to let, together with one fronting the Sea, with a large Bow-window.
>
> Also a Suite of Rooms to let to a large Family, or Party, consisting of a Dining Room twelve Yards by seven, a Drawing Room over it, both which have Bow-windows, containing eleven best Beds, and as many Servants' Beds as may be required.[11]

As trade directories became more comprehensive during the 19th century, two general trends can be established: over the course of the century the numbers of lodgings grew rapidly and the status of the buildings in which lodgings were available broadened, reflecting the growing democratisation of the seaside holiday. For example, Weston-super-Mare in 1804 was a small village of just over 100 people, but it was already described as having several lodging houses that had recently been built. By 1822 there were 12 available in the town, which had a population of 738 people in 126 houses; thus 10 per cent of the houses were in use as lodgings, approximately one for every 60 inhabitants.[12] By 1894, 158 lodging houses and apartments were listed in the town, which by then had a population of 15,864: one per 100 inhabitants. Ilfracombe saw a similar expansion in its lodgings provision during the 19th century: a directory of 1830 listed 18 houses where lodgings were available, and the number had increased to 54 by 1850.[13] By the end of the 19th century a huge increase had taken place: a directory of 1889 included 249 lodging houses, 7 boarding houses and 12 hotels, while in 1902 there were 399 apartments, 21 boarding houses and 7 hotels available.[14]

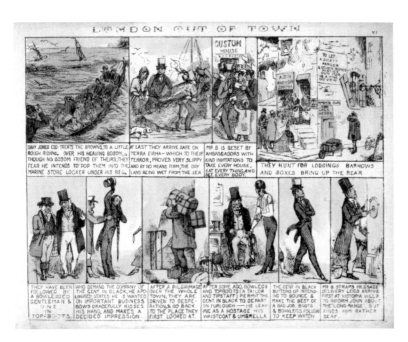

Fig 7.1
Page 6 from Leighton 1847

On arrival at the resort 'Mr B is beset by ambassadors with kind invitations to take every house', but prefers to set off in search of lodgings. However, after looking through the whole town he goes back to the first place he looked at.
(Courtesy of Bryn Mawr College Library, Pennsylvania)

In the 18th and 19th centuries any house could provide lodgings, so how did visitors find rooms to suit them? In 1787 a guidebook to Scarborough outlined the main ways to find lodgings: 'Securing a particular house, apartment or situation, which may be preferred, by letter to the proprietor, or a friend. Others rather choose for themselves, on the spot: and accordingly drive immediately to the situation they wish for; and if a board with lodgings written on it is affixed, alight, visit, and treat for them' (Fig 7.1).[15] Some holidaymakers also tried to stay in the same lodgings each year. For example, Daniel Benham describes how he and his family visiting Ramsgate in 1829 '[f]ound our old lodgings engaged, therefore took a sitting room and 2 bedrooms at Mr Cullen's in Hertford Place which was erected in 1813'.[16]

The 1787 guidebook mentioned that lodgings could be recognised by boards attached to buildings. Mrs Parry Price, travelling through Devon in 1805, wrote that she 'passed a most beautiful cottage enclosed in pleasure ground with a board fastened to a pole to say it was to be let. We then got out of the carriage & desired to look at it & a sweet pretty place it is & very genteelly furnished'.[17] Genteel houses had more discrete means of indicating to visitors that lodgings were available. For example, in *Sanditon*, Mr Parker arriving at the original village at Sanditon sees small 'Lodgings to Let' signs in cottage windows, and Lady Denham describes the 'lodging papers' in the windows of the higher-status terrace.[18]

Visitors could also consult lists of lodgings kept in circulating libraries and published in newspapers and guidebooks. By the middle of the 19th century, house agents had begun to appear at resorts, and as well as keeping lists of houses for sale they also had lodgings to rent.[19] For instance, by 1840 Hastings already boasted two lodging-house agents in prominent streets, where new visitors would be likely to find them on arrival in the resort.[20]

The economics of lodgings

The price of lodgings depended on the location in the town, the size of the house and the standard of the rooms. Houses located on the coast, with a sea view or in a prestigious location were more expensive than lodgings inland. In 1789 at Brighton one author noted that 'Of Lodging-Houses, those erected on the Stein, being most beautifully situated, are consequently most expensive; but there are others suitable to Persons of all Ranks and Fortunes.'[21] At Weymouth in about 1800 a guidebook noted that there were excellent lodging houses in the interior of the town, but those on the seafront were 'esteemed the most desirable lodgings'.[22]

Prices also depended on the time of year:

The houses in Brighthelmston, as is common at watering places, are usually let by the week or month, agreeably to the wish and stay of the visiting applicants, and the prices vary according to the season in which they are engaged; as for instance, buildings that command from five to fifteen guineas per week, during the months of June, July, August, September, and October, may be had for considerably less than a moiety of those prices at almost any other period of the year.[23]

A business card for Daniel Wonham's Rock Crescent at Bognor listed the prices for each month.[24] Number nine, which had eleven bedrooms, two parlours and a drawing room could be rented weekly for:

January £2 12s 6d	July 11 guineas
February £2 12s 6d	August 11 guineas
March £2 12s 6d	September 11 guineas
April 4 guineas	October £8 18s 6d
May 5 guineas	November 4 guineas
June £7 17s 6d	December £2 12s 6d

Renting out lodgings provided landlords with significant incomes. For example, in

1777 William Stane bought and converted a house into lodgings for £645, 9s 11d, and by 1796 he had received rent of £1,124, providing a profit of over £25 per year.[25] Stane was already a wealthy man: as well as earning money from his house, he owned hundreds of pounds of stocks and was lending money to people to buy houses.

Most lodging-house keepers needed a second source of income, and directories show that any tradesperson might offer rooms to visitors. A Scarborough guidebook of 1797, for example, reveals that some lodgings were provided by people involved in businesses catering for visitors, including a hairdresser and perfumer and a musician and dancing master.[26] However, most lodging-house keepers were grocers, butchers, drapers, and so forth: the types of occupation found in every town. At some addresses more than one trade was being practised. For example, in 1840 Maria Banks – in her house in Marine Terrace, Herne Bay – provided visitors with lodgings and a library, as well as serving as the postmistress and a perfumier (Fig 7.2).[27] Many 19th-century directories indicate that women kept substantial numbers of lodging houses and boarding houses. At the time this was considered a socially acceptable occupation for a woman, which exploited their domestic skills.[28] However, it is also likely that many women were listed because they were at home while their husbands were working.

On the other hand, some men were listed as providing lodgings, though their wives may have been responsible for the guests.

Most keepers of lodgings operated a single house, but some people made a business from renting out a number of properties, such as Mrs Mary Kingman, who, in 1874, was listed in a Bognor directory as running a lodging house at 1 Marine Parade, but by 1903 was also letting out apartments at 2, 9 and 10 Rock Gardens. Whole families seem to have become involved in letting rooms. In 1874 the building firm of Booker Brothers of Glamis Street in Bognor appears in a directory and Edwin, George and Henry Booker are listed as offering lodgings in Alexandra Terrace in Clarence Road: by 1878 four Bookers resided at 1, 3, 5 and 6 and offered lodgings. It is tempting to suggest that the family building firm erected the terrace as a speculation, with a view to letting out rooms and selling two of the houses (Fig 7.3).

These examples at Bognor also reveal something about the status of those who provided lodgings. Mrs Kingman's status rose in the late 19th century, so that she became eligible to appear in the private citizens section, though her lodgings were still itemised in the commercial section. In 1878 the two houses in Alexandra Terrace not occupied by the Booker family were in the hands of Major John Morton Jeffery and the Reverend William Jones, who were listed in

Fig 7.2
Marine Terrace, Herne Bay, Kent; 1816–1830s
In an ordinary house in this seafront terrace, Maria Banks provided a number of facilities for visitors. Frustratingly, the Herne Bay books of the 1841 census are missing and in 1851 she is not recorded in the terrace. Marine Terrace is a haphazard terrace of substantial houses that was part of the first, unsuccessful development undertaken by Sir Henry Oxenden in 1816. (AA053018)

Fig 7.3
Alexandra Terrace,
Clarence Road,
Bognor Regis, West
Sussex; pre-1878
It is the ordinariness of
these houses that is their
most obvious feature. In
plan they appear originally
to have had two rooms on
each floor. A blue plaque
commemorates the fact that
James Joyce wrote part of
Finnegans Wake *in the*
end house in 1923.
(DP022339)

Fig 7.4 *(opposite, top)*
Union Crescent,
Margate, Kent; *c.*1800
In this very plain terrace
Mary Figgins lodged for a
month in c.1828. In her
diary she describes how she
and her brother Vincent
suffered at the hands of the
house owner, a music
teacher, and another
lodger: 'whenever he is in,
he is what Vincent calls
tormenting the violin.
Mr Wilson likewise plays
so that between the two we
have scraping nearly all
day.'
(DP026090)

Fig 7.5 *(opposite,*
bottom)
Belvidere, The
Esplanade,
Weymouth, Dorset;
1818 onwards
The seafront at Weymouth
is dominated by tall
terraced houses, and it is
clear from early guidebooks
that most provided lodgings
for visitors. In the 20th
century many were
converted into bed and
breakfasts while others were
subdivided into flats. It is
rare for a large seaside
house still to be occupied by
a family.
(AA037433)

the private residents section of the directory. However, by 1890 both houses had been converted into lodgings run by George Day and Mrs Elizabeth Dicker, who appear in the commercial section of the directory. As in *Nicholas Nickleby*, the houses had 'gone down in the world' to become lodgings.

The form of lodgings

Most lodgings in the 18th and 19th centuries were in standard houses, often in long undifferentiated terraces. In 1810 the French-American merchant Louis Simond stayed in lodgings in a family home in London and described the house, the form of which echoes those in contemporary resorts:

> It may be a matter of curiosity in France to know how the people of London are lodged … . These narrow houses, three or four stories high – one for eating, one for sleeping, a third for company, a fourth under ground for the kitchen, a fifth perhaps at top for the servants – and the agility, the ease, the quickness with which the individuals of the family run up and down, and perch on the different stories, give the idea of a cage with its sticks and birds. The plan of these houses is very simple, two rooms on each story; one in the front with two or three windows looking on the street, the other on the yard behind, often very small; the stairs generally taken out of the breadth of the back-room.[29]

Although the Georgian and Victorian terrace house has a rigid exterior and plan form, diaries reveal great flexibility in the way rooms were used (Fig 7.4). Simond ascribed functions to each floor, but at the seaside it was common in lodgings to have services in the basement or on the ground floor, the landlord's family on the ground floor while the upper floors were used for whatever purpose suited the visitors. In Georgian houses with a tall *piano nobile*, these rooms on the first floor were the most prestigious, and therefore the most expensive.

New seaside houses were never the grandest buildings of their period, but they could be as substantial as all but the largest houses in London. The most imposing would best be described as being second or third class in terms of the classifications of the London Building Act of 1774.[30] The architectural writer Stefan Muthesius placed these houses in the categories that included the homes of professionals, lawyers and doctors through to those of lower-paid professionals, successful clerks and shopkeepers (Fig 7.5).[31]

Houses built to be used as lodgings seem to have followed the plans used in contemporary town houses. For instance, wherever houses were built on the seafront at Weymouth, their plans seem to have employed forms similar to contemporary urban houses (Fig 7.6). They were usually one room wide and two rooms deep, with the stairs normally

Fig 7.6
Late 18th- and early
19th-century House
Plans, Weymouth;
from RCHME 1970
*Seaside houses employed
the types of plan found in
towns throughout England,
but the way they were used
was very different. Instead
of being family homes with
functions ascribed to each
room, these houses were
used flexibly to meet the
needs of visitors.*

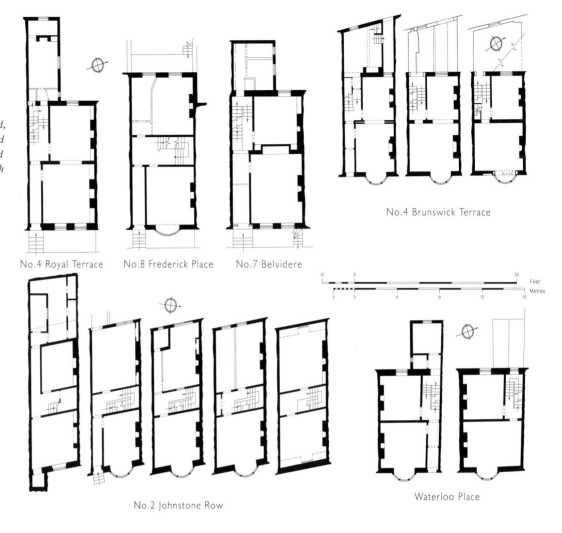

No.4 Royal Terrace   No.8 Frederick Place   No.7 Belvidere

No.4 Brunswick Terrace

No.2 Johnstone Row

Waterloo Place

at the rear of the buildings, though in John-stone Row, for example, they were between the front and rear rooms. On the upper floors the plan was similar to the ground floor but the space above the entrance hall was incorporated into a larger front room. Comparison of the number of rooms speci-fied in an early 19th-century directory with the houses described indicates that there was some subdivision of large rooms to increase the number of bedrooms.[32]

The general form of seaside lodging houses may follow that of houses through-out England, but within resorts there are important differences between some houses at the heart of resorts and houses in less central streets. The most obvious difference is in the height of the houses. There are more four-storied houses near the seafront, the additional storey providing extra lucra-tive bedrooms to let. Although a taller house would be more expensive to build, this addi-tional cost would be recouped within a few

years. As was noted in chapter 4, there was also a greater preoccupation with providing balconies and bay windows to exploit the virtues of the location. These attractive architectural features may have also served as adverts to passing visitors.

Most lodgings were in buildings designed as houses, but some were built in conjunction with the new facilities required in an expanding resort. In 1736 Thomas Barber advertised his new bath at Margate and noted that 'There are in the same House convenient Lodgings to be Lett'.[33] A fuller description of the facilities on offer appeared in an advertisement in the follow-ing year: 'Lodging Rooms, Dressing Rooms, and a handsome large sash'd Dining Room' and 'a Summer House, ... which affords a pleasant Prospect out to Sea.'[34]

The new baths on Knightstone Island in Weston-super-Mare, built in the 1820s, included lodgings in the bath house, and houses that were used as lodging houses

(Fig 7.7).[35] An advertisement for the sale or lease of these properties in 1847 described some of the accommodation as follows:

> The Bath House consists on the ground floor of an Entrance Hall; spacious Room, now used as Reading Room; 8 Bath Rooms, properly fitted up with hot, cold and shower baths, with anterooms and water closets. On the first floor, three sitting rooms, 7 bedrooms, and water closet, with an underground kitchen, Scullery etc. Servants Hall, Boiler for Hot Baths, steam apparatus and Drying and Hot Air Stores...
>
> The Sitting Room and bedrooms are so arranged as to form 3 sets of Apartments for the accommodation of invalids or small families who may wish to avail themselves of the Baths; they were fitted up at a great expense by the late Proprietor, and the whole forms one of the most complete Bathing Establishments in England.[36]

Lodgings combined with baths also existed at Great Yarmouth and Lyme Regis, and in some resorts lodgings were incorporated into other buildings.[37] At Margate the new Assembly Room, built in 1769, had a tavern behind it, but in the main block, above the first-floor Assembly Room, there was a 'Flight of Bed-chambers neatly furnished, for the Accommodation of such Persons as are not provided with other Lodgings at their first coming'.[38] Engravings and photographs, taken prior to a fire in 1882, show that the west face of the building had small attic windows, lighting what were presumably fairly rudimentary rooms (*see* Fig 6.9).

Life in lodgings

What could a visitor to a resort expect from his or her lodgings? Wealthy visitors might have exclusive use of the house and there would be no need for a resident landlord to provide domestic services as the occupiers had their own servants. However, some visitors could not rent a whole floor, either because of the cost or because of a lack of rooms to rent: for example, when the Benham family took lodgings at Torquay in 1849 they stayed on the floor above their host and his family.[39] On 16 August 1849 Daniel Benham described how they were sharing the first floor of a house in Ilfracombe with

Fig 7.7
Knightstone Baths, Knightstone Island, Weston-super-Mare, Somerset; 1832

Alongside the baths that were built by Dr Fox, a house was built to accommodate visitors. Providing rooms may have been a convenience for guests but this would also have been an important additional source of income.
(DP022324)

other lodgers, while on 31 August he recorded that 'The gentleman occupant of the first floor left today to make room for the ladies in the parlour'.[40]

Lodgings could be rented unfurnished for wealthy visitors expecting to spend long periods in a resort. At Teignmouth in 1805, for instance, the best lodging houses were said to be in East Teignmouth and the houses could be hired furnished or unfurnished depending on the choice of the tenant.[41] Many lodgings used folding furniture or furniture that could be moved easily. Folding tables could be set up to play cards or eat meals, and light tables and chairs could be moved to a window for light and air, and to the fire for warmth.[42]

Guests in lodgings had a range of options for dining, from providing their own food to what was effectively full board. For example, the author of a guide to Margate in 1797 described how he had found lodgings that included the use of a kitchen for one guinea per week,[43] and at Margate in about 1828 Mary Figgins regularly went to the market in the morning to buy her family's food, but her landlady prepared it.[44] Another option was to hire a cook and other servants for the length of the holiday: in Scarborough in 1797 'Cooks may be had, to attend a family, at half-a-guinea per week; and, as far as plain living, will be found competent'.[45] Hastings had Goodenough's Servants Agency, whose sign recorded that it also had branches at Margate, Folkestone and Dover, but not in any inland towns.[46] Guests in lodgings could also arrange for meals to be delivered to their rooms. For example, in 1797 at Scarborough dinners were 'served at lodging houses from the coffee-house, and many of the inns, upon reasonable terms'.[47]

Some lodgings, although described as such, were almost indistinguishable in their function from boarding houses as the landlord or landlady provided meals for the guests. By 1770, boarding houses for small families or single persons who required meals had begun to appear in Margate, and Scarborough had two boarding houses by 1797.[48] Mr Day, a grocer, ran one in Newborough Street and in Hardings Walk 'Mr Husband's Boarding House is considerably enlarged; and terms as follows: Board 1L per week; Lodgings, 10s. Servants, 15s board and lodging. The company find their own tea, sugar, wine &c'.[49] In 1808 at Weymouth, rooms were available at 26s per week excluding tea, sugar and wine, with the two best boarding houses being Scriven's on the Esplanade and Dymond's behind the church.[50] In 1824 William Moss, writing about Hastings, believed that boarding houses 'comprise all the advantages of hotels, without their noise and bustle, possessing all the comforts of private houses, without any attendant inconveniences'.[51] Suspiciously similar sentiments were expressed about Brighton's boarding houses:

> No town in the kingdom can be better furnished with those convenient accommodations for visitants, called Boarding-houses, than Brighton is; and those in our town, from their judicious management, may be said to include all the advantages of inns without their bustle, and all the comforts of private houses, without the inconvenience of being engaged in domestic concerns.[52]

Hotels

The wealthy visitors of the 18th and early 19th centuries spent weeks in seaside resorts and therefore usually stayed in rented houses; the alternative of a luxury hotel did not yet exist. For them an inn was an uncomfortable overnight stay to be endured while travelling or before finding suitable lodgings. A 1787 guide book to Scarborough noted that 'Some, especially such as arrive towards the evening, find it eligible to make an inn their residence for the night; and next morning deliberately seek a more permanent abode, entirely adapted to their inclination and convenience'.[53] An 1817 guidebook described Torquay's two inns as 'but tolerable' and other, early writers noted the expense that would be incurred by a prolonged visit to an inn: 'As for the Inns you cannot be at all decently accommodated in them. They are stinking filthy places, not fit for a pig … . They are besides hyperextravagantly dear & according to my calculation, had we gone there it would have cost us at least £100 per month.'[54]

Purpose-built hotels began to appear at seaside resorts in the 1820s, but before this they had begun to emerge in name, once assembly rooms or similar polite facilities were added to inns or taverns. For example, in 1769 a large assembly room was built as part of Fox's Tavern in Cecil Square in Margate; in 1794 it was renamed the Royal Hotel in honour of the visit of George Prince of Wales.[55] There is no indication of substantial changes to the buildings, the

Fig 7.8
Former Royal Hotel,
The Beach, Hayling
Island, Hampshire;
begun 1825, Robert
Abraham

This early hotel was part of the ill-fated scheme to make Hayling Island a major resort. The central, seven-bay section is the original building, flanked by two, asymmetrical additions.
(DP022325)

renaming simply implying a building of higher status and comfort (*see* Fig 6.9).

The word 'hotel' was in use in its older sense (to mean an inn with rudimentary catering facilities) by the 1760s, for example on the Lincolnshire Coast. There was also a purpose-built 'hotel', at least in name, at Bognor: one of the key buildings of Sir Richard Hotham's ill-fated Hothamton was a building described in contemporary guides as a 'commodious Hotel', though it does not seem to have had the range of facilities associated with modern hotels (*see* Fig 2.11).[56] But the first full-scale, purpose-built hotel was probably the Royal Hotel at Plymouth, which was completed in 1819;[57] by the 1820s a number of substantial purpose-built hotels were being built at resorts. In

1818–19 Dr Hall combined his two houses into the Royal York Hotel at Brighton, and in 1826 the Albion Hotel opened on the site of Dr Russell's house: its creation may have prompted the addition to the Royal York of a new, large, central block.[58] The development of Hayling Island in the mid-1820s included a new hotel, the foundation stone of which was laid on 16 December 1825 (Fig 7.8). At Teignmouth, Andrew Patey built Cockram's Hotel on the Den in 1825 while he was erecting Den Crescent and the assembly rooms; this hotel closed in 1988 and was replaced by a block of flats.[59] The Royal Victoria Hotel was at the heart of St Leonards in the late 1820s, and another early substantial, purpose-built seaside hotel is the Norfolk Hotel at Bognor (Fig 7.9).

Fig 7.9
Norfolk Hotel,
Aldwick Road,
Bognor Regis, West
Sussex; after 1826

In June 1826 a fire destroyed the forerunner of this hotel. By 1838 a guidebook described how 'A very handsome and capacious hotel' had been built. Like the Hayling Island hotel, this was extended later in the 19th century.
(DP018033)

Fig 7.10
Bristol Hotel, Marine
Parade, Brighton, East
Sussex; illustration
from Horsfield 1835
*This terrace of three houses
had become a hotel by
1835, but it is now three
buildings again, subdivided
into flats.*
(DP022326)

Fig 7.11
Royal Exeter Hotel,
Exeter Road,
Bournemouth,
Dorset; 1811–12 and
later additions
*At the heart of the Royal
Exeter Hotel, under the
battlemented tower of
1870, sits Lewis
Tregonwell's 'The
Mansion', the first house
built on this once relatively
desolate stretch of Dorset
coast. In a similar vein to
Southport's William
Sutton, Tregonwell has
been credited as 'The
Founder of Bournemouth'.*
(DP001321)

Railways stimulated the erection of major hotels in coastal towns, which were built at ports with resort functions, where they acted as places to wait between travelling by train and boat. A guide to Folkestone bemoaned the lack of accommodation in 1839, and it was the arrival of the railway and the start of the cross-channel steamer service that prompted the construction of the Pavilion Hotel in 1843.[60] Dickens described the hotel: 'at the Great Pavilionstone Hotel, you walk into that establishment as if it were your club and find ready for you your newsroom, dining-room, smoking-room, billiard room, music-room, public dinner twice a day (one plain, one gorgeous) hot baths and cold baths.'[61] In 1883 local historian SJ Mackie noted that it 'attracts year after year crowds of visitors that make it their abode frequently for months together during the summer season'.[62]

Sir Peter Hesketh-Fleetwood commissioned Decimus Burton to build a new town at Fleetwood to coincide with the establishment of a railway line which opened in 1840.[63] He included a number of hotels in the scheme, including the North Euston Hotel with its long, semicircular, convex frontage. Architecturally, it is only the absence of doorways on the façade that distinguishes the structure from a conventional, Georgian terrace. Before the middle of the 19th century there is often little else to distinguish hotels from groups of terraced houses. Confusingly, many modern hotels have been formed by merging a number of adjacent terraced houses (Fig 7.10).

Early hotels also resembled substantial houses (Fig 7.11). The Norfolk Hotel at Bognor Regis, prior to its extension, was described as a 'gentleman's mansion' and at some resorts the first hotels provided the centrepieces of long terraces or crescents (Fig 7.12).[64] However, by the 1860s the largest seaside hotels were striving to emulate the grandest, palatial hotels being built in London. These introduced a new scale of construction and helped to establish a version of the style being adopted in Second Empire Paris, combining elements of the Italian Renaissance with French detailing, particularly in the rooflines.[65] One such was Brighton's Grand Hotel, which opened in 1864, and which was the first to adopt the name that associated it with the Grand Hotel du Louvre in Paris (opened in 1855) (Figs 7.13, 7.14). Smaller resorts could not support such huge institutions, but still aspired to provide visitors with something of the same grandeur. For example, the Zetland Hotel, at the heart of the new resort of Saltburn, was built in 1863 in the form of a small Italianate palace (*see* Fig 2.20).[66] These hotels provided visitors with a range of facilities in which to relax and dine. In addition, at hydropathic hotels health treatments were also part of a visitor's stay: Blackpool Imperial Hydropathic Hotel of 1867 included 10 types of baths (Fig 7.15), and the Eastbourne Hydro, which opened in 1896, published its own newspaper to proclaim its bathing and hotel facilities, as well as describing excursions that might interest its guests.

During the late 19th century, large hotels with extensive facilities were built at every resort, though none could compete with the scale of Scarborough's Grand Hotel. A plan of the Cavendish Hotel at Eastbourne, which opened in 1873, shows that the ground floor was dominated by a large number of small, private sitting rooms as well as a bar, coffee room, billiard rooms, a smoking room and a commercial room.[67] There was only a small dining room, and

Fig 7.12
Hesketh Crescent,
Torquay, Devon;
1845–8, John Tapley
Harvey and William
Harvey
*Some of the first hotels were
located within a long,
prestigious terrace or a
crescent. This crescent of
houses with a central hotel
was the largest building in
Torquay when it was built.
(DP001355)*

Fig 7.13
Grand Hotel, King's
Road, Brighton, East
Sussex; 1862–4, John
Whichcord Junior
*The Grand originally had
260 bedrooms served by
early hydraulic lifts. At the
heart of the building there
is a huge, open-well stair.
An extension to the west
has destroyed the symmetry
of the original design.
(DP022327)*

Fig 7.14
Grand Hotel,
St Nicholas Cliff,
Scarborough, North
Yorkshire; opened in
1867, Cuthbert
Brodrick

*Scarborough's Grand
Hotel, which contained 300
bedrooms, dominates the
heart of the resort. When it
was built it was reputed to
be the largest hotel in
Europe. Cold sea water
could be drawn directly
from the sea for customers'
baths. (DP006187)*

few lavatories. The Metropole at Folkestone contained the services in the basement, while on the ground floor there was a dining room, ballroom, lounge, drawing room, smoking room, reading room and billiard room.[68] On the three floors above there were a mixture of suites, bedrooms, dressing rooms and some rooms that could be used as either bedrooms or sitting rooms. Compared to modern hotels, the toilet and bathing facilities were limited in number: they were located flanking the stairs at the centre of the building, and at the rear ends of both wings (Fig 7.16).

Around 1900, an era when some of the largest hotels were built, the palatial style of the 1860s received an infusion of newly fashionable detailing. As well as the Metropole at Folkestone, the huge Felix Hotel at Felixstowe (1900–3) was built within extensive grounds, and the Headland Hotel at Newquay (opened 1900) was erected on an

isolated site above the resort. New types of facilities were also provided, including central heating and increasing numbers of bathrooms. Many hotels were also provided with winter gardens and palm courts where the warmth nurtured exotic plants and where guests were provided with a warm place to relax and listen to music (*see* Fig 6.39).

These grand Victorian hotels may have been comfortable, but they soon began to seem old-fashioned, so between the wars there were some attempts to renew the formula. The North Western Hotel at Morecambe had opened in 1848 and was renamed the Midland Hotel in 1871.[69] In the early 1930s Oliver Hill was commissioned by the London Midland and Scottish Railway to design a replacement and Lord Clonmore described how its construction meant that Morecambe would be 'well emancipated from Victorian gloom' (*see* Fig 4.38).[70]

Fig 7.15
Imperial Hotel,
Promenade,
Blackpool,
Lancashire; 1867,
Clegg and Jones

*The Blackpool Seawater
Company supplied
hydropathic hotels such as
the Imperial with sea
water. The popularity of
the hotel is demonstrated by
additions in 1875 and
1904.*
(AA053237)

Fig 7.16
Metropole, the Leas,
Folkestone, Kent;
1895–7, TW Cutler

*The hotel has now been
converted into a block of
flats with a health club,
gym, restaurant, bar and
art gallery.*
(DP022340)

Fig 7.17
Cliftonville Hotel,
Ethelbert Crescent,
Margate, Kent; 1868
(BL 22782)

By the beginning of the 20th century most resorts could boast large, luxury hotels. However, the arrival of the Art Deco equivalents of the grand hotel at Morecambe and Saltdean could not disguise the decline that was under way, one which accelerated rapidly after the Second World War. One reason for the decline was the outdated facilities at the large seaside hotels, which had been conceived during an era when cheap, female servants were plentiful. In addition, in 1936 one writer believed that the expensive hotels on the south coast were also under threat because: 'The petrol engine and the electric train more than the vagaries of fashion or the ill-deserved reputation of our climate, have driven wealthy and aristocratic England to Continental places.'[71] Today there are modernised grand hotels that have been retained at a few resorts, but some have gone to seed and others have been demolished or converted into flats.[72] For example, post-war demolitions have removed Margate's grandest hotels: The Queen's Highcliffe Hotel, built in about 1890, was taken over by Butlins in 1955, and after two fires it was demolished and replaced in 1993 by the Queen's Court apartments.[73] The 300-room Cliftonville Hotel, which was built in 1868, was demolished in 1962 and its site is now occupied by

a bowling alley and bar (Figs 7.17, 7.18).[74] The White Hart Hotel, built in 1876, was demolished in 1967 and the White Hart Mansions now occupy the site.[75]

At some resorts, new hotels have been built, two of the most recent being in association with major attractions. The Big Blue Hotel was built recently beside the Pleasure Beach at Blackpool, which owns it; the most popular rooms are not those with a sea view, but those with views over the adjacent park. Butlins has recently returned to hotel management by opening its Shoreline Hotel at Bognor Regis, allowing guests to enjoy the facilities of the adjacent holiday park while staying in a comfortable hotel.

The car was hailed as a threat to the survival of hotels, but the freedom it provided inspired the motel in the USA. American models had relatively little impact on the English seaside resort, the type of environment where they might have been expected to thrive, but its influence can nevertheless be found in places.[76] A short distance outside Weymouth, at Bowleaze Cove, the Riviera Hotel was built in 1937 (Fig 7.19); in name it is a hotel, but in its form it is attempting to echo design principles that appear in motels abroad. Another quirky nod to the car in hotel design can be found in Bournemouth's Roundhouse Hotel,

Fig 7.18
Cliftonville Hotel,
Ethelbert Crescent,
Margate, Kent; 1868
(BL 22785)
These Bedford Lemere
photographs, along with
figure 6.39, offer an insight
into the elegance of hotel
living at the end of the
19th century. This was one
of the hotels run by
Frederick Gordon, whose
empire included hotels in
London, in France and at
a number of resorts.

Fig 7.19
Riviera Hotel,
Bowleaze Coveway,
Weymouth, Dorset;
1937, L Stewart
Smith
The hotel consists of a
central block containing
amenities and offices, with
the accommodation being
housed in a pair of
flanking two-storied wings.
Individual hotel rooms are
entered from the arcaded
external walkways.
(AA050669)

where guests check in on the ground floor, park their cars on the floors immediately above, then retire to their rooms in the top four floors.

Accommodation in the 20th century

At the end of the 19th century the majority of visitors to the seaside without local relatives took rooms in lodgings and boarding houses and a smaller, though still significant, number stayed in hotels. The situation changed markedly during the 20th century as new options appeared including bed and breakfasts, the holiday camp and the caravan. These extended choice for visitors and each offered their customers a distinctive product. The bed and breakfast, like its predecessor the boarding house, offered some of the comfort of hotels, but with less formality and at a lower price. Holiday camps provided a package of accommodation and entertainment that was within the reach of most families. At the beginning of the 21st century there are more than 90 holiday camps in England and Wales, although in recent years the definition of what constitutes a holiday camp has become blurred with the creation of residential caravan sites with substantial entertainment facilities.

Early holiday camps

The origin of the holiday camp can be traced back to 19th-century traditions of religious and political philanthropy. In 1894 Joseph Cunningham established what is accepted as Britain's first holiday camp when he leased a piece of land on the Isle of Man and attracted campers from a number of Sunday Schools, clubs and temperance leagues from around Liverpool.[77] His camp could house 600 men in tents, but, as the land was leased, any communal buildings that were erected had to be temporary.[78] In 1904 Cunningham bought another site and immediately built a 100-foot-long (30m-long) dining and social room and erected 1,500 four-person tents set on wooden floors.[79] Campers could enjoy activities such as billiards, mini-golf, tennis, a bowling green, a 90-foot-long (27m-long) covered swimming pool and a concert hall. To cater for visitors there were shops, a bank, a post office, a bakehouse, photographic darkrooms and a chaplain.[80]

Gradually, a series of increasingly grand and elaborate buildings was erected. In 1907 a miniature castle housing washrooms and latrines was added and other buildings were created with minarets, in a mock-Tudor style, and, after the First World War,

Fig 7.20
Leicester Children's Holiday Centre, Quebec Road, Mablethorpe, Lincolnshire

In 1936 a two-storied permanent building was built to house up to 80 children. Today it is still used as a holiday home for children from the east Midlands.
(DP022328)

some neo-classical forms were employed. The camp had some of the atmosphere of a grand hotel, with a palm court, fernery, an orchestra and waiters, but by staying in tents, and, later, in bungalows and dormitories, the cost of the holiday could be kept within the reach of large numbers of visitors. Although increasingly sophisticated facilities were provided, the camp remained a temperance institution with set meal times and lights-out marked by bugle calls. 'Tentmen', who were responsible for each camping ground, organised sports events and the camp issued its own badge.[81] When Billy Butlin visited the camp in the 1930s he saw many features that he adapted and introduced into his own camps.

The camp on the Isle of Man is rightly celebrated as the first holiday camp in Britain but a range of other organisations, such as the Children's Country Holidays Fund, the Boys Brigade, the Catholic Church and, most famously, the Boy Scouts created rudimentary, temporary camps for children. Some early permanent camps were created to allow children from industrial cities the opportunity to enjoy fresh, sea air, such as the Wood Street Mission in Manchester, which established a holiday camp in 1897 at St Anne's-on-Sea for children from the slums of central Manchester and Salford. In

the 1890s a boys' club in Leicester created a charity to pay for trips to the seaside, and by about 1900 longer holidays were being organised (Fig 7.20).[82] A newspaper report described the trip in 1911: 20 boys and 20 girls, described as 'weakly children', showed significant improvements after their stay – 'The children, greatly improved in manners, gained in weight, and returned wonderfully benefited.'[83] A children's holiday camp was also opened by the City of Salford at Prestatyn in 1928.[84] The main T-shaped block contained a dining room, which was also used for recreation activities, a large kitchen and accommodation for the superintendent.[85] There were also two pairs of single-storied dormitory blocks, and a small sanitary block containing showers, baths and washing facilities (Fig 7.21).

Although local authorities had found ways to establish camps, it was not until 1937 that an Act of Parliament explicitly stated that 'A local authority may acquire, layout, provide with suitable buildings and otherwise equip, and maintain lands ... for the purpose of gymnasiums, playing fields, holiday camps or camping sites'.[86] In 1938 Lambeth decided to establish a municipal holiday camp and by June 1939 a site had been found at Herne Bay; a design for a camp for 400 children reached the model

Fig 7.21
Salford Holiday Camp, 86 Victoria Road West, Prestatyn, Clwyd

Despite modern rebuilding the broad outline of the plan of the original camp of 1928 survives today. Children still sleep in dormitories in large huts, which have been modernised or rebuilt. (DP022329)

171

stage, but the war prevented its construction.[87] Camps for children from municipalities were always rare and after the Second World War no more were founded. However, before and after that war 'holiday camps' appeared throughout Western Europe. Like these rare examples in England and Wales, they were predominantly intended to remove children from polluted, urban environments, rather than for family holidays.[88] They were run by inland municipal authorities or occasionally by large companies, and are distinct from the commercial, family-oriented holiday camps common in England.

Some early holiday camps emerged from a political or trade-union background. For example, a camp was established at Caistor-on-Sea in 1906 by John Fletcher Dodd for the Independent Labour Party, but due to its lack of entertainment facilities it never prospered. Roseland Summer Camp at Rothesay, which opened in 1911, was run as a cooperative camp. The Workers' Travel Association established Rogeston Hall Camp at Corton (Norfolk) in 1938, and the National Association of Local Government Officers (NALGO) had two camps that opened in the 1930s at Scarborough and Croyde Bay (Devon), the latter still being open as a camp run by the union's successor, UNISON. In 1939 the Derbyshire Miners' Association opened a holiday centre for 900 visitors a week at Ingoldmells, beside Skegness, adjacent to its 1928 convalescent home (*see* Figs 5.36, 5.37).[89]

Fig 7.22
Brighstone Camp, Military Road, Brighstone, Isle of Wight; opened 1932
Between the wars a number of the commercial chains of holiday camps were created. This was also a period when single family-run holiday camps were established. This camp has retained some of its early chalets, but parts of the site are under threat from the erosion of the cliffs on which it is located.
(DP005028)

Commercial holiday camps

In 1939 there were 116 permanent holiday camps and 59 temporary ones in England (Fig 7.22).[90] From the 1920s, in addition to philanthropic and politically motivated camps, commercial holiday camps were beginning to be established. In 1920 Herbert Potter and his brother Arthur opened a camp at Caister in Norfolk, and Herbert opened a second in 1924 at Hopton-on-Sea near Great Yarmouth.[91] In 1925 Captain Harry Warner retired from the Royal Artillery and opened a seaside restaurant,[92] then in 1931 he opened his first holiday camp on Hayling Island and by the outbreak of the Second World War he owned four camps. After the war the company expanded until it had 14 camps. Fred Pontin began to provide holiday camps to cater for demobbed members of the armed forces, with the first being created at a former military site at Brean (Somerset) and a pre-war holiday camp at Osmington Bay near Weymouth.[93]

Butlins

William 'Billy' Butlin (1899–1980) began his career in 1921 with a single hoop-la stall, and in 1928 he took a huge gamble by investing £2,000 in the first batch of Dodgem cars to arrive in Britain.[94] By 1934 he ran eight seaside amusement parks and operated most of the attractions at several big Christmas fairs. In the mid-1930s he decided to diversify into holiday camps. He

Fig 7.23
Skyline Pavilion,
Butlins, Bognor Regis,
West Sussex; late
1990s

*The creation of undercover
facilities began with the
provision of indoor pools,
both to extend the season
and to make campsites
more attractive to visitors
who could be tempted by
the sun of the
Mediterranean. In the late
1990s Butlins introduced
'Skyline Pavilions' to its
three camps. These link the
existing entertainment
buildings and create a
central forum where visitors
can congregate regardless of
the weather.*
(DP022330)

visited Cunningham's camp on the Isle of Man to learn about the practicalities of the business and although the family could not prevent him from seeing the public areas of the camp, they barred him from visiting the private areas such as the kitchens.[95] Butlin saw the potential of a self-contained, holiday village for middle-income families, with chalets set in landscaped gardens and a range of sports and entertainment facilities,[96] so building work began in October 1935 at Ingoldmells, near Skegness, and the camp opened to its first 500 visitors on Easter Saturday 1936.[97] The site was to accommodate 1,000 people in 600 chalets and 250 bathrooms; set within the landscaped grounds were 'all the amenities of a first-class Hotel. Free Golf, Tennis, Bathing, Bowls, Dancing and Concert Parties, Boating Lake and Licensed Club'.[98]

A key to the success of Butlins was the creation of a strong brand. In the 1920s he had issued his staff with coats with an embroidered 'B' badge, and his stalls and lorries bore the slogan 'Hurrah! It's Butlin's'.[99] This was superseded at Skegness by the slogan on the reception block 'OUR TRUE INTENT IS ALL FOR YOUR DELIGHT', a slight misquote from *A Midsummer Night's Dream* lifted from the side of a fairground organ.[100] Butlin was convinced that he had provided

the infrastructure to guarantee a happy holiday, but he sensed that something was missing.[101] Bored campers, keeping to their own family groups, were not getting involved with activities: a new type of participatory culture was needed, and to achieve this the 'redcoats' were created. Butlin and Norman Bradford, one of his staff, were behind this innovation and it was Bradford who first uttered the immortal, pre-breakfast greeting 'Good morning campers'. By 1939 Butlin had two camps and a third was being built at Filey. He managed to get an agreement with the War Ministry to finish this camp and build two others, which the military would use until the war was over.[102] After an unsuccessful venture into the US market, Butlin opened a new camp at Bognor Regis in 1960, followed by camps at Minehead in 1962 and Barry Island in 1966.[103] By this time the need for a change in the atmosphere of the camps was recognised and gradually some of its distinctive features were relaxed. By 1977, Radio Butlin, the nickname of the camp tannoy systems, was recognised as archaic and began to be phased out.[104] Today the three remaining Butlins holiday villages have large, modern, tented structures at their hearts, linking existing entertainment buildings and providing new, undercover facilities (Fig 7.23).

Fig 7.24
Butlins, Ingoldmells, Lincolnshire; 1936

'Cosy Elizabethan Chalets with electric light, carpeted floors, running water, baths and first-class sanitary arrangements. This will be the solution to your holiday problem – for many holidays to come.' This was the original description of the chalets on offer at Skegness. They were timber-framed, with asbestos panels, and a slate roof with overhanging eaves and bargeboards, creating a small veranda at the front of the chalet. (DP022331)

The buildings of holiday camps

Holiday-camp buildings fall into two categories: the small-scale accommodation which was consciously conservative in design, and the facility buildings that were substantial structures erected in various contemporary styles. This applies equally to the camps of the 1930s or those of the 1960s, though the style of individual buildings had changed. What camps of all dates share is the desire to create an escapist atmosphere, where campers can forget their daily lives and enjoy a taste of something different on their holiday.

By the 1930s camps were being built with wooden and even brick chalets and substantial communal buildings. In 1930, when Potters Camp moved to its present site, it boasted 'brick chalets with running water, electric light and modern toilet facilities' as well as 'a brick sun-lounge, lavishly furnished with expensive carpets and modern easy chairs'.[105] The early chalets at Butlins at Skegness were built in a homely, mock-Tudor style at a cost of only £10 each; one of the chalets has been preserved and is now a listed building (Fig 7.24). However, Butlins was not the first camp to provide this type of single chalet, and photographs from all over England show a similar design employed from the 1920s to the 1960s. For example, on the Isle of Wight, the Bembridge Chalet Hotel offered accommodation set in '20 acres of beautiful seashore grounds', while the Golden Sands at Hopton (Norfolk) had a 'crescent of comfortable wooden chalets'.[106] The original timber chalets in Butlins, like those at many other sites, have gradually been replaced by more substantial single-storey brick buildings, often built in long rows, or by two-storied blocks of flats with modern facilities. The 40-watt bulb and cold tap of the 1930s have now been superseded by the widescreen TV, microwave and bathroom (Fig 7.25).

The buildings housing facilities at Butlins holiday camps were predominantly large, almost industrial in scale, with steel-framed or concrete structures. Although they had to be cost-effective, this did not

Fig 7.25
Starfish Quay, Butlins, Ingoldmells, Lincolnshire

Today visitors to holiday camps have higher expectations and want modern facilities comparable to those they might enjoy at home. Long lines of chalets have now been replaced by apartment blocks in an attractive campus layout. (DP022332)

mean that they lacked decorative flourishes. The original white concrete blocks at Skegness and the façade of the main buildings at Clacton reflected current Art Deco tastes; the Gaiety Theatre at Clacton had a crow-step gable decorated with herms treated as toy soldiers standing to attention. At a holiday camp at Prestatyn, which opened in 1939, the London Midland & Scottish Railway and Thomas Cook consciously tried to echo the form of an ocean-going liner. William Hamlyn, the architect for the railway company, who was responsible for its design, even included a mock-up of a liner's deck including masts and flags.[107] At Middleton Tower Holiday Camp, near Morecambe, which also opened in 1939, its founder Harry S Kamiya took the allusion to liners one stage further:[108] he acquired fittings from three ships to include in the main entertainment building, which was christened SS Berengaria. Many of the post-war buildings were built using pier-and-panel construction, to maximise the area of fenestration, and in their form they resembled contemporary buildings, especially schools. Communal buildings were essentially blank canvases on which, and into which decorative themes of the current fashion could be introduced (Fig 7.26).

Caravan holidays

Horse-drawn carriages as homes, described as 'caravans', have existed since at least the 17th century, and Napoleon even took one on his ill-fated march on Moscow. During the 19th century, they were adopted by travelling menageries, circuses and gypsies. As a boy in the 1830s, the circus proprietor 'Lord' George Sanger had travelled around fairs with his family in a caravan and Roger Fenton, the photographer, took a converted delivery van to the Crimea in 1855 to use as a darkroom as well as living accommodation.[109] By the end of the 19th century many private citizens were using horse-drawn caravans for leisure.

By the outbreak of the First World War, the first motor homes resembled a caravan on a lorry chassis, but the first motor-towed caravans had to be small as the cars that towed them were not particularly powerful.[110] Between the wars caravans became increasingly sophisticated and more comfortable, but remained an expensive item restricted to wealthy travellers, though an extensive hire trade developed. By the mid-1930s there were about 3,500 caravans in

use and the first caravan rallies were taking place,[111] although at this time there were no designated caravan sites and people had to negotiate with a friendly farmer for the use of a corner of a field. Formal caravan sites only began to appear after the Second World War, and in 1960 these became regulated by the Caravan Sites and Control of Development Act.[112] Before the Second World War the caravan holiday was confined to people able to afford a car, but after the war cheaper vehicles brought the activity within the reach of most of the populace. By the mid-1950s static caravans to rent had been established at many resorts: these were often privately owned and rented out for an income as well as providing the owner with a place for their own holiday (Fig 7.27).

Caravan numbers grew rapidly after the Second World War: in 1939, 2,500 were produced each year, but by 1966 this figure had risen to 65,000.[113] Membership of the two

Fig 7.26
Butlins, Bognor Regis, West Sussex
The facilities of holiday camps were in substantial, but usually fairly plain buildings that could be adapted, internally or externally, as tastes changed. A room housing an Irish theme pub could previously have been a Bier Keller decorated with steins or a Beachcomber Bar complete with flotsam and jetsam.
(DP022333)

Fig 7.27
Skegness Sands
Caravan Site,
Winthorpe Avenue,
Ingoldmells,
Lincolnshire
*Static caravans have
evolved into substantial
chalets. Some designs
employ architectural
detailing, such as
pediments and a version of
the Venetian window,
which help to distance them
from their caravan origins.*
(DP022334)

major caravan clubs also grew rapidly: membership of the Caravan Club trebled from just over 100,000 at the end of the 1960s to around 300,000 by the 1990s.[114] The Camping and Caravan Club enjoyed a similarly rapid rise: in 1960 it had 51,000 members, rising to 301,849 at the end of 1999.[115] As a consequence of this boom in popularity, some parts of the coast are now dominated by caravan sites. For example, by the late 1980s of the 120,000 bed spaces available on the Lincolnshire coast from Skegness to Mablethorpe, 90 per cent were in caravans and chalets (Fig 7.28, *see also* Fig 3.43).[116] In 1967, Kent and Sussex had 32 licensed sites housing 3,468 caravans, and by 1969 there were 487 static caravan sites, 398 touring caravan sites and 177 campsites in Dorset, Somerset, Devon and Cornwall.[117] Despite regulation, it is difficult to disguise the visual impact of caravan sites on the countryside and the coastline. History professor James Walvin, writing in 1978, barely disguised his dislike of these new additions to resorts: 'One by-product of the advance of the pri-

vate car was the rash of caravan parks which erupted around the coast'.[118]

Conclusion

The accommodation needs of visitors have probably had a more profound affect on the appearance of resorts than any other aspect of holiday activity. At the heart of resorts, tall 18th- and 19th-century houses dominate much of the seafront, as well as some of the streets stretching inland or around a high-status square. During the past two centuries these may have been used as houses, lodgings, boarding houses and during the 20th century as bed and breakfast accommodation, but the majority are too large to have avoided subdivision. In former houses on the seafront, the ground floors have often been converted into shops or amusement arcades, while the upper floors are often now unoccupied. Duality of function is not just a modern phenomenon, houses in the earliest resorts having provided not just lodgings, but also services such as libraries,

shops and even baths. While the tall houses in the centre of resorts provided the more polite accommodation, more frugal rooms were available throughout towns. For example, in 1822 Richard Ayton recorded that at Scarborough 'there are other houses of the same kind, in different parts of the town, that offer accommodations adapted to the various classes of visitors'.[119]

During the 19th century, the rudimentary facilities of the inn evolved into the opulent hotel. Most resorts still have at least one substantial hotel or hydro, but their clientele is no longer the wealthy who once relaxed in the palm courts, dined in comfort and bathed in mineral water and seawater without having to leave the grounds of their hotel; it is now coach parties and travelling businessmen that provide the backbone of the business of many large hotels, with families often selecting smaller, quieter hotels and guest houses.

Families are also attracted to the caravan parks, campsites and holiday camps that have provided a challenge to the character of the fringes of resorts. They offer a safe environment for children and a range of activities to entertain all the family, even when the British summer weather inevitably plays its tricks. Although these places may be regarded by some people as an eyesore, they are, nevertheless, an essential part of the accommodation sought by tourists and an established aspect of the resort townscape.

Fig 7.28
Caravan Site, Roman Bank, Ingoldmells, Lincolnshire
This view, in conjunction with the aerial photograph of Ingoldmells (see Fig 3.43), illustrates how prevalent the caravan has become on some stretches of the English coastline.
(DP022335)

8
Conclusion

'Special' was the first word used in this book to describe the seaside resort. The ensuing chapters have explored the characteristics of seaside towns, from the vibrant to the mundane, and considered the factors that gave rise to these special qualities. Although the stories of individual resorts share many of these influences with comparable non-resort towns, the arrival of holidaymakers and the creation of associated facilities have defined the English seaside town. The rate of visitor growth and the evolving needs of the holidaymaker determined both the speed at which resorts grew and the nature of their expansion. The first resorts developed at small working towns, places that, often, were suffering economic hardship, and therefore the rising fashion for the seaside provided a new, important source of income and employment. By the end of the 18th century, the lure of the sea had gained sufficient momentum to allow the creation of new resorts independent of existing towns, either near pre-existing, inland villages or on virgin stretches of coastline. By the early 19th century the majority of today's modern resorts had been created and, often, their tone had been established. For instance, Margate was the first resort to cater for large numbers of tourists from London, and Blackpool was already attracting working people from Lancashire towns, though its rapid expansion did not begin until the late 19th century. At the other extreme, in the early 19th century Brighton was the refuge for the Prince Regent, his entourage and a host of camp followers, and although Queen Victoria deserted it in favour of Osborne House and the Isle of Wight, Brighton still retains something of this higher-status reputation.

Exclusivity inevitably came into conflict with the growth in England's population in the 19th century. The seaside holiday gradually extended from the realm of a small aristocratic elite, first to the middle-class family, by the early 19th century, and then to the mass of working people by the close of the century. This was an expression of increasing mobility, in social and economic terms, as well as a reflection of the provision of rapid and affordable means of travel.

The impact, on resorts, of the growth of the seaside holiday was immediate and dramatic. The first effect was to improve the houses of the existing town, replacing small, vernacular buildings with more spacious, comfortable and, perhaps most importantly, fashionable houses. Modest entertainment facilities were created in association with inns or in buildings that were little more than capacious agricultural buildings, but by the early 19th century the permanence of the taste for the seaside brought greater investment in purpose-built facilities.

Margate experienced rapid growth due to the impact of steamers operating along the Thames, but for most resorts the first phase of major expansion coincided with the arrival of the railways. Modest growth, the addition of a few houses or a terrace, was supplanted by developments that might take place a field at a time, as large areas of land were released for construction. This often occurred first along the seafront, but subsequently affected inland areas, utilised for less affluent visitors and for residents. Wealthy visitors were gradually forced from the heart of resorts to the edges, and the terrace, once the lodgings of the 'Company', was deserted in favour of villas further along the coast, around inland parks or on the wooded hillsides above the resort. The small social institutions of the 18th-century resort proved unsuitable for the growing numbers of holidaymakers arriving by railway, so the exclusivity of the assembly rooms and circulating library shifted to the golf clubhouse and the yacht club, where membership fees and the cost of equipment excluded the hordes that were being disgorged from steamers and trains.

An important part of the story of resorts is about tensions. In the 18th century, the working life of the precursor town was often in conflict with the whims of its visitors, the Steyne at Brighton and the east end of Hastings beach showing two possible outcomes

of such struggles. In the 18th century there was also a perceived conflict between the health-giving properties of the coastal environment and the temptations of the entertainments that were on offer. By the 19th century new tensions, between residents and visitors and between wealthier visitors and the day trippers, had become obvious. Estates were created at some resorts to keep delicate residents and polite visitors apart from the throngs invading the central areas of resorts. The houses that once provided lodgings for long-term visitors became rooms rented out for families, and today many are simply storage spaces above shops and amusement arcades (Fig 8.1). A constant theme in resort history is that of balancing the need to cater for visitors while providing facilities for residents, and today resorts are recognising that a good place to live will create a good place to visit. However, the economic boost of a holiday season is no longer necessarily as big an advantage as it was at the beginning or middle of the 20th century, therefore some local authorities are placing a greater emphasis on developing the year-long economy of their towns.

The seasonal influx of holidaymakers meant that resorts were able to sustain a range of facilities far beyond levels that would have been viable in non-resort towns of comparable sizes; entertainment venues in particular benefitted from this, and a number of purpose-built venues appeared around the beginning of the 20th century. Notable amongst these are cinemas and theatres, and although their numbers have

declined since the Second World War, many survive in use as bars, nightclubs and bingo halls (Fig 8.2). Houses in resorts broadly followed the architectural forms evolving in London and its suburbs, but they were often used for dual purposes, serving as homes and also providing accommodation and services for visitors during the summer. The most obvious impact on house forms was to do with height, the provision of an extra storey often creating additional rooms that could be let out during the season. Another difference is in fenestration, especially on or near the seafront: bay windows and balconies exploited the natural virtues of the location and served to entice possible lodgers, as well as allowing the occupants to observe the life of the resort taking place in the streets below (Fig 8.3).

Seaside houses adopted styles prevalent throughout England, but many tended towards the more colourful end of the prevailing fashion. However, the seaside town developed its own architectural flavour, which appears predominantly in its major facilities. This style can be described as a lively, almost chaotic, blend of the exotic that first appeared in the Royal Pavilion in Brighton, combined with rather more conventional architectural styles, as were used in the more sober institutions of major towns. The taste for the exotic and the exuberant came to epitomise seaside-

Fig 8.1
143–5 Promenade, Blackpool, Lancashire.
This 19th-century house is a rare survival amid the entertainment complexes that dominate the central part of Blackpool's seafront. Although the ground floor is now occupied by a shop and a take-away, there is no significant use of the upper floors.
(AA058329)

Fig 8.2
Former Central Picture Theatre, Central Drive, Blackpool, Lancashire; 1913
This is one of two early cinemas that have survived in Blackpool. It was converted into a bingo hall while the other, on the Promenade near the Metropole Hotel, is now a night club.
(AA052999)

Fig 8.3
Borough Street,
Brighton, East Sussex
Whether streets face the sea
or are perpendicular to it,
houses near the seafront
employ the bay window as
an architectural decoration
as well as a means of
enjoying sea air and, with
luck, some view of the sea.
(DP017961)

entertainment buildings and the spirit of the promenade. In the 20th century, this trend embraced new technologies, especially electric lighting, to create a sense of the unusual, the exhilarating and the fun. Novel architectural designs and motifs were augmented by applied fascias, often illuminated with arrays of multi-coloured lights. The constant is that architecture was used as entertainment and mood-setter, as a backdrop to the frivolities of the seaside holiday and as a tool of the entertainment industry to lure visitors: bigger and brighter equated with more fun.

Buildings and open spaces define the special character of resorts and they hint at how seaside holidays have changed, but diaries, letters and other literary sources help to bring this story to life. One of the earliest accounts of seaside holidays can be found in the diary of John Baker, who spent a month in Brighton in 1771 and a month at Margate in 1777. The first action of his first holiday, after finding lodgings, was to visit the assembly room, circulating library and coffee house to pay his subscriptions. In 1777 he spent three days travelling from London and took lodgings at Hall's library,

then the day after his arrival he met the hoy that had brought his maid to the resort. His days on both holidays included some bathing, card games, dances, meals with fellow members of the 'Company', and walking on the beach (Fig 8.4). At Margate he visited the theatre, a precursor of the current Theatre Royal, which he described as 'a vile house' with 'vile acting'.[1]

The early journals that feature seaside holidays were predominantly penned by wealthy gentlemen and leading socialites, the type of people who could afford a holiday and had the education and free time to indulge in diary keeping. The first accounts of what is recognisable as the family seaside holiday begin to appear in the early 19th century, when two very different accounts offer complementary pictures of a seaside holiday around the start of Queen Victoria's reign. In 1836 Charles Dickens published 'The Tuggses at Ramsgate', which includes a description of their month-long holiday, and John Leighton's 'London Out of Town' in 1847 is a cartoon story of a brief seaside holiday along the Thames.[2]

Dickens' Mr Tuggs, a grocer, took his family to Ramsgate by steamer and took

Fig 8.4
Characters at the
Steyne, Brighton, East
Sussex; 1824
*This engraving provides an
impression of the lively
social scene enjoyed by the
wealthy well-dressed
visitors to the resort. Most
people depicted are simply
socialising, though one
braver lady is starting a
donkey ride.*

lodgings for a month. On the first morning after their arrival the family went to a crowded beach and settled into rush-covered chairs to watch what was going on:

> The ladies were employed in needlework, or watch guard making, or knitting, or reading novels; the gentlemen were reading newspapers and magazines; the children were digging holes in the sand with wooden spades, and collecting water therein; the nursemaids with their charges in their arms, were running in after the waves, and then running back with the waves after them; and, now and then, a little sailing boat either departed with a gay and talkative cargo of passengers, or returned with a very silent and particularly uncomfortable looking one.[3]

Dickens soon realised that seaside holidays settle into a familiar, largely repetitive pattern after the initial change of scene: 'Thus passes the evening; thus passed the days and evenings of the Tuggses, and the Waterses, for six weeks. Sands in the morning – donkeys at noon – pier in the afternoon – library at night – and the same people everywhere.'[4]

In John Leighton's story, the Brown family take the steamer down the Thames, but the journey proves to be a challenge. Mrs Brown 'faints in the presence of a vulgar London mob' and 'Davy Jones Esq treats the Browns to a little rough riding'. After a struggle to find lodgings they end up in a house with a view over the railway station, the bone-crushing mill, the Billy-Boy pub, the Brick-Bat Hotel and, through a gap between two houses, the sea. On the first

day the family go on a trip into the countryside in a landau, and take part in some archery and donkey riding and in the evening they promenade on the pier. The next day brings rain, forcing them to stay in their lodgings, but on the third day they are able to visit the beach to build sand castles and catch crabs. After lunch they go for a sail and, in the evening, go to the library, where they win a silver tobacco box in a raffle. The evening ends with them watching the dancing and 'Ethiopian' entertainers from London (Figs 8.5, 8.6).

These accounts described the holiday as it existed before the rapid growth in holiday-making during the later 19th century. By the end of the 19th century, a holiday or at least a day trip, was within the reach of most people, either travelling independently or on organised excursions. For example, on Friday 24 July 1914 the brewing firm Bass, Ratcliff and Gretton provided an excursion to Scarborough for their workers. The company thoughtfully provided its staff with a timetable and a guidebook to the resort, and it had also arranged preferential rates for entry to many of the leading attractions.[5] Through this guide it is possible to reconstruct a specific day out during the last summer before the First World War.

Fourteen trains, consisting of 225 carriages, brought the company's employees from Burton-upon-Trent to the excursion station at Scarborough (*see* Fig 3.32). The last summer of peace is often depicted in romantic dramas as sunny and warm, but on this day at Scarborough it was cool, with sunshine and showers, scarcely the best

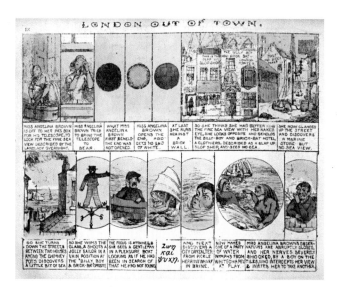

Fig 8.5

Page 9 from Leighton 1847

Miss Brown uses her father's new telescope to look out at the resort. She turns her gaze from the motley collection of buildings which surround her lodgings to a tantalising sea view through a gap between buildings.

(Courtesy of Bryn Mawr College Library, Pennsylvania)

Fig 8.6

Page 12 from Leighton 1847

After enjoying a 'Gipsey Party' during the afternoon, they walk on the pier in the evening. The next day is wet and so they try to borrow books from the library, but all the good books are out because of the weather. Bored and trapped in her lodgings, Miss Brown is reduced to writing poetry in the condensation on the window. Her naughty brother carves his name into the table, costing his father £2 2s!

(Courtesy of Bryn Mawr College Library, Pennsylvania)

weather for swimming or sitting on the beach;[6] the arrangements that the company made with indoor entertainments at the resort seem to have been prudent.

The guide listed the main attractions awaiting the excursionists, including the recently enlarged spa, where programmes of orchestral and light operatic music were provided. They could also enjoy a visit to the People's Palace and Aquarium, which had opened in 1877. Although it was still an aquarium in name, many of the fish tanks had been removed to be replaced by stalls selling fancy goods, and in 1913 a zoo with 20 cages had been created. At the People's Palace, visitors could also enjoy the recently created skating rink, along with concerts, variety shows, slide shows, dancing and swimming exhibitions being held in the complex. A 'People's Palace' by name, this three-acre complex was effectively a kursaal.[7]

The day trippers were also directed to other theatrical entertainments and the cinemas that had appeared in recent years: for example 'Caitlin's Arcadia', which was one of the largest theatres in England with over 3,000 seats, and was home to a famous pierrot troupe. It was located next to one of the four cinemas listed in the guide, The Palladium, which survives today as the Futurist Theatre, albeit with a new façade (Fig 8.7). A few yards away from these on the seafront was a set of baths, which have now been converted into Corrigan's amusements. The excursionist's guide also included a description of the simpler pleasures of the harbour, castle, parish church and parks and gardens, and provided details of steamer trips and the locations of various sports facilities. Any hardy trippers intending to go into the sea

were provided with instructions, including advice about avoiding bathing after a hearty meal. The guide ended with details of the basics of the visit, including transport around the resort, the location of the post office, lavatories and a list of hotels and restaurants, including those that served Bass beer.

After the Second World War, the summer holiday became an annual event for most families. The beach holiday is a common childhood experience for most English people, including the authors of this book, indulging in the same type of activities that the Tuggses, the Browns and the workers of Bass would recognise. The popularity of the seaside holiday peaked in the 1970s, when one of the seeds of its decline had already begun to emerge: English holidaymakers began to head south to the Mediterranean in the 1960s, and by the end of the 20th century some media reports and official publications were beginning, erroneously, to pronounce the end of the English seaside holiday.

A decline in the popularity of seaside towns as the primary holiday destination has had an impact on their economic state. In the Multiple Deprivation Indices prepared by the Department for Communities and Local Government (formerly the Office of the Deputy Prime Minister), a number of resorts that might appear prosperous to visitors feature among the 100 most deprived local authorities.[8] The indices list the 354 local authorities in England, in which Blackpool ranks 24th, Hastings 38th, Brighton 83rd and Thanet, which includes Margate, 85th. In this broad measure Blackpool ranks alongside Lambeth, Rochdale and Gateshead, while Hastings appears alongside Wolverhampton, St Helens, Doncaster and Westminster. Using the narrower measure of unemployment, Brighton is rated 43rd, between Ealing and Oldham. Yet by some other measures these resorts may be described as successful. For instance, Brighton's economy grew from £2.7 billion in 1996 to £3.2 billion by 2004 and the town has thriving universities with over 30,000 students between them.[9]

The Deprivation Index figures appear gloomy, but a recent study by Sheffield Hallam University has shown that seaside towns have prospered more in recent years than these statistics might suggest.[10] Their research has revealed that employment is relatively strong in resorts, and that there is a net outward flow of people from resorts to work in nearby towns. Commuting has taken place in some form since the 19th century, but has grown in significance with improvements in train services. Many companies, particularly those in the service sector, have also recognised that a coastal location is not a hindrance, with all the technological provision of modern communications. Recent surveys of house prices, which indicate that there is a premium to be paid for houses in many seaside towns, support the assertion that resorts are doing well economically, at least in terms of their resident population.

The report also revealed that the rate of employment is a few per cent lower in resorts due to the presence of significant numbers of retired people. In 2006 Southend-on-Sea was named as the best place to retire to, based on factors such as the absence of hills, bus services, the level of council tax, the cost of houses and the availability of NHS services.[11] In the late 20th century, many developers recognised the market for seaside retirement facilities; most are new and purpose-built, but some historic buildings, such as the former Royal National Sanatorium for Consumption and Diseases of the Chest at Bournemouth, have been converted into retirement apartments (*see* Fig 5.29).

A history inevitably dwells on the past, but contained within it are lessons that can inform speculation about the future. The primary lesson of this study is that the history of seaside resorts is a story of change, with the towns adapting to new challenges. Instead of seeing the seaside resort as being in decline, it may be more accurate to consider it as being in transition. Previous steps in the seaside story have been accompanied by, and triggered by, changes in the means of transport for holidaymakers, and the advent of cheap flights to overseas resorts is a further important element in this process, marking a shift in holiday patterns. However,

Fig 8.7
Futurist Theatre, Foreshore Road, Scarborough, North Yorkshire; pre-1914
The upper part of the façade provides a hint of what the Palladium was like when the workers of Bass had their day out in Scarborough in July 1914.
(DP006185)

will flying remain as affordable in the future if new levies are imposed to mitigate its effects on climate change? Although there will not be a return to the 'holidays at home' of wartime, environmental concerns and accompanying taxes may again redirect interest to England's own beaches.

Local authorities and a wide range of public bodies and private organisations now recognise that change is under way and that if resorts are to prosper they must evolve. A number of ways forward are beginning to be identified. The former English Tourism Council's *Sea Changes: Creating World-class Resorts in England* in 2001 pointed to ways in which resorts can try to tempt back visitors:

The English resort determined to similarly reinvent itself and evolve into a modern successful business will need to combine the original strengths that made it appealing and which differentiated it in that era (the sea, the beach, promenades, the sea air etc), along with new or evolved aspects which will again give it some form of differentiation. The successful resort will need to differentiate not only from its peer resorts, but from the spectrum of other leisure and tourism experiences with which it is competing both domestically and abroad.[12]

Most resorts still provide a range of popular attractions for family entertainment and in recent years some have become popular destinations for hen and stag nights, with a consequent increase in adult venues. A potential forthcoming attraction for a number of resorts will be the presence of large casinos. Rather than looking to Las Vegas and Atlantic City for inspiration, England's resorts might create facilities more analogous to those that already occupy the heart of many French resorts (Figs 8.8, 8.9).

As well as trying to create and maintain venues for mass entertainment, some resorts have recognised that developing their own niche, or exploiting an existing phenomenon, may be a path to success. Newquay is now the surf capital of England, and Padstow, a picturesque Cornish town around a harbour, enjoys particular success due to its present association with the chef Rick Stein (*see* Fig 1.2). Culture is also seen at some resorts as a driver for economic development. For example, the Tate Gallery at St Ives has provided a focus for art-loving visitors and Margate has a scheme for the Turner Contemporary gallery beside the harbour as the centrepiece of efforts to regenerate the oldest part of the town. Similarly, a combination of five-star accommo-

Fig 8.8
Casino and Grand Hotel, Cabourg, Calvados, France
The casino in the foreground and the larger Grand Hotel behind are at the heart of this elegant resort. Most French seaside towns have a casino of some sort and its status and form depends on the character and size of the resort's clientele.
(DP022336)

Fig 8.9
Luxor Casino, 3900
Las Vegas Boulevard
South, Las Vegas,
Nevada, USA
*The Strip at Las Vegas is
lined with a series of vast
casino hotels, some of
which are designed using
exotic architectural forms.
In the space of a few miles
it is possible to travel from
Egypt to New York to Paris
and Venice, where gondola
trips are available around
the hotel.*
(DP022337)

dation, fine cuisine and culture underpins the redevelopment of the Midland Hotel at Morecambe, which, it is hoped, will be a key element in the future prosperity of the town.

At the centre of most regeneration strategies is a recognition that the seafront itself is the most precious asset of the seaside resort. Architectural critics may reel with horror at some new structures being built on seafronts, or at how some historic buildings have been adapted to serve the needs of visitors, but this is not a new concern. In 1912 Brook Kitchin wrote in the *Architectural Review* that:

> We seem to have touched the lowest depths of architectural baseness in catering for a pleasure-seeking, holiday-making public. … It is not necessary to seek very far for the causes that have produced the failure of our sea-frontages. The people who go to the sea do not really care so long as they are amused; the railway companies, who largely exploit the seaside towns, do not care so long as there are attractions that will fill their trains; the residents do not care so long as business flourishes; … The fact that the 'season' is short and that profits have to be made in a limited space of time produces a cheap and showy type of architecture, the main object of which is to draw attention to itself and to shout down everything near it.[13]

Twenty years later the architectural correspondent of *The Times* wrote that 'No part of England has suffered more from indiscriminate building than have the sea-fronts of popular resorts'.[14] In an effort to guide developers towards more discriminating buildings, the Commission for Architecture and the Built Environment (CABE) and English Heritage published *Shifting Sands*, illustrating how good design and sensitive reuse of buildings could contribute to the regeneration and revitalisation of resorts.[15] Local authorities are conscious of the need to improve the seafront, although there is often little that can be done to improve the standard of privately owned buildings that line the promenade. On seafront open spaces, however, art has a key role to play in enhancing the local environment, in schemes such as those at Blackpool and Bridlington, or Morecambe, where Eric Morecambe's statue is now a place of pilgrimage (Fig 8.10).

Perhaps it is fitting to end where the story of the seaside began, with another such pilgrimage site. The patients who made the first tentative visits to a nearby stretch of coastline in search of a magical cure could not have realised that, centuries later, millions of people would head to the seaside annually for sun, sea and sand, pursuing the formula for a successful holiday. It

Fig 8.10
Eric Morecambe
Statue, Seafront,
Morecambe,
Lancashire; 1999,
Graham Ibbeson
… bring me sunshine,
bring me love.
(MF99-0632-37)

is difficult to envisage a time when people in England did not go to the seaside, and it is inconceivable that the seaside will entirely lose its appeal, but without public and private investment, sensitive restoration and appropriate new buildings the glories of the English seaside resort may lose some of their lustre. However, whatever challenges face the seaside resort in the future, it will always retain a special place in this island nation's affections.

Notes

1 Introduction

1 Brodie, Sargent and Winter 2005.
2 Mason 2003.
3 Gilbert 1939.
4 Lancaster 1936.
5 Pearson 1991.
6 Lindley 1973.
7 Gray 2006.
8 Braggs and Harris 2000.
9 Pimlott 1947.
10 Walton 1983; Walton 2000.
11 Farrant 1980; Farrant and Farrant 1980; Farrant 1987; Berry 2002; Berry 2005.
12 Cannadine 1980.
13 Perkin 1976.
14 Lewis 1723; Lewis 1736.
15 Relhan 1761.
16 Sickelmore 1827.
17 Anon 1734b.
18 Lyons 1763.
19 For instance, at Margate there is much in common between various editions of guidebooks – Anon 1770a, Hall 1790, Anon 1797b, Anon 1809, Anon 1822, Kidd 1831.
20 Carey 1799.
21 Russell 1752; Awsiter 1768.
22 Clark 1829.
23 East Kent Archives R/TR 2188/2 Extracts from Journals and Letters of Lady Mary Coke 1780, 1783, 1788, 1820; R/U127/1 Diary of Mary Figgins at Margate c.1828.
24 Palmer 1943; Palmer 1944; Whyman 1980.
25 www.britishpathe.com (accessed 11 September 2006).
26 www.imagesofengland.org.uk; www.pastscape.org.uk/homepage; http://viewfinder.english-heritage.org.uk.
27 English Tourism Council 2001, 23.

2 A brief history of seaside resorts

1 Butler 1980, 5–12; Goodall 1992, 8; Fisher (ed.) 1997, 60.
2 www.healthsystem.virginia.edu/internet/library/historical/artifacts/antiqua/healer cults.cfm (accessed 11 September 2006).
3 Osler 1921, 49.
4 www.fordham.edu/halsall/ancient/suet-nero-rolfe.html (accessed 11 September 2006).
5 Miller 1926, 143; Shelton 1950, Chapter XXXVIII, cited from www.soilandhealth.org/02/0201hyglibcat/020127shelton.III/020127.ch38.htm (accessed 11 September 2006).
6 Hembry 1990, 6–7.
7 Turner 1562.
8 Vicary 1587, 55.
9 www.departures.com/he/he_1100_thalassotherapy.html (accessed 11 September 2006); www.thalassofederation.com/page_menu_e.php?page=histo2#egypte (accessed 11 September 2006).
10 Mulcaster 1581, 95.
11 Markham 1610, 167.
12 Leland 1964, 43–4: 'Olde Finiox buildid his faire house on purchasid ground for the commodite of preserving his helth. So that afore the phisisians concludid that it was an exceding helthfulle quarter.'
13 Manship 1854, 104.
14 The year 1626 is suggested by Robert Wittie, who in his *Scarbrough Spaw*, … of 1660, states that 'It was found by accident about thirty four years ago'. Wittie 1660, 7.
15 ibid, 36; Wittie 1667, 172.
16 Colbatch 1696, 138–41.
17 ibid, 107.
18 Floyer 1702, 191.
19 Floyer and Baynard 1706, 26.
20 Floyer 1702, 193.
21 Blundell 1968 volume I, 181.
22 ibid, 225.
23 Bailey 1955, 31; Jones 1718.
24 Neller 2000, 13, citing Lincolnshire Record Office LAO, MASS 13/16.
25 Anon 1734b, 31.
26 Anon 1732, 1ff.
27 Anon 1734b, 37.
28 ibid, 40.
29 *The Kentish Post, or Canterbury News Letter* 14 July 1736, cited in Whyman 1985, 160.
30 Morley 1966, 12.
31 Evans 1821, 37.
32 Berry 2005, 2ff.
33 Farrant 1980, 15; Berry 2005, 29.
34 Pococke 1889, 104.
35 Berry 2002, 99.
36 Schopenhauer 1988, 130.
37 Bread 1859, 4.
38 Smith 1991, 3.
39 Parkin 1776, 400.
40 Pococke 1888, 92–3.
41 Harvey 1800, 17.
42 Boddy and West 1983, 61; ibid 1800, 17.
43 Burney 1988, 252ff.
44 Smollett 1995, 65.
45 'I went on to Star Cross, and crossed over the river to Exmouth, situated near the place where the river Ex empties itself into the sea, and is chiefly inhabited by fishermen and publicans, it being a place to which the people of Exeter much resort for diversion and bathing in the sea'. Pococke 1888, 102.
46 Pococke 1889, 6; Walton 1998, 13. Walton dismisses claims by some early writers of bathing being practised much earlier in the century.
47 Hutton 1789, 4.
48 ibid, 28.
49 Ayton, 1815 volume II, 116.
50 Floyer 1702, A4; Walton 1983, 10; Walton 1992, 10.
51 Pevsner et al. 1989, 619; Robinson 1981, 57.
52 Lackington 1974, 312; Bennett and Bennett (eds) 1993, 122.
53 Gawthern 1980, 71.
54 Neller 2000, 14; Bennett and Bennett (eds) 1993, 122; Kime 2005, 21–2.
55 Park nd, 1.
56 Bailey 1955, 29, 34; Glazebrook 1826, 59–64; Alsop 1832, 39; Robinson 1848, 25.
57 ibid 1955, 36.
58 Brannon 1867, 9.
59 Sherry 1972, 129.
60 Anon 1825, 478.
61 Brannon 1867, 10.
62 Granville 1971 volume II, 512.
63 Anon 1838, 5; Butler 1984, 2; Young 1983, 1–8.
64 Hay 1794, 45.
65 Young 1983, 47.
66 Kent Archives Service, K/Herne Bay, Herne Bay Pier Company Prospectus 1831.
67 Coulson 1984, 8–9.
68 Scott 1974, 7.
69 Dale 1967, 113–19.
70 Baines 1990, 9, 11.
71 Colvin 1995, 194.
72 Anon 1831, cited in Baines 1990, 9.
73 Southend also had a few buildings on the shore by the late 18th century, some of which have survived.

74 Borsay (ed.) 1990, 133.
75 Chalklin 2001, 59; Clark 2000 (ed.), 531. Seaside resorts that were medieval boroughs included East and West Teignmouth, Sidmouth, Lyme Regis, Melcombe Regis (Weymouth), Dover, Great Yarmouth, Southwold, Hastings, Bridlington, Scarborough, Whitby. Beresford and Finberg 1973.
76 Clarke 1955, 9; Smellie 1968, 12–14.
77 Ray 1989, 213.
78 16 Geo III c. 57.
79 3 Geo. IV c. lvii.
80 6 Geo. IV c. cxxxv.
81 5 & 6 Will. IV c. ci.
82 For instance at Deal 36 Geo. III c. 45 and Folkestone 36 Geo III c. 49.
83 5 & 6 Will. IV c. ci, section CIX; East Kent Archives FO/AM4/1.
84 27 Geo III c. 45, 52 Geo III c. clxxxvi.
85 Austin 1992, 15–23.
86 White 1867, 305; Walton 1983, 143, 146.
87 Guilmant 1982, no pagination; Griffiths 1965, 89.
88 Post Office Directory of Essex 1874, 198.
89 Clarke 1975, 1.
90 Young 1983, 150.
91 Albert 1972, 14, 44, 49.
92 ibid, 205, 206, 211.
93 Austen 1975, 1.
94 Baker and Gerhold 1995, 37.
95 Walton 1983, 21.
96 Ayton 1815 volume II, 102.
97 Albert 1972, 219.
98 Anon 1810, 304.
99 Grandfield 1989, 65, 66.
100 Anon 1770a, 22; Scurrell 1982, 60.
101 Walvin 1978a, 22.
102 Lyons 1763, 15.
103 Anon 1810, 307.
104 Ransom 1984, 124; Bagwell and Lyth 2002, 24.
105 Kidd 1831, 1; Camden 1835, 27; Whyman 1985, 24.
106 Whyman 1981, 124; ibid 1985, 78.
107 East Kent Archives R/U127/1.
108 Anon 1865, frontispiece.
109 Kellett 1969, 90. First class sales rose from 7.1 million to 27 million, second class from 22.8 million to 66.7 million, third class from 28.5 million to 194.8 million.
110 Walton 1983, 22.
111 Ekberg 1986, 60.
112 Walton 1983, 23.
113 Whyman 1980, 185–225; Palmer 1943, 211–43.
114 Baker 1990, 154; Sigsworth (ed.) 1980, 128; Simmons and Biddle (eds) 1999, 51.
115 Ibid 1980, 129.
116 Granville 1971, 346–7.
117 Walvin 1978b, 81.

118 Simmons 1986, 244–5.
119 Cannadine 1980, 237–8.
120 Walton 1979, 195; Biddle 1990, 132.
121 ibid 1990, 132–3; Simmons 1986, 255.
122 Walton 1979, 197–8, 200–1, 205, 208; ibid 1990, 133.
123 Simmons 1986, 257.
124 Biddle 2003, 381–3; ibid 1986.
125 Jordan and Jordan 1991, 233, Biddle 1990, 132; Ekberg 1986, 60.
126 Cannadine 1980, 410–11.
127 Walton 1981, 249–65; Poole 1994, 3; Barton 2005, 74.
128 Cunningham 1980, 15.
129 Smee 1871, 3–4.
130 The Bank Holidays Act, 1871, 34 Vict c. 17.
131 Simmons and Biddle (eds) 1999, 150; Jordan and Jordan 1991, 11–12.
132 ibid 1999, 112; Horn 1999 127; ibid 1991, 13.
133 ibid 1999, 150; Walton 1983, 28.
134 Anon 1977; ibid 1999, 151.
135 Jordan and Jordan 1991, 159.
136 Perkin 1976, 184.
137 Jordan and Jordan 1991, 35.
138 ibid 1991, 37.
139 Barton 2005, 113–14; Pimlott 1976, 155.
140 Report of the Committee on Holidays with Pay 1937–8 Cmd 5724, 7; ibid 1976, 215.
141 1 & 2 Geo 6 c. 70. Bills were introduced in 1925, 1929, 1936 and 1937.
142 Report of the Committee on Holidays with Pay 1937–8 Cmd 5724, 21.
143 Brunner 1945, 13; Pimlott 1976, 221–2; Shaw and Williams (eds) 1997, 58.
144 Lancaster 1936a, 12. Monthly rail figures published in a parliamentary debate on 6 April 1938 were – June 56 million, July 60 million, August 72 million, September 52 million.
145 House of Commons Journal 27 April 1938, column 367–8.
146 Brenan 1936, 15.
147 Anon 1938c, 15; Pimlott 1947, 225ff. Pimlott even devoted an appendix to a description of his visit to Butlins at Clacton in 1946, 276–83.
148 Baker 1990, 151; Walton 1998, 139.
149 www.dft.gov.uk/stellent/groups/dft_transstats/documents/downloadable/dft_transstats_609987.pdf, table 6.1 (accessed 11 September 2006).
150 Brunner 1945, 6.
151 Lavery (ed.) 1974, 100; www.staruk.org.uk//webcode/contents.asp?id=657&parentid=469&bg=white (accessed 11 September 2006).
152 Morton 1927, vii.
153 Roberts 1976, 212.
154 Gilbert 1939, 20.
155 Shaw and Williams (eds) 1997, 29.

156 ibid, 40.
157 Walton and Walvin (eds) 1983, 141.
158 Shaw and Williams (eds) 1997, 21–48, 43.
159 Pimlott 1976, 244–5; Braggs and Harris 2000, 72.
160 Farrant 1987, 137–62; ibid 1976.
161 *The Times*, 31 August 1943, 3.
162 Stafford and Yates 1985, 157.
163 Walton 1998, 137.
164 Shaw and Williams (eds) 1997, 50. In 1978, 9 million holidays of four nights or more were taken abroad, but nine years later this had risen to 20 million. Shaw and Williams (eds) 1997, 59.
165 English Tourism Council 2001, 4.

3 The form of resorts

1 For the purpose of this study the central area of 27 towns were examined using English Heritage's Geographical Information System, including 13 resorts, 5 spa towns and 9 other towns with comparable areas and comparable populations.
2 Horn 1999, 13.
3 Anon 1793, 4, 14.
4 Boddy and West 1983, 81.
5 Whyman 1980, 191, 197.
6 Lucking 1971, 11, 12, 19.
7 Gawthern 1980, 116.
8 Leach 1999, 12–13.
9 Giles 2000, 248.
10 Saunders 1989, 117, 119.
11 'I took a ride to Seaford, where we took a walk by the seaside, and took a view of two forts newly erected there, one of which has 24-pounders mounted, and the other five 12-pounders.' Turner 1979, 55, Sunday 1 August 1762.
12 Douet 1998, 82; Longstaff-Tyrell 2002, 12.
13 Sutcliffe 1972, 59–61.
14 East Kent Archives FO/S1/3/1 is a set of 1917 photographs of the damage done by the air raid including a school, the Central Station approach, the top floor of Osborne Hotel in Bouverie Road West, the Bouverie Hotel and a number of shops in Tontine Street.
15 Bridgeman and Drury 1977, 95.
16 Bartley 1971, 125.
17 White 1855, 550.
18 Anon 1800, 21.
19 Miller 1888, 7.
20 Jordan and Jordan 1991, 24–5.
21 Simmons 1986, 248; Whitney 1986, Introduction; Farrant 1987, 148.
22 Thompson 1839, 152.
23 Griffiths 1965, 47.
24 Bulley 1956, 151.
25 East Kent Archives R/U127/1. Diary of Mary Figgins at Margate *c*.1828.

26 Capper 1833, 11.
27 Morrison 2003, 93.
28 'What was but two years ago the mere face of a pile of rocks, is now an extensive "Bazaar" to be surmounted by a magnificent crescent, with a chapel; the carriage road to which, incredible as it may seem, winds over the top of the Bazaar!!!' Diplock nd, 52.
29 Whyman 1985, 314.
30 Morrison 2003, 102ff.
31 Camden 1835, 32.
32 Walton 2000, 96.
33 Anon 1733, 26; Anon 1734a, 28; Anon 1770b, 22–3.
34 Anon 1835, 12.
35 Kidd 1831, 8.
36 Anon 1835, 13.
37 Berry 2005, 179; Rutter 1829, 20.
38 Le Bas 1802, 77–8.
39 www.jewishgen.org/jcr-uk/Community/br5-early/index.htm (accessed 11 September 2006); Berry 2005, 182.
40 Kellett 1993, 187.
41 Appleton 1968, 103.
42 The streets appear on the 1907 Ordnance Survey map, but on the 1898 edition the same area is a field.
43 Biddle 2003, 111; Simmons 1986, 237.
44 Lee 1974, 18.
45 Hardy and Ward 1984, 72.
46 Joad 1957, 88.
47 Thorold 2003, 155; Mason 2003, 22–3.
48 Hardy and Ward 1984, 90.
49 Thoms et al. 1998, 43.
50 Anon 1938b, 240.
51 Brenan 1936, 15.
52 Maitland 1936, 19.
53 ibid, 20.
54 Thorold 2003, 108.
55 Calladine and Morrison 1998; Walton 1998, 132.

4 The architectural styles of seaside buildings

1 Anon 1908, 57.
2 Anon 1809, 14; Anon 1770a, 12; Hall 1790, 9; Cozens 1793, 24.
3 Kidd 1831, 8; Anon 1835, 13.
4 Perkin 1976, 184–7.
5 Torrington 1934 volume 1, 87.
6 Lewis 1723, 87.
7 The town in the 16th century was illustrated in a plan/view of the French attack, in a manuscript of c.1539–45. British Library Cotton MS Augustus I. i. 18.
8 Relhan 1761, 15.
9 ibid.
10 Clarke 1793, 39–40.
11 Thornber 1837, 226, 207.
12 Anon 1770a, 12–13.

13 Schopenhauer 1988, 130.
14 Hunter 1998, 135–8. The author did not include Leasowe Castle, which dates from the late 16th century and was apparently built to make use of the sea.
15 Miele 1998, 149, 156.
16 Colvin 1995, 710–11; Anon 2003, 17.
17 Bridlington, Folkestone, Weston-super-Mare, Great Yarmouth, Exmouth, Morecambe, Llandudno, Blackpool, etc.
18 Arnold (ed.) 1995, 57.
19 Burney 1988, 275.
20 King 1984, 1.
21 Plan of Freehold Bungalow situate at Westgate-on-Sea…To be sold…1887, British Library Maps 137.c.4. (3.).
22 Harrison 1909, 33–5.
23 Granville Illustrated News, 25 October 1879, cited in King 1984, 73.
24 King 1984, 86, 274.
25 Wolters 1985, 9.
26 ibid, 10.
27 King 1984, 171.
28 Pigot 1832, 1007–8.
29 Morley 1984, 13, 32ff; Brighton Polytechnic School of Architecture and Interior Design 1987, 26–30; Berry 2005, 46–62.
30 Summerson 1949, 169.
31 The impact of electricity will be considered in detail in chapter 6.
32 Anon 1938b, 294.
33 Brook 1997, 24; Fairley 2001, 33–4.
34 Bexhill Observer, 16 September 1933, cited in Brook 1997, 25.
35 Brook 1997, 30.
36 Information from the hotel; Taylor 1998, 8.
37 Anon 1935a, 167–73.
38 Clonmore 1933, 93–9.
39 Smith 2005, 24, 146ff; Longstaff-Tyrell 2002, 68–9; Braggs and Harris 2000, 77.
40 Powers 2005, 104–5. Some of the best information about the site comes from plaques containing historical facts placed on each of the old rides.
41 Dawe and Powell 2001, 75, 102, 112, 148, 170.
42 Martin Hall sees Las Vegas as 'a series of massive, decorated sheds' providing 'a three dimensional stage set' – Casella and Symonds (eds) 2005, 263.

5 The health of visitors

1 Shaw 1735, 36–8.
2 Russell 1752, v–vi.
3 Awsiter 1768, 5.
4 Parry 1983, 25.
5 Pearce 2000, 23.
6 Shaw 1735, 36.
7 Blundell 1972 volume III, 52.
8 Anderson 1795, 32.

9 Awsiter 1768, 4–5.
10 Smollett 1995, 166–7.
11 Cozens 1793, 3.
12 Schofield 1787, 20.
13 Angerstein 2001, 69.
14 Whyman 1980, 198–9.
15 La Rochefoucauld 1988, 217.
16 Cited in Hart 1981, 70.
17 Parkes 2001, 59–60.
18 The Times, Thursday 22 July 1920, 10.
19 Longmate 1991, 486.
20 Lyons 1763, 12.
21 Carey 1799, 5.
22 Anon 1809, 50.
23 Walton 1983, 159.
24 Reid 1795, 70.
25 Anon 1797a, 70.
26 Hawkins 1991, 55, 57.
27 Whyman 1990, 39.
28 Clarke 1975, 30.
29 Kay and Kay 1998, 33.
30 JK Laughton, 'Knowles, Sir Charles, first baronet (d. 1777)', rev. Richard Harding, Oxford Dictionary of National Biography, Oxford University Press, 2004: www.oxforddnb.com/view/article/15765 (accessed 11 September 2006).
31 Anon 1810; Wallis 1836, 57.
32 The Kentish Post, or Canterbury News Letter, 14 July 1736, cited in Whyman 1985, 160.
33 The Kentish Post, or Canterbury News Letter, 27 April 1737, cited in ibid, 161.
34 Awsiter 1768, 15–18.
35 Berry 2002, 103–4; Farrant 1980, 15, 19, 21.
36 ibid 1980, 21.
37 NMR Buildings File 86314.
38 Mahomet 1997, 161–2.
39 ibid, 165.
40 Anon 1822, 67.
41 Pigot 1826/7.
42 Whyman 1985, 170–2; Post Office 1851.
43 Pearce 2000, 6.
44 ibid, 13.
45 Sickelmore 1827, 66–7.
46 East Kent Archives F1954/2/B2 The Folkestone Bathing Establishment Company Limited Minute Book 1878–1890.
47 Easdown 1998, 36.
48 Kelly 1889a, 546.
49 Carey 1799, 92.
50 Hart 1981, 70.
51 Kelly 1924, 195.
52 Durie 2002, 38–9.
53 Curtis 1888 (ed.), 31.
54 ibid 1888, 31–2; Anon 2002, 2–3.
55 Blundell 1968 volume I, 257, 263; Torrington 1935 volume II, 386.
56 Reid 1795, 12.
57 Bartholomew c.1870, 93–4.

58 Rollier 1927, 1; Miller 1926, 143.
59 ibid 1927, 1.
60 Saleeby 1928, xi.
61 Rollier 1927, 263–5, 269, 271–3; Miller 1926, 143–5.
62 Clark 1830, 29.
63 Barker 1860.
64 Brannon 1867.
65 Anon 1891, 16. The pines were even celebrated in song in *The City of Pines: Or, Beautiful Bournemouth*, written in 1912.
66 Richardson (ed.) 1998, 127; St Clair Strange 1991, 19.
67 Original minutes manuscript printed in St Clair Strange 1991, 20–2.
68 Richardson (ed.) 1998, 127.
69 St Clair Strange 1991, 66.
70 Whyman 1981, 728; ibid 1991, 37, 51, 62.
71 ibid 1991, 104, 183.
72 ibid, 170.
73 Hobday 1997, 456–7.
74 Ransome 1903, 62–3.
75 While the majority of institutions with multiple wards canted the wings 'inwards', generally towards the south and south-east, St Anne's Sanatorium at Poole in Dorset (1909–12) incorporated wings that splayed in the opposite direction and gave greater vistas towards Poole Bay at the south-east end of the institution's grounds.
76 NMR Buildings File 100243.
77 Anon nd(b).
78 Nightingale 1863, 113.
79 *The Builder*, 21 December 1872, 1003.
80 NMR Buildings File 102493.
81 *The Builder*, 25 September 1869, 769.
82 *Shields Daily News*, 15 September 1869; *The Builder*, 25 September 1869, 769–70.
83 This building was demolished in *c*.1985. Whitehouse 1986, 1–2.
84 *Building News*, 5 November 1897; ibid 1986, 7.
85 ibid 1986, 11, 12.
86 ibid, 13–14.
87 ibid, 35–41.
88 ibid, 45.
89 NMR Buildings File 91077; Richardson (ed.) 1998, 188.
90 NMR Buildings File 91077; *The Builder*, 6 July 1928, 9–11; Anon 1929, 43.
91 Anon 1938–9, 347-52.
92 Kelly 1939b, 773.
93 Kime 1988, 33.
94 An open-air seawater baths was built on the banks of the River Test at Southampton in 1853, but Scarborough South Bay Pool (1914–15) was the first of the grand, seaside open-air pools.
95 Braggs and Harris 2000, 72.
96 Smith 2005, 130.
97 *Morecambe Visitor*, 22 July 1936.
98 Smith 2005, 129.
99 Belisario 1959, 17; Paul 1918, 16.
100 www.thalassofederation.com/page_menu_e.php?page=savoir_faire (accessed 11 September 2006).

6 Entertaining the visitor

1 Anderson 1795, 63–6.
2 East Kent Archives Service R/TR 2188/2, Extracts from Journals and Letters of Lady Mary Coke.
3 Kielmansegge 1902, 117. When he died on 12 February 1761 his body lay in state for four days for mourners to pay their last respects, a fitting end to the life of a self-proclaimed monarch. Poole 1976, 63.
4 Walters 1968, 43–7; ibid 1976, 15.
5 Connely 1955, 29.
6 Love 1788, 46; Harvey 1800, 81; Anon 1815, 51–2.
7 Anon 1809, 21.
8 Anon 1793, 14.
9 *The Times* 26 August 1803, 2.
10 Anon 1734b, 41.
11 Schopenhauer 1988, 118.
12 Travis 1993, 74.
13 Commins 1836, book plate and 22.
14 RCHME 1970, 340.
15 Travis 1993, 74; Colvin 1995, 833; Bulley 1956, 158.
16 Whyman 1985, 268; Anon 1822, 36.
17 Anon 1809, 23.
18 Hall 1790, 10; Cozens 1793, 25.
19 ibid 1790, 10–11.
20 Whyman 1985, 269.
21 Anon 1797b, 47.
22 Anon 1809, 24–5; Whyman 1985, 279.
23 Cunningham 1980, 153; Stewart-Murphy 1992, 16.
24 Anon 1793, 7–8.
25 Anon 1734b, 38–9; Hazard, a dice game similar to craps, and Faro, a version of roulette, were the favourite forms of gambling. Murray 1998 162–4.
26 Lyons 1763, 16; Clarke 1975, 76; Baines 1986, 304–5; Moss 1824, 168.
27 Anon 1770b, 13–14.
28 ibid, 13.
29 Hyett 1805, 39.
30 Carrington *c*.1840, 9.
31 ibid; Griffiths 1965, 88.
32 Kelly 1889a, 545 states 1869; Griffiths offers the date of 1871.
33 Kelly 1900–1, 96. It opened on 8 August 1898. Clements 1992, 118.
34 Anon 1793, 16.
35 Morley 1966, 12–17.
36 Anon 1734b, 41; Berry 2002, 105.
37 Hutton 1789, 37–8.
38 10 Geo II c.19; Trussler 1994, 191; Natan 1961, 166, 182.
39 Trussler 1994, 192.
40 Staelens 1989, 31.
41 Carey 1799, 113.
42 Adams 1967, 302–13.
43 ibid, illustrations on 308, 313.
44 Ryall 1800, 9; Commins 1836, 29; Anon 1846, 32; ibid, 303–5.
45 Whyman 1985, 295.
46 Baines 1986, 307–9.
47 Busson 1985, 37.
48 Bailey (ed.) 1986, 4; Mander and Mitchenson 1974, 17–18; Delgado 1971, 49, 53.
49 Walvin 1978b, 110.
50 Pigot 1824, 253; Bulley 1956 157; Griffiths 1965, 89.
51 Speaight 1981, 43; Manser 1987, 108.
52 Sanger 1966, 142.
53 Speaight 1981, 50, 191.
54 Anon 1895, no pagination.
55 Bratton (ed.) 1986, 70; Toll 1974, 28, 196; Leighton 1847. This amusing cartoon book includes a scuffle among the crowd at a performance of 'Ethiopian' entertainers from London.
56 Walvin 1978b, 75; Bridgeman and Drury 1977, 62; Pertwee 1999, 11.
57 Adams and Leach 1978, 4; Speaight 1970, 39. Byrom 1972, 8–9.
58 Charlton 1779, 333
59 Speaight 1970, 124.
60 Whyman 1985, 220 citing *The Thanet Itinerary* 1819, 42–3. A report in *The Times* in 1805 described a standard day at Brighton: 'The amusements of today have been, as usual with the fashionables, bathing in the morning, at noon driving over the Downs, donkey-trotting on the cliffs, or sauntering on the sun-scorched Steine.' *The Times* 20 August 1805, Brighton, 2; Searle 1977, 81.
61 Whyman 1985, 195–7; Whyman 1980, 190 n12: 'I must not omit to notice Ramsgate Sands [where] for the accommodation of visitors, a number of chairs (some hundreds) have been placed on them, to a considerable distance – the charge being only 1d. per day, for each person' (*Sea Side Reminiscences c*.1835). 'There were old gentlemen, trying to make out objects through long telescopes; and young ones, making objects of themselves in open shirt-collars; ladies, carrying about portable chairs, and portable chairs carrying about invalids; parties, waiting on the pier for parties who had come by the steam-boat; and nothing was to be heard but talking, laughing, welcoming, and merriment.' Dickens 1994, 333.
62 Giraldus 1937, 35.
63 Hull (ed.) 1955, 175.
64 Roberts 1823, 141; Roberts 1830, no pagination.

65 Anon 1734b, 30–1. Brighton's races were inaugurated in 1783.
66 Burney 1988, Volume I, 290.
67 ibid, 291.
68 Grandfield 1989, 80.
69 Hull (ed.) 1966, 112–14.
70 Grandfield 1989, 78.
71 Hull (ed.) 1966, 109–17.
72 'Maidstone seems a large town and the Jail a large, strong, melancholy and clean place of punishment … we all walked to the New Jail, a fine stone building – went into the wards and chapel – saw the prisoners spinning, weaving, making mats, string, ropes, etc., then we came in to dinner.' Hull (ed.) 1966, 110.
73 Sex Pistols, *Holidays in the Sun*, released 15 October 1977; Whyman 1980, 200.
74 Storry nd, 54–6.
75 Furby 1846, 6; Lewis 1840 volume II, 377.
76 Cross (ed.) 1990, 88.
77 Plumb 1980, 30; Burke 1946, 124.
78 Anon 1834, 4–6.
79 John R. Lloyd, 'Birch, Eugenius (1818–1884)', rev. Mike Chrimes, *Oxford Dictionary of National Biography*, Oxford University Press, 2004 www.oxforddnb.com/view/article/37193 (accessed 11 September 2006). Birch's piers were built at Margate, Blackpool (North), Weston-super-Mare (Birnbeck Pier), Deal, Brighton (West Pier), Aberystwyth, Lytham, New Brighton, Scarborough, Eastbourne, Hastings, Bournemouth, Hornsea and Plymouth.
80 Gordon 1869, 25.
81 www.theheritagetrail.co.uk/cliff_trams/ southend_cliff_railway.htm (accessed 11 September 2006).
82 Jackson 1993, 3–7.
83 ibid, 16–18.
84 Braithwaite 1976, 19.
85 Bennett 1998, 18.
86 Parry 1983, 133–5.
87 ibid, 146–52.
88 In recent years the parks at Morecambe, Southport and Folkestone have closed.
89 Braithwaite 1976, 37; National Fairground Archive: The history of fairground rides www.shef.ac.uk/nfa/history/rides/index.p hp (accessed 11 September 2006).
90 Wyatt 1996, 13. It was reused in 1904 in the St Louis exhibition, but scrapped in 1906.
91 Hill 1978, 36; Curtis 1988, 31–2.
92 Preedy 1996, 38.
93 Crowe 2003, 11.
94 Ware 1977, Plate 32; Butlin and Dacre 1993, 88–9.
95 Cartmell 1987, 42; Preedy 1996, 2; Wyatt 1996, 10; Bennett 1998, 15.

96 Preedy 1996, 2; Easdown 1998, 67.
97 Bishop 1974, 117.
98 Clements 1992, 126; Bennett 1998, 23, 187.
99 Humphreys 1857, 19; Blunt 1976, 86; Kisling (ed.) 2000, 40–1, 70.
100 Anon 1871, 11–18.
101 Clunn 1929, 45.
102 Walton 1983, 170–1.
103 Kelly 1883, 574; Lewis 1980, 22.
104 Anon 1890, 1043.
105 Hammond 1981, 116.
106 Gray 1996a, 10.
107 Gray 1996(b), 17, 22–3.
108 Anon 1977.
109 Gray 1996a, 18.
110 NMR Report 94780.
111 Gray 1996a, 18; Bennett 1998, 21.
112 Curtis 1988, 11; Cross (ed.) 1990, 216.
113 Parry 1983, 144.
114 The title of the oldest glass-roofed cast-iron greenhouse in Britain appears to belong to Chiselhampton, which dates from *c*.1800. Woods and Warren 1990, 88.
115 Hix 1974, 114.
116 *The Times* 2 September 1833, 4.
117 Lewis 1980, 21–2.
118 Whitney 1986, Fig 109.
119 Pearson 2002, 25, 27.
120 The Winter Garden was demolished in 1962.
121 Walton 1998, 87–90.
122 Williams and Savage 1992, 3–4.
123 Avon County Council Planning Department 1991, 46; Harding and Lambert (eds) 1994, 99.
124 ibid 1991, 46.
125 Young 1983, 215.
126 Guilmant 1982, no pagination.
127 Kelly 1906, 459; Crowe 2003, 3, 9. Today the site of the outdoor rides is occupied by modern housing.
128 Young 1983, 194. It was demolished in 1975. Wales 1997, 21.
129 Coleman and Lukens 1956, 28–9; Evans 2003, 5; Clements 1992, 125.
130 Morley 1966, 93; Evans 2003, 7–8; Clements 1992, 125; Mirams 1984, 4.
131 Evans 2003, 8.
132 Walvin 1978b, 75.
133 Anon 1895, no pagination.
134 Pearson 2002, 27.
135 In 1914 an underground passage joined the Tower and Palace. The Palace was demolished in 1961.
136 Cross (ed.) 1990, 128.
137 Maitland 1936, 22.
138 Braggs and Harris 2000, 86.
139 Anon 1732, 1, 7.
140 www.archiveshub.ac.uk/news/ 04062901.html (accessed 11 September 2006); www.mac.ndo.co.uk/a%20brief% 20history.htm (accessed 11 September 2006).

141 Kelly 1939a, 6, 254.
142 Noall 1977, 111; Baker 2000, 8, 31.

7 Staying at the seaside

1 Berry 2005, 89.
2 Dickens 1999, 22.
3 Stockdale 1817, Powell 1825.
4 Evans 1821, 38.
5 Bread 1859, 4; Lyons 1763, 11.
6 Austen 1975, 22.
7 Torrington 1934 volume 1, 87, 26 August 1782.
8 Anon 1765, 11.
9 Anon 1797a, 71.
10 Bulley 1956, 151.
11 *The General Evening Post* (London) June 19–21 1792 – Extract from St Anne's Express dated 24 August 1910 in Blackpool Central Reference Library M851 (p) C R 17 971.
12 Brown and Loosley 1985, 19–22.
13 Pigot 1830; White 1850.
14 Kelly 1889a, Kelly 1902.
15 Schofield 1787, 16.
16 Whyman 1980, 187.
17 Gray 1996b 83.
18 Austen 1975, 22, 44.
19 Gowler 1998, 57.
20 Pigot 1840b, 690.
21 Wigstead and Rowlandson 1790, no pagination.
22 Ryall 1800, 4–5.
23 Sickelmore 1827, 100.
24 Young 1983, 79–80.
25 East Kent Archives U1453/A2 *An Acct of the Pirchis of My New Dwelling And Additions made to the same in the year 1777.*
26 Hatfield 1797, 37–40.
27 Pigot 1840a.
28 Wojtczak 2002, 35; Kay 2003, 41 53.
29 Simond 1968, 36–7.
30 Guillery 2004, 282–4.
31 Muthesius 1982, 43–5.
32 Anon 1815, 86.
33 *The Kentish Post, or Canterbury News Letter* 14 July 1736, cited in Whyman 1985, 160.
34 *The Kentish Post, or Canterbury News Letter* 27 April 1737, cited in ibid, 161.
35 Rutter *c*.1840.
36 Knightstone Baths & Lodging Houses, *Bristol Mirror* 9 January 1847. Notes taken from photocopy of museum sheet from NMR buildings file 86314.
37 Utting 1846, 63.
38 Anon 1770a, 13.
39 Palmer 1943, 213.
40 ibid, 226, 231, 233.
41 Hyett 1805, 39.
42 Girouard 1992, 261. In *Sanditon* Jane Austen described how Mr and Mrs Parker had moved their furniture in the

evening to benefit from the fire: 'They were in one of the Terrace houses; and she found them arranged for the evening in a small neat drawing room with a beautiful view of the sea if they had chosen it; but though it had been a very fair English summer day, not only was there no open window, but the sofa and the table and the establishment in general was all at the other end of the room by a brisk fire.' Austen 1975, 57.

43 Whyman 1985, 113.
44 East Kent Archives Service R/U127/1.
45 Hatfield 1797, 24–5.
46 Haines 1989, 106.
47 Hatfield 1797, 24.
48 Anona 1770, 15.
49 Hatfield 1797, 37–8.
50 Anon 1808, 381.
51 Moss 1824, 168.
52 Sickelmore 1827, 99.
53 Schofield 1787, 16.
54 Anon 1817, 81; Neller 2000, 14.
55 Clarke 1975, 72.
56 Hay 1794, 45.
57 Pevsner 1976, 173–4.
58 Bishop 1880, 138.
59 Barber and Barber 1993, 6.
60 Pigot 1839, 293.
61 Nevill 2002, 12.
62 Mackie 1883, 94.
63 Pardon 1857, 54–5.
64 Anon 1852, 35.
65 D'Ormesson 1984, 17; Pevsner 1976, 189–90.
66 Carter 1989, 37.
67 Elleray 1995, no pagination.
68 The plans survive in the East Kent Archives signed by Cutter, dated 8 July 1895 East Kent Archives FO PS 7/3-11.
69 Carter 1989, 36.
70 Clonmore 1933, 94.
71 Brenan 1936, 14.
72 Shaw and Williams (eds) 1997, 87–90.
73 Kay and Kay 1998, 49; Clements 1992, 116.
74 Kay and Kay 1998, 8, 50; Clements 1992, 113; Clements, 1997, 31.
75 Clements 1997, 19; Kay and Kay 1998, 53.
76 Jakle et al. 1996, 19ff.
77 Drower 1982, 9–10; www.isle-of-man.com/manxnotebook/tourism/ccamp

(accessed 11 September 2006).
78 Drower 1982,15, Kniveton et al. 1996, 37.
79 International Young Men's Holiday Camp (DOUGLAS) 1904, 3, 7; Kniveton et al. 1996, 37 www.isle-of-man.com/manxnotebook/tourism/ccamp (accessed 11 September 2006).
80 Anon 1935b, 762; Drower 1982, 16.
81 Drower 1982, 19, 25, 35, 61.
82 www.childrensholidaycentre.co.uk/history.html (accessed 11 September 2006).
83 The Times 29 February 1912, 14.
84 Wilkinson 2002, 82.
85 ibid, 35, plate opposite 39.
86 Physical Training and Recreation Act 1937 1 Edw 8 and 1 Geo 6 c. 46, s. 4.
87 Anon 1938d, 5; Anon 1939a, 6; Anon 1939b, 30.
88 Balducci (ed.) 2005.
89 The Times 17 May 1939, 9; Gration 2000, 11, 13.
90 Hardy and Ward 1984, 119.
91 www.starmakers.connectfree.co.uk/htmfiles/pothis01.htm (accessed 11 September 2006); www.pottersholidays.com/history.aspx (accessed 11 September 2006).
92 www.butlinsmemories.com/2/id183.htm (accessed 11 September 2006).
93 Willsher 2003, 6, 37.
94 Butlin and Dacre 1993, 88.
95 Read 1986, 7; every week they prepared 2,750 loaves, 700 hams, 3½ miles of sausages and 7 tons of potatoes. Gravy and Custard were prepared in 100-gallon pans and the kitchen had a dishwasher that could clean 20,000 plates after every meal. Drower 1982, 57.
96 Butlin and Dacre 1993, 31.
97 ibid, 105.
98 Anon 1937, 462.
99 Butlin and Dacre 1993, 79.
100 ibid, 109–10. A Midsummer Night's Dream, Act V Scene I: ' We do not come, as minding to content you, / Our true intent is. All for your delight / We are not here. That you should here repent you, / The actors are at hand:'
101 ibid, 113–14.
102 ibid, 130.

103 ibid, 188, 190, 191, 193.
104 ibid, 163.
105 www.butlinsmemories.com/2/id130.htm (accessed 18 September 2006).
106 www.butlinsmemories.com/19/id95.htm (accessed 11 September 2006); www.butlinsmemories.com/19/id85.htm (accessed 11 September 2006).
107 Braggs and Harris 2000, 116.
108 www.butlinsmemories.com/2/id203.htm (accessed 11 September 2006).
109 Sanger 1966, 44; Whiteman 1973, 9–19.
110 Jenkinson 2003, 6; Jenkinson 1998, 7.
111 Jenkinson 1998, 34; Braggs and Harris 2000, 39.
112 Caravan Sites and Control of Development Act 1960 8 & 9 Eliz II c. 62.
113 Whiteman 1973, 261.
114 Jenkinson 1999, 24.
115 Constance 2001, 187, 235, 264.
116 Mills (ed.) 1989.
117 ENGLAND. National Parks Commission 1967, 35; Shaw and Williams (eds) 1997, 62.
118 Walvin 1978a, 146.
119 Ayton 1814–25, volume VI 1822, 67.

8 Conclusion

1 Baker 1931, 419.
2 Dickens 1994, 330ff describes the holiday; Leighton 1847.
3 ibid, 335.
4 ibid 341.
5 Anon 1977.
6 Information supplied by Philip Eden at www.weather-uk.com.
7 Anon 1890, 1043.
8 www.communities.gov.uk/index.asp?id=1128444 (accessed 22 January 2007); www.communities.gov.uk/index.asp?id=1128445#P200_14232 (accessed 22 January 2007)
9 Crockett 2004.
10 Beatty and Fothergill 2003.
11 Anon 2006, 97–100.
12 English Tourism Council 2001, 5.
13 Kichin 1912, 18–22.
14 The Times 19 February 1934, 15.
15 Mason 2003.

Bibliography

Adams, A and Leach, R 1978 *The World of Punch & Judy*. London: Harrap

Adams, VJ 1967 'Weymouth Theatricals'. *Dorset Natural History and Archaeological Society* 89, 302–313

Albert, W 1972 *The Turnpike Road System in England, 1663–1840*. London: Cambridge University Press

Alsop, W 1832 *A Concise History of Southport, etc.* Southport: William Alsop

Anderson, J 1795 *A Practical Essay on the Good and Bad Effects of Sea-water and Sea-bathing*. London: C Dilly, etc.

Angerstein, RR 2001 *RR Angerstein's Illustrated Travel Diary, 1753–1755: industry in England and Wales from Swedish perspective / translated by Torsten and Peter Berg with an introduction by Professor Marilyn Palmer*. London: Science Museum

Anon 1732 *The Scarborough Miscellany. An original collection of poems, odes, tales, songs, epigrams, &c. None of which ever appear'd in print before. … By several hands*. London

Anon 1733 *The Scarborough Miscellany for the Year 1733*. London

Anon 1734a *The Scarborough Miscellany for the Year 1734*. London

Anon 1734b *A Journey from London to Scarborough, in Several Letters. ….* London

Anon 1765 *A Description of the Isle of Thanet, and Particularly of the Town of Margate, etc.* London

Anon 1770a *The Margate Guide. Containing a particular account of Margate, … to which is prefix'd, a short description of the Isle of Thanet ….* London

Anon 1770b *The New Brighthelmstone Directory: or, Sketches in miniature of the British shore*. London: T Durham

Anon 1793 *A Poetical Description of New South-End*. London

Anon 1797a *The Hastings Guide … To which is added, some account of the Cinque Ports, and … of the … battle of Hastings. The second edition. By an Inhabitant … With … plates and a map, etc.* Hastings: J Barry

Anon 1797b *The Margate Guide, a descriptive Poem, with … notes. Also a general account of Ramsgate, Broadstairs, &c. By an Inhabitant*. Margate

Anon 1797c *A New Weymouth Guide, etc.* Dorchester

Anon 1800 *A Companion to the Watering and Bathing Places of England … London*: HD Symonds

Anon 1808 *Guide to Watering and Sea Bathing Places*. London

Anon 1809 *Picture of Margate, being a guide to all persons visiting Margate, Ramsgate, and Broadstairs ….* London

Anon 1810 *A Guide to all the Watering and Sea Bathing Places, with a description of the Lakes; a sketch of a tour in Wales, and Itineraries … Illustrated with maps and views. By the Editor of the Picture of London*. London

Anon 1815 *A New Weymouth Guide: exhibiting the ancient and present state of Weymouth and Melcombe Regis …* Weymouth

Anon 1817 *A Guide to the Watering Places, on the Coast, between the Exe and the Dart, including Teignmouth, Dawlish, and Torquay, etc.* Teignmouth: E Croydon

Anon 1822 *The Thanet Itinerary*. Margate

Anon 1825 *A Guide to all the Watering and Sea Bathing Places, with a description of the Lakes; a sketch of a tour in Wales, and Itineraries … London*

Anon 1831 *The Watering Places of Great Britain and Fashionable Directory, etc.* London: IT Hinton

Anon 1834 *Holidays at Brighton; or, Sea-side Amusements*. London: Darton & Harvey

Anon 1835 *A Picture of the New Town of Herne Bay, its beauties, history, and the curiosities in its vicinity, including some particulars of the Roman town called Reculver*. London: John Macrone

Anon 1838 *The Bognor Guide, containing the history of Bognor, and the history and antiquities of several adjoining parishes …* Petworth: John Phillips

Anon 1846 *A Guide Book to Weymouth and Melcombe Regis, with the adjacent villages and the Island of Portland*. Weymouth

Anon 1852 *The Visitor's Guide to Bognor and its Vicinity; or An account of its history and advantages as a watering place and marine residence … .* Bognor: J Osborn

Anon 1865 *All about Margate and Herne Bay*. London

Anon 1871 *Life Beneath the Waves, and a Description of the Brighton Aquarium*. London

Anon 1890 *History, Topography, and Directory of North Yorkshire*. Preston: T Bulmer & Co.

Anon 1891 *Apartment, Hotel and Trade Guide for Hampshire. Description of the watering places and pleasure resorts. (Section 1.)* Southampton: Petford and Co.

Anon 1895 *Illustrated Guide to the Blackpool Tower, and programme of amusements* Blackpool: WH Southern & Co.

Anon 1908 'Notes of the month. Seaside Architecture'. *The Architectural Review* **24** (August), 57

Anon 1929 *Miners' Welfare Fund Seventh Report of the Committee appointed by the Board of Trade to Allocate the Fund, together with the Second Report of the Selection Committee appointed to Administer the Miners' Welfare National Scholarship Scheme, 1928*. London

Anon 1935a 'Embassy Court, Brighton'. *The Architectural Review* **78** (November), 167–73

Anon 1935b 'By Loch, Mountain and Sea.' *Holiday and Health Resorts Guide (Holidays by L.M.S.), etc.* London

Anon 1937 'By Loch, Mountain and Sea.' *Holiday and Health Resorts Guide (Holidays by L.M.S.), etc.* London

Anon 1938a 'Folkestone and its Foreshore'. *The Architectural Review* **83** (January), 15–26

Anon 1938b 'Leisure as an Architectural Problem'. *The Architectural Review* **84** (December), 231–310

Anon 1938c *Holiday Camp Review* **1**, no 1 (April). London

Anon 1938d *Holiday Camp Review* **1**, no. 5 (August–September). London

Anon 1938–9 'Communal Mothercraft'. *Mother and Child* **9**, 347–52

Anon 1939a *Holiday Camp Review* **2**, no. 1 (May). London

Anon 1939b *Holiday Camp Review* **2**, no. 2 (June). London

Anon 1977 *Bass, Ratcliff & Gretton Limited Excursion to Scarborough.* Burton upon Trent

Anon 2002 *Hotel in the Glen: A History of the Town Hall (1881–2002).* Bournemouth

Anon 2003 'Fortfield Terrace'. *The Picturesque* 44 (autumn 2003), 16–17

Anon 2006 'The Great Retirement Guide'. *Yours* (29 March–25 April), 95–118

Anon nd(a) *A Butlin's History.* Typescript from Butlins Museum

Anon nd(b) *The Mundesley Sanatorium Prospectus*

Appleton, JH 1968 'Railways and the morphology of British towns', in RP Beckinsale and JM Houston (eds) *Urbanization and its Problems.* Oxford: Basil Blackwell, 82–118

Arnold, D (ed.) 1995 *The Picturesque in Late Georgian England: papers given at the Georgian Group Symposium, 22nd October 1994.* London: Georgian Group

Austen, B 1966 'The impact of the mail coach on public coach services in England and Wales'. *The Journal of Transport History* 3 ser **2** (1), 25–37

Austen, J 1975 *Sanditon.* London: Mandarin

Austin, B 1992 *Tales Of Old Weston Volume 1: Weston To 1842 & Dredge's Pier (1845–1848).* Weston-super-Mare: Woodspring Museum Service

Avon County Council Planning Department 1991 *Gazetteer Of Historic Parks & Gardens In Avon.* Bristol: County of Avon Public Relations and Publicity

Awsiter, J 1768 *Thoughts on Brightelmston. Concerning sea-bathing, and drinking sea-water. With some directions for their use.* London: J Wilkie

Ayton, R 1814–25 *A Voyage Round Great Britain Undertaken in the Summer of the Year 1813.* 8 vols. London: Longman

Bagwell, P and Lyth, P 2002 *Transport in Britain from Canal Lock to Gridlock*, London: Hambledon and London

Bailey, FA 1955 *A History of Southport.* Southport: A Downie

Baines, JM 1986 *Historic Hastings* St Leonards-on-Sea: Cinque Port
——1990 *Burton's St Leonards.* Hastings: Hastings Museum

Baker, DV 2000 *Britain's Art Colony by the Sea.* Bristol: Sansom

Baker, J 1931 *The Diary of John Baker ...* London: Hutchinson & Co

Baker, MHC 1990 *Railways to the Coast: Britain's Seaside Lines Past and Present.* Wellingborough: Stephens

Baker, T and Gerhold, D 1995 *The Rise and Rise of Road Transport, 1700–1990.* Cambridge: Cambridge University Press

Bailey, P (ed.) 1986 *Music Hall: The Business of Pleasure.* Milton Keynes: Open University Press

Balducci, V (ed.) 2005 *Architecture per le colonie di vacanza.* Florence: Alenia

Barber, C and Barber, S 1993 *Around & About Teignmouth and Shaldon.* Pinhoe: Obelisk

Barker, WG 1860 *On the Climate of Worthing: its remedial influence in disease, especially of the lungs.* London: John Churchill

Bartholomew, C c.1870 *The Turkish Bath: Mr Bartholomew's evidence before the doctors on the prevention and cure of diseases by the use of Turkish, oxygen, ozone, and electric baths, and medicated atmospheres with reports on places*, 6th edn., Bristol

Bartley, LJ 1971 *The Story of Bexhill.* Bexhill-on-Sea: FJ Parsons

Barton, S 2005 *Working-class Organisations and Popular Tourism, 1840–1970.* Manchester: Manchester University Press

Beatty, C and Fothergill, S 2003 *The Seaside Economy: The Final Report of the Seaside Towns Research Project.* Sheffield: Centre for Regional Economic and Social Research, Sheffield Hallam University

Beckinsale, RP and Houston, JM (eds) 1968 *Urbanization and its Problems. Essays in honour of E.W. Gilbert.* Oxford: Basil Blackwell

Belisario, JC 1959 *Cancer of the Skin.* London: Butterworth & Co.

Bennett, D 1998 *Roller Coaster: Wooden and Steel Coasters, Twisters and Corkscrews.* London: Aurum

Bennett, S and Bennett, N (eds) 1993 *An Historical Atlas of Lincolnshire.* Hull: University of Hull Press

Beresford, MW and Finberg, HPR 1973 *English Medieval Boroughs: A Hand-list.* Newton Abbot: David and Charles

Berry, S 2002 'Myths and reality in the representation of resorts'. *Sussex Archaeological Collections* **140**, 97–112
——2005 *Georgian Brighton.* Chichester: Phillimore & Co. Ltd

Biddle, G 1990 *The Railway Surveyors: The Story of Railway Property Management 1800–1990.* London: Ian Allen: British Rail Property Board
——2003 *Britain's Historic Railway Buildings: An Oxford Gazetteer of Structures and Sites.* Oxford: Oxford University Press

Bishop, CH 1974 *Folkestone: The Story of a Town.* London: CH Bishop

Bishop, JG 1880 *A Peep into the Past: Brighton in the Olden Time.* Brighton: JG Bishop

Blundell, N 1968–72 *The Great Diurnal of Nicholas Blundell of Little Crosby, Lancashire ... Transcribed and Annotated by Frank Tyrer ... Edited ... by J. J. Bagley.* 3 vols, Manchester: Record Society of Lancashire & Cheshire

Blunt, W 1976 *The Ark in the Park: The Zoo in the Nineteenth Century.* London: Hamilton: Tyron Gallery

Boddy, M and West, J 1983 *Weymouth: An Illustrated History.* Wimborne: Dovecote

Boniface, P 1981 *Hotels & Restaurants: 1830 to the Present Day.* London: HMSO

Borsay, P (ed.) 1990 *The Eighteenth-century Town: A Reader in English Urban History 1688–1820.* London: Longman

Braggs, S and Harris, D 2000 *Sun, Fun and Crowds: Seaside Holidays Between the Wars.* Stroud: Tempus

Braithwaite, D 1976 *Fairground Architecture*, 2nd edn revised. London: Hugh Evelyn

Brannon, P 1867 *The Illustrated Historical and Picturesque Guide to Bournemouth and the Surrounding Scenery.* London

Bratton, JS (ed.) 1986 *Music Hall: Performance and Style.* Milton Keynes: Open University Press

Bread, O 1859 *Bread's New Guide and Hand-Book to Worthing and its Vicinity. With Illustrations.* Worthing

Brenan, HB 1936 'The Visitor'. *The Architectural Review* **53** (July), 14–16

Bridgeman, H and Drury, E 1977 *Beside the Seaside: A Picture Postcard Album.* London: Elm Tree Books

Brighton Polytechnic School of Architecture and Interior Design 1987. *A Guide to the Buildings of Brighton*, Macclesfield: McMillan Martin for the South East Region of the Royal Institute of British Architects

Brodie, A, Sargent, A and Winter, G 2005 *Seaside Holidays in the Past.* London: English Heritage

Brook, J 1997 'The story of the De La Warr Pavilion' in *Erich Mendelsohn 1887–1953: A touring exhibition organised by Modern British Architecture.* Bexhill-on-Sea: Modern British Architecture in conjunction with A3 Times, 23–33

Brown, BJH and Loosley, J 1985 *Yesterday's Town: Weston-Super-Mare*. Buckingham: Barracuda

Brunner, E 1945 *Holiday Making and the Holiday Trades*. Oxford: Oxford University Press

Bulley, JA 1956 'Teignmouth as a Seaside Resort'. *Reports and Transactions of the Devon Association* **88**, 143–62

Burke, T 1946 *Travel in England: From Pilgrim and Pack-horse to Light car and Plane*. New York: Charles Scribner's sons

Burney, F 1988 *The Early Journals and Letters of Fanny Burney*. Edited by Lars E. Troide. Oxford: Clarendon Press

Busson, C 1985 *The Book of Ramsgate*. Buckingham: Barracuda

Butler, C 1984 *The Bognor Estate of Sir Richard Hotham MP*. Bognor: Bognor Regis Local History Society

Butler, RW 1980 'The concept of a tourist area cycle of evolution: implications for management of resources'. *Canadian Geographer* **24** (1), 5–12

Butlin, B and Dacre, P 1993 *The Billy Butlin Story: A Showman to the End*. London: Robson

Byrom, M 1972 *Punch and Judy: Its Origin & Evolution*. Aberdeen: Shiva Publications

Calladine, T and Morrison, K 1998 *Road Transport Buildings: A Report by RCHME for the English Heritage Post-1939 Listing Programme*. Cambridge: Royal Commission on the Historical Monuments of England

Camden, W 1835 *The Steam-Boat Pocket Book: a descriptive guide from London Bridge to Gravesend, Southend, the Nore, Herne Bay, Margate, and Ramsgate, etc*. London: B Steill; G Berger

Cannadine, D 1980 *Lords and Landlords: The Aristocracy and the Towns 1774–1967*. Leicester: Leicester University Press

Capper, BP 1833 *The Herne Bay Guide*. London

Carey, GS 1799 *The Balnea, or, an impartial description of all the popular watering places in England: interspersed with original sketches and incidental anecdotes, in excursions to Margate [etc.] ...* London: W West

Carrington, NT *c*.1840 *The Teignmouth Guide, containing a description of the town, ... the excursions and walks, climate, ... etc etc. By several literary gentlemen*. Teignmouth: Edward Croyden

Carter, O 1989 *An Illustrated History of British Railway Hotels, 1838–1983*. St Michael's: Silver Link

Cartmell, R 1987 *The Incredible Scream Machine: A History of the Roller Coaster*. Fairview Park, OH: Amusement Park Books; Bowling Green, OH: Bowling Green State University Popular Press

Casella, EC and Symonds, J (eds) 2005 *Industrial Archaeology: Future Directions*. New York: Springer

Chalklin, C 2001 *The Rise of the English Town, 1650–1850*. Cambridge: Cambridge University Press

Charlton, L 1779 *The History of Whitby, and of Whitby Abbey*, etc. York: A Ward

Clark, J 1829 *The Influence of Climate in the Prevention and Cure of Chronic Diseases, more particularly of the chest and digestive organs*. London: T & G Underwood

——1830 *The Influence of Climate in the Prevention and Cure of Chronic Diseases, more particularly of the chest and digestive organs ...* 2nd edn. London: T & G Underwood

Clark, P (ed.) 2000 *The Cambridge Urban History of Britain. Vol. II. 1540–1840*. Cambridge: Cambridge University Press

Clarke, ED 1793 *A Tour through the South of England, Wales and part of Ireland, made during the summer of 1791*. London: R Edwards

Clarke, GE 1975 *Historic Margate*. Margate: Margate Public Libraries

Clarke, JJ 1955 *A History of Local Government of the United Kingdom, etc*. London: Herbert Jenkins

Clements, R 1992 *Margate in Old Photographs*. Stroud: Alan Sutton

——1997 *Margate: A Second Selection* Stroud: Sutton

Clements, WH 1999 *Towers of Strength: The Story of the Martello Towers*. Barnsley: Leo Cooper

Clonmore, The Lord 1933, 'London, Morecambe & elsewhere'. *The Architectural Review* **74** (September), 93–9

Clunn, H 1929 *Famous South Coast Pleasure Resorts Past and Present, etc*. London: T Whittingham & Co

Cobbett, W 1958 *Rural Rides ...* London: Macdonald

Colbatch, J 1696 *A Physico Medical Essay, concerning Alkaly and Acid, so far as they have relation to the cause or cure of distempers ...* London: Dan Browne

Coleman, GS and Lukens, J 1956 *The Sanger Story*. London: Hodder & Stoughton

Colvin, HM 1995 *A Biographical Dictionary of British Architects, 1600–1840*, 3 edn. New Haven, CT; London: Yale University Press for the Paul Mellon Centre for Studies in British Art

Commins, J 1836 *Commins's Improved Weymouth Guide*. Weymouth: J Commins

Connely, W 1955 *Beau Nash, Monarch of Bath and Tunbridge Wells*. London: Werner Laurie

Constance, H 2001 *First in the Field: A Century of the Camping and Caravanning Club*. Coventry: Camping and Caravanning Club

Corfield, PJ 1990 'Walking the City Streets'. *Journal of Urban History* **16** (2) (February), 132–74

Coulson, RLH 1984 *A Chronology of Herne Bay to 1913*. Herne Bay: Kent County Council

Cozens, Z 1793 *A Tour through the Isle of Thanet, and some other parts of East Kent, etc*. London

Crockett, T 2004 *The Story of Brighton: Is it a Model for the South Coast?* Conference paper at The First Annual South Coast Towns Conference (9 July)

Cross, G (ed.) 1990 *Worktowners at Blackpool: Mass-Observation and Popular Leisure in the 1930s*. London: Routledge

Cross, GS and Walton, JK 2005 *The Playful Crowd: Pleasure Places in the Twentieth Century*. New York; Chichester. Columbia University Press

Crowe, K 2003 *Kursaal Memories: A History of Southend's Amusement Park*. St Albans: Skelter Publications

Cunningham, H 1980 *Leisure in the Industrial Revolution, c.1780– c.1880*. New York: St Martin's Press

Curtis, B 1988 *Blackpool Tower*. Lavenham: Dalton

Curtis, CHO (ed.) 1888 *Bright's Illustrated Guide To Bournemouth, Christchurch, New Forest, Poole, Wimborne, Swanage, Corfe Castle, Etc*. London

Dale, A 1967 *Fashionable Brighton 1820–1860*. 2 edn. Newcastle upon Tyne: Oriel Press

Dawe, N and Powell, K 2001 *The Modern House Today*. London: Black Dog

Delgado, A 1971 *Victorian Entertainment*. Newton Abbot: David & Charles

Dickens, C 1994 'The Tuggses at Ramsgate', *in* Michael Slater (ed.), *The Dent Uniform Edition of Dickens' Journalism*. Columbus: Ohio State University Press

——1999 *Nicholas Nickleby*. London: Penguin

Diplock, W nd *The Hastings Guide*. Hastings

D'Ormesson, J 1984 *Grand Hotel: The Golden Age of Palace Hotels. An Architectural and Social History.* London: Dent

Douet, J 1998 *British Barracks 1600–1914: Their Architecture and Role in Society.* London: Stationery Office

Drower, J 1982 *Good Clean Fun: The Story of Britain's First Holiday Camp.* London: Arcadia Books

Durie, AJ 2002 'The business of hydropathy in the north of England, c.1850–1930'. *Northern History* **39** (March), 37–58

Easdown, M 1998 *Victoria's Golden Pier: The Life and Times of the Victoria Pier, Folkestone and Other Attractions on Folkestone Seafront.* Seabrook: Marlin

Ekberg, C 1986 *The Book of Cleethorpes.* Buckingham: Barracuda

Elleray, DR 1995 *Eastbourne: A Pictorial History.* Chichester: Phillimore

ENGLAND. National Parks Commission 1967. *The Coasts of Kent and Sussex Report of the Regional Coastal Conference Held in London on May 27th 1966,* London: HMSO

English Tourism Council 2001 *Sea Changes: Creating World-class Resorts in England: A Strategy for Regenerating England's Resorts.* London: English Tourism Council

Evans, J 1821 *Recreation for the Young and the Old. An excursion to Brighton, with an account of the Royal Pavilion, a visit to Tunbridge Wells, and a trip to Southend. In a series of letters, etc.* Chiswick

Evans, N 2003 *Dreamland Remembered: 140 Years of Seaside Fun in Margate.* Whitstable: Nick Evans

Fairley, A 2001 *Bucking the Trend: The Life and Times of the Ninth Earl De La Warr 1900–1976.* Bexhill-on-Sea: The Pavilion Trust

Farrant, S 1980 *Georgian Brighton 1740–1820.* Brighton: Centre for Continuing Education, University of Sussex

——1987 'London by the sea: resort development on the south coast of England 1880–1939'. *Journal of Contemporary History* **22,**137–62

——and Farrant, JH 1980 'Brighton, 1580–1820: from Tudor town to Regency resort'. *Sussex Archaeological Collections* **118,** 331–50

Fisher, S (ed.) 1997 *Recreation and the Sea.* Exeter: University of Exeter Press

Floyer, J 1702 *The Ancient Ψυχρολουσια revived: or, an essay to prove Cold Bathing both safe and useful.* London: S Smith and B Walford

——and Baynard, E 1706 *Ψυχρολουσια: or, the history of cold bathing: both ancient and modern* 2 edn. London: S Smith and B Walford

Fowles, J 2000 *A Short History of Lyme Regis.* Stanbridge: The Dovecote Press

Furby, J 1846 *Furby's Hand-book for Strangers visiting Bridlington Quay, etc.* Bridlington

Gawthern, A 1980 *The Diary of Abigail Gawthern of Nottingham 1751–1810.* Edited by Adrian Henstock. Nottingham: Thoroton Society

Gilbert, EW 1939 'The growth of inland and seaside health resorts in England'. *Scottish Geographical Magazine* (January), 16–35

Giles, JA 2000 *The Diary and Memoirs of John Allen Giles.* Taunton: Somerset Record Society

Giraldus, C 1937 *The Autobiography of Giraldus Cambrensis.* Edited and translated by HE Butler. London: Jonathan Cape

Girouard, M 1992 *Town and Country.* New Haven, CT; London: Yale University Press

Glazebrook, TK 1826 *A Guide to Southport, North Meols in the County of Lancaster: with an account of the places in the immediate neighbourhood* 2 edn. London

Goodall, B 1992 'Coastal resorts: development and redevelopment'. *Built Environment* **18** (1), 5–11

Gordon, S 1869 *The Watering Places of Cleveland; being descriptions of these and other attractive localities in … Yorkshire.* Redcar

Gosling, T and Marshall, L 1993 *Lyme Regis.* Stroud: Alan Sutton

Gowler, MAH 1998 *Bognor's Early Trades and Traders.* Bognor Regis: Bognor Regis Local History Society

Grandfield, Y 1989 'The holiday diary of Thomas Lott: 12–22 July, 1815'. *Archaeologia Cantiana* **107**, 63–82

Granville, AB 1971 *Spas of England and Principal Sea-bathing Places.* 2 vols. Bath: Adams & Dart

Gration, G 2000 *The Best Summer of our Lives: A Photographic History of the Derbyshire Miners' Holiday Camp.* Derby: Breedon

Gray, F 2006 *Designing the Seaside: Architecture, Society and Nature.* London: Reaktion

Gray, R 1996a *Cinemas in Britain: One Hundred Years of Cinema Architecture.* London: Lund Humphries

Gray, T 1996b 'The travels of Mrs Parry Price through Devon in 1805'. *Transactions of the Devon Association for the Advancement of Science* **128**, 65–89

Griffiths, G 1965 *History of Teignmouth.* Teignmouth: Brunswick Press

Guillery, P 2004 *The Small House in Eighteenth-century London: A Social and Architectural History.* New Haven, CT; London: Yale University Press

Guilmant, A 1982 *Bexhill-on-Sea: A Pictorial History.* Chichester: Phillimore

Haines, P 1989 *Hastings in Old Photographs.* Gloucester: Sutton

Hall, J 1790 *New Margate and Ramsgate guide … : and a general account of the Isle of Thanet.* Margate

Hammond, JH 1981 *The Camera Obscura: A Chronicle.* Bristol: Hilger

Harding, S and Lambert, D (eds) 1994 *Parks and Gardens of Avon.* Bristol: Avon Gardens Trust

Hardy, D and Ward, C 1984 *Arcadia for All: The Legacy of a Makeshift Landscape.* London: Mansell

Harrison, PT 1909 *Bungalow Residences: a handbook for all interested in building … Illustrated by twenty-two plates and numerous text diagrams.* London: Crosby, Lockwood & Son

Hart, HW 1981 'A transport curiosity. Walter Fagg's broad-gauge line. Notes concerning a Folkestone innovation'. *The Journal Of Transport History*, 3 ser, **2** (1) (March 1981), 69–74

Harvey, J 1800 *Harvey's Improved Weymouth Guide, etc.* Dorchester

Hatfield, J 1797 *A New Scarborough Guide, containing customs, amusements, lodging-houses, &c. … .* London: J Hamilton

Hawkins, J 1991 *Herne Bay in Old Photographs.* Stroud: Sutton

Hay, A 1794 *The Chichester Guide: containing, an account of the antient and present state of the City of Chichester and its neighbourhood, etc.* Chichester: J Seagrave

Hembry, P 1990 *The English Spa 1560–1815: A Social History.* London: Athlone

Hern, A 1967 *The Seaside Holiday. The History of the English Seaside Resort.* London: Cresset Press

Hill, CW 1978 *Edwardian Entertainments: A Picture Post Card View.* Burton upon Trent: MAB Publishing

Hix, J 1974 *The Glass House.* London: Phaidon

Hobday, RA 1997 'Sunlight therapy and solar architecture'. *Medical History* **41**, 456–7

Horn, P 1999 *Pleasures and Pastimes in Victorian Britain*. Stroud: Sutton

Horsfield, TW 1835 *The History, Antiquities and Topography of the County of Sussex*. Lewes: Sussex Press

Hull, F (ed.) 1955 'A Tour in Kent 1759'. *Archaeologia Cantiana* **69**, 171–8

——(ed.) 1966 'A Kentish Holiday, 1823'. *Archaeologia Cantiana* **81**, 109–17

Humphreys, HN 1857 *Ocean Gardens: the history of the marine aquarium, and the best methods … for its establishment and preservation*. London

Humphreys, R 1991 *Thanet at War 1939–45*. Stroud: A Sutton

Hunter, M 1998 'The first seaside house?'. *The Georgian Group Journal* **8**, 135–42

Hutchins, J 1774 *The History and Antiquities of the County of Dorset; … with a copy of Domesday Book, and the Inquisito Gheldi for the County; … 2 vols*. London: W Bowyer and J Nichols

Hutchinson, G 1994 *Martello Towers: A Brief History*. Rye: G Hutchinson

Hutton, W 1789 *A Description of Blackpool, in Lancashire; frequented for sea bathing*. Birmingham

Hyett, W 1805 *A Description of the Watering Places on the South East Coast of Devon, from the river Exe to the Dart inclusive, etc*. Exeter

International Young Men's Holiday Camp (DOUGLAS) 1904, *The Camp Herald*, Douglas

Jackson, AA 1993 *Volk's Railways, Brighton: An Illustrated History*. Brighton: Plateway Press

Jakle, JA et al. 1996 *The Motel in America*. Baltimore: Johns Hopkins University Press

Jenkinson, A 1998 *Caravans, The Illustrated History – 1919–1959*. Dorchester: Veloce Publishing

——1999 *Caravans, The Illustrated History – From 1960*. Dorchester: Veloce Publishing

——2003 *Motorhomes – The Illustrated History*. Dorchester

Joad, CEM (ed.) 1957 *The English Counties*. London: Odhams Press

Jones, S 1718 *Whitby, a poem. Occasioned by Mr Andrew Long's recovery from the jaundice, by drinking of Whitby spaw-waters*. York: Tho. Hammond

Jordan, A and Jordan, E 1991 *Away for the Day: The Railway Excursion in Britain, 1830 to the Present Day*. Kettering: Silver Link

Kay, AC 2003 'A little enterprise of her own: lodging-house keeping and the accommodation business in nineteenth-century London'. *London Journal* **28** (2), 41–53

Kay, A and Kay, I 1998 *Margate: Then & Now*. Stroud: Tempus

Kellett, JR 1969 *The Impact of Railways on Victorian Cities*. London: Routledge & Kegan Paul; Toronto: University of Toronto Press

——1993 'The railway as an agent of internal change in Victorian Cities', *in* RJ Morris and R Roger (eds) *The Victorian City: A Reader in British Urban History 1820–1914*. London: Longman, 181–208

Kelly 1846 *Post Office London Directory, 1846* (facsimile edn King's Lynn: Michael Winton, 1994)

——1883 *Kelly's Directory of Cambridge, Norfolk and Suffolk: with coloured maps, 1883*. London: Kelly & Co

——1889a *Kelly's Directory of Devonshire, 1889*. London: Kelly & Co

——1889b *Kelly's Directory of Kent, 1889*. London: Kelly & Co

——1900–1 *Kelly's Directory of the Isle of Thanet, 1900–1*. London: Kelly's Directories Ltd

——1902 *Kelly's Directory of Kent, 1902*. London: Kelly's Directories Ltd

——1906 *Kelly's Directory of Essex, 1906*. London: Kelly's Directories Ltd

——1924 *Kelly's Directory of Lancashire (exclusive of the cities of Manchester and Liverpool) 1924*. London: Kelly's Directory Ltd

——1939a *Kelly's Directory of Cornwall, 1939*. London: Kelly's Directories Ltd

——1939b *Kelly's Directory of Devonshire, 1939*. London: Kelly's Directories Ltd

Kichin, B 1912 'The architectural treatment of sea-fronts'. *The Architectural Review* **32** (188) (July), 18–22

Kidd, W 1831 *The Picturesque Pocket Companion to Margate, Ramsgate, Broadstairs, and the parts adjacent …* London: William Kidd

Kielmansegge, F von 1902 *Diary of a Journey to England in the Years 1761–1762 … Translated by Countess Kielmansegg*. London: Longmans & Co

Kime, W 1986 *The Book of Skegness, Ingoldmells, Addlethorpe and Chapel St Leonards*. Buckingham: Barracuda

——1988 *Skegness in the 1920s and '30s*. Skegness: CH Major

——2005 *The Lincolnshire Seaside*. Stroud: Sutton

King, AD 1984 *The Bungalow: The Production of a Global Culture*. London: Routledge & Kegan Paul

Kisling, VN (ed.) 2000 *Zoo and Aquarium History: Ancient Animal Collections to Zoological Gardens*. Boca Raton, FL; London: CRC Press

Kniveton, G et al. 1996 *Centenary of the Borough of Douglas 1896–1996: A Celebration*. Douglas: Manx Experience

Lackington, J 1974 *Memoirs of the First Forty-five Years of James Lackington*. New York; London: Garland Publishing

Lancaster, O 1936a *Progress at Pelvis Bay*. London: John Murray

——1936b 'The English at the seaside'. *The Architectural Review* **80** (July), 8–14

La Rochefoucauld, François, duc de 1988 *A Frenchman's Year in Suffolk: French Impressions of Suffolk Life in 1784 … .* Translated and edited by Norman Scarfe. Woodbridge: Boydell

Lavery, P (ed.) 1974 *Recreational Geography*. Newton Abbot: David and Charles

Leach, N 1999 *For those in Peril: The Lifeboat Service of the United Kingdom and the Republic of Ireland, Station by Station*. Kettering: Silver Link

Le Bas, Charles 1802 *The New Margate, Ramsgate and Broadstairs Guide*. Margate

Lee, L 1974 *As I Walked out One Midsummer Morning*. London

Leighton, J 1847 *London Out of Town: or, the adventures of the Browns by the sea-side. By Luke Limner, Esq*. London

Leland, J 1964 *The Itinerary of John Leland in or about the Years 1535–1543*. Edited by Lucy Toulmin Smith. London: Centaur Press

Lello, J 1999 *Lyme Regis Past*. Lyme Regis: Lello Publishing

Lewis, C 1980 *Great Yarmouth: History, Herrings and Holidays*. Cromer: Poppyland

Lewis, J 1723 *The History and Antiquities, Ecclesiastical and Civil, of the Isle of Tenet in Kent*. London

——1736 *The History and Antiquities, as well Ecclesiastical and Civil, of the isle of Tenet, in Kent*. London

Lewis, S 1840 *A Topographical Dictionary of England … and the Islands of Guernsey, Jersey and Man … with maps … and a plan of London, etc.* 4 edn. 4 vols. London

Lindley, K 1973 *Seaside Architecture.* London: Hugh Evelyn

Longmate, N 1991 *Island Fortress: The Defence of Great Britain 1603–1945.* London: Hutchinson

Longstaff-Tyrell, P 2002 *Barracks to Bunkers: 250 Years of Military Activity in Sussex.* Stroud: Sutton

Love, J 1788 *The new Waymouth Guide, or useful pocket companion: containing a description of Waymouth, the mineral spring at Nottington, etc.* Weymouth: J Love

Lucking, JH 1971 *The Great Western at Weymouth: A Railway and Shipping History.* Newton Abbot: David & Charles

Lyons, JA 1763 *A Description of the Isle of Thanet, and particularly of the town of Margate; … .* London

Mackie, SJ 1883 *A Descriptive and Historical Account of Folkestone and Its neighbourhood.* 2 edn. Folkestone: J English

Mahomet, SD 1997 *The Travels of Dean Mahomet: An Eighteenth-century Journey through India.* Edited with an introduction and biographical essay by Michael H Fisher. Berkeley, CA; London: University of California Press

Maitland, P 1936 'The architect'. *The Architectural Review* **80** (July), 18–28

Mander, R and Mitchenson J, 1974 *British Music Hall.* Revised edn. London: Gentry Books

Manser, RN 1987 *Circus.* Blackburn: Richford

Manship, H, 1854 *The History of Great Yarmouth, edited by C.J. Palmer.* Great Yarmouth: LA Meall

Marchant, R 1997 *Hastings Past.* Chichester: Phillimore

Markham, G 1610 *Markhams Maister-Peece, or, What doth a Horse-man lacke. Containing all possible knowledge whatsoeur … touching the curing of all maner of diseases or sorrances in horses, etc.* London

Marrat, W 1814 *The History of Lincolnshire, topographical, historical and descriptive.* Boston

Mason, T 2003 *Shifting Sands: Design and the Changing Image of English Seaside Towns.* London: English Heritage; CABE

Miele, C 1998 'The first architect in the world in Brighton'. *Sussex Archaeological Collections* **136**, 149–75

Miller, JW 1926 'History of Heliotherapy in Tuberculosis'. *Medical Life* **33**, 143–6

Miller, W 1888 *Our English Shores: being recollections of watering places on the coasts of England … Illustrated, etc.* Edinburgh: Oliphant, Anderson & Co

Mills, DR (ed.) 1989 *Twentieth Century Lincolnshire.* Lincoln: History of Lincolnshire Committee for Lincolnshire History and Archaeology

Mirams, MD 1984 *Old Margate.* Rainham: Meresborough

Morley, J 1984 *The Making of the Royal Pavilion Brighton: Designs and Drawings.* London: Published for Sotheby Publications by Philip Wilson

Morley, M 1966 *Margate and its Theatres, 1730–1965.* London: Museum Press

Morris, RJ and Roger, R (eds) 1993 *The Victorian City: A Reader in British Urban History, 1820–1914.* London: Longman

Morrison, KA 2003 *English Shops and Shopping: An Architectural History.* New Haven, CT; London: Yale University Press

Morton, HV 1927 *In Search of England.* London: Methuen & Co

Moss, WG 1824 *The History and Antiquities of the Town and Port of Hastings, illustrated by a series of engravings, etc.* London: WG Moss

Mulcaster, R 1581 *Positions wherein those primitive circumstances be examined, which are necessarie for the training up of children, either for skill in their booke, or health in their bodie, etc.* London: T Vautrollier

Murray, V 1998 *High Society: A Social History of the Regency 1788–1830.* London: Viking

Muthesius, S 1982 *The English Terraced House.* New Haven, CT; London: Yale University Press

Natan, A (ed.) 1961 *Silver Renaissance. Essays in Eighteenth-century English History.* London: Macmillan & Co; New York: St Martin's Press

Neller, RM 2000 *The Growth of Mablethorpe as a Seaside Resort 1800–1939.* Mablethorpe: SBK Books

Nevill, A 2002 *Dickens in Folkestone.* Folkestone: Folkestone and District Local History Society

Nightingale, F 1863 *Notes On Hospitals: being two papers read before the National Association for the promotion of social science, … 1858; with evidence given to the Royal Commissioners on the state of the Army in 1857.* 3 edn, enlarged and for the most part rewritten. London

Noall, C 1977 *The Book of St Ives: A Portrait of the Town.* Chesham: Barracuda Books

Osler, W 1921 *The Evolution Of Modern Medicine … Lectures, etc.* New Haven, CT: Yale University Press

Palmer, MG 1943 'A diarist in Devon'. *Report and Transactions of the Devonshire Association* **75**, 211–43

——1944 'A diarist in Devon'. *Report and Transactions of the Devonshire Association* **76**, 215–47

Pardon, GF 1857 *Porter's Guide to Blackpool, with notes of Fleetwood, Lytham, &c., and a directory of Blackpool.* Blackpool & Fleetwood: W Porter

Park, S nd *A Brief History of the Vine Hotel.* Typescript

Parkes, WH 2001 *Guide to Thorpeness (Leiston Station, G.E.R.).* Aldeburgh: Meare

Parkin, C 1776 *The History and Antiquities of Yarmouth.* London

Parry, K 1983 *Resorts of the Lancashire Coast.* Newton Abbot: David & Charles

Paul, CN 1918 *The Influence of Sunlight in the Production of Cancer of the Skin.* London: HK Lewis & Co

Pearce, F 2000 *The Torquay Marine Spa 1853–1971.* Chudleigh: Orchard Publications

Pearson, LF 1991 *The People's Palaces: The Story of the Seaside Pleasure Buildings of 1870–1914.* Buckingham: Barracuda

——2002 *Piers and other Seaside Architecture.* Princes Risborough: Shire

Perkin, HJ 1976 'The "social tone" of Victorian seaside resorts in the north-west'. *Northern History* **11**, 180–94

Pertwee, B 1999 *Beside the Seaside: A Celebration of 100 Years of Seaside Entertainment.* London: Collins & Brown

Pevsner, N 1976 *A History of Building Types.* London: Thames and Hudson

——et al. 1989 *Lincolnshire.* 2 edn, revised. Harmondsworth: Penguin

Pigot 1824 *Pigot and Co.'s London and Provincial New Commercial Directory, For 1823–4 [Devonshire].* London: J Pigot

——1826/7 *Directory of Kent.* London

——1830 *Directory of Devon.* London

——1832 *Directory of Sussex*. London

——1839 *Directory of Kent*. London

——1840a *Directory of Kent*. London

——1840b *Directory of Sussex*. London

Pimlott, JAR 1947 *The Englishman's Holiday: A Social History*. London: Faber & Faber

——1976 *The Englishman's Holiday: A Social History*. 1 edn, reprinted. Hassocks: Harvester Press

Plumb, JH 1980 *Georgian Delights*. London: Weidenfield and Nicholson

Pococke, R 1888 *The Travels through England of Dr Richard Pococke … Volume I*. Edited by JJ Cartwright. London

——1889 *The Travels through England of Dr Richard Pococke … Volume II*. Edited by JJ Cartwright. London

Poole, KB 1976 *The Two Beaux*. Wakefield: EP Publishing

Poole, R 1994 *The Lancashire Wakes Holidays*. Preston: Lancashire County Books

Post Office 1851 *Directory of Kent 1851*. London

——1874 *Directory of Essex 1874*. London

Powell, 1825 *The Hastings Guide*. Hastings

Powers, A 2005 *Modern: The Modern Movement in Britain*. London: Merrell

Preedy, RE 1996 *Roller Coasters: Shake, Rattle and Roll!* Leeds: RE Preedy

Pulling, J 1983 *Volk's Railway Brighton 1883–1983 Centenary*. Brighton: Brighton Borough Council

Ransom, PJG 1984 *The Archaeology of the Transport Revolution 1750–1850*. Tadworth: World's Worth

Ransome, A 1903 *The Principles of 'Open-Air' Treatment of Phthisis and of Sanatorium Construction*. London: Smith, Elder & Co

Ray, M 1989 'Who were the Brunswick Town Commissioners? A study of a Victorian urban ruling elite 1830–1873'. *Sussex Archaeological Collections* **127**, 211–28

Read, S 1986 *Hello Campers!: Celebrating 50 Years of Butlins*. New York; London: Bantam Press

Reid, T 1795 *Directions for Warm and Cold Seabathing; with observations on their application and effects in different diseases*. London: T Cadel & W Davies; Ramsgate: P Burgess

Relhan, A 1761 *A Short History of Brighthelmston, with remarks on its air, and an analysis of its waters, particularly of an uncommon mineral one, etc.* London: W Johnston

Richardson, H (ed.) 1998 *English Hospitals 1660–1948: A Survey of their Architecture and Design*. Swindon: RCHME

Roberts, G 1823 *The History of Lyme Regis, Dorset, from the earliest periods to the present day*. Sherborne

——1830 *A Guide Descriptive of the Beauties of Lyme-Regis … with … a description of the great storm in 1824*. Lyme

Roberts, R 1976 *A Ragged Schooling: Growing up in the Classic Slum*. Manchester: Manchester University Press

Robinson, D 1981 *The Book of the Lincolnshire Seaside: The Story of the Coastline from the Humber to the Wash*. Buckingham: Barracuda

Robinson, F 1848 *A Descriptive History of Southport, … on the western coast of Lancashire*. London: Hall & Co

Rollier, HA 1927 *Heliotherapy*. 2 edn. Translated by G de Swietochowski. London: Humphrey Milford

Rooney, ED, Taylor, AF and Whitney, CE 1990 *Folkestone in Old Photographs*. Stroud: Alan Sutton

Royal Commission on the Historical Monuments of England (RCHME) 1970 *An Inventory of Historical Monuments in the County of Dorset. Volume Two: South-east*. London: HMSO

Russell, R 1752 *A Dissertation on the use of Sea-Water in the diseases of the Glands … Translated from the Latin of R. Russell, MD, by an eminent Physician*. London

Rutter, J 1829 *The Westonian Guide: intended as a Visitor's Companion to that favourite watering place (Weston super Mare), and its vicinity, etc.* Shaftesbury: J Rutter

——c.1840 *A new Guide to Weston-super-Mare*. Weston-super-Mare: J Whereat

Ryall, I 1800 *Ryall's New Weymouth Guide, containing a description of Weymouth the mineral spring at Nottington, and whatever is worthy of notice at … Portland, Abbotsbury, Bridport …* Weymouth

Rymer, J 1777 *A Sketch of Great Yarmouth, in the County of Norfolk; with some reflections on Cold Bathing*. London

St Clair Strange, FG 1991 *The History of the Royal Sea Bathing Hospital, Margate 1791–1991*. Rainham: Meresborough Books

Saleeby, CW 1928 *Sunlight and Health*. 4 edn. London: Nisbet & Co Ltd

Sanger, G 1966 *Seventy Years a Showman. With an introduction by Colin MacInnes*. London: MacGibbon & Kee

Saunders, A 1989 *Fortress Britain: Artillery Fortification in the British Isles and Ireland*. Liphook: Beaufort

Schofield, J 1787 *An Historical and Descriptive Guide to Scarborough and its Environs*. York: W Blanchard

Schopenhauer, J 1988 *A Lady Travels: Journeys in England and Scotland. From the diaries of Johanna Schopenhauer; translated from the German and edited by Ruth Michaelis-Jena and Willy Merson*. London: Routledge

Scott, R 1974 *A Topographical and Historical Account of Hayling Island, Hants*. Petersfield: Frank Westwood

Scurrell, D 1982 *The Book of Margate*. Buckingham: Barracuda

Searle, M 1977 *Bathing-machines and Bloomers*. Tunbridge Wells: Midas Books

Shaw, G and Williams, A (eds) 1997 *The Rise and Fall of British Coastal Resorts: Cultural and Economic Perspectives*. London: Mansell

Shaw, P 1735 *A Dissertation on the Contents, Virtues and Uses, of Cold and Hot Mineral Springs; particularly, those of Scarborough …* London: Ward and Chandler

Shelton, HM 1950 *The Hygienic System Vol. III Fasting and Sun Bathing*. 3 edn, revised. San Antonio, TX: Dr Shelton's Health School

Sherry, D 1972 'Bournemouth: a study of a holiday town'. *The Local Historian* **10** (3), 126–34

Sickelmore, R 1827 *History of Brighton and its Environs, from the earliest period to the present time*. Brighton: C & R Sicklemore

Sigsworth, EM (ed.) 1980 *Ports and Resorts in the Regions*. Hull: School of Humanities and Community Education, Hull College of Higher Education

Simmons, J 1986 *The Railway in Town and Country, 1830–1914*. Newton Abbot: David & Charles

——and Biddle, G (eds) 1999 *The Oxford Companion to British Railway History, from 1603 to the 1990s*. Oxford: Oxford University Press

Simond, L 1968 *An American in Regency England. The Journal of a Tour in 1810–1811*. Edited and with an introduction and notes by Christopher Hibbert. London: Robert Maxwell

Smee, WR 1871 *National Holidays, and in reference to Sir J. Lubbock's Bank Holiday Bill*. London

Smellie, KB 1968 *A History of Local Government*. London: Allen & Unwin

Smith, J 2005 *Liquid Assets: The Lidos and Open Air Swimming Pools of Britain* London: English Heritage

Smith, JR 1991 *The Origins and Failure of New South-End*. Chelmsford: Essex Record Office

Smollett, T 1995 *The Expedition of Humphry Klinker*. Ware: Wordsworth Classics

Speaight, G 1970 *Punch & Judy: A History*. Revised edition. London: Studio Vista

——1981 *A History of the Circus*. London: Tantivy

Staelens, Y 1989 *Weymouth through Old Photographs*. Exeter: Dorset Books

Stafford, F and Yates, N 1985 *Kentish Sources. 9, The Later Kentish Seaside (1840–1974): Selected Documents*. Gloucester: Sutton for Kent Archives Office

Stewart-Murphy, CA 1992 *A History of British Circulating Libraries: The Book-labels and Ephemera of the Papantonio Collection*. Newtown: Bird & Bull

Stockdale, FWL 1817 *A Concise Historical & Topographical Sketch of Hastings, Winchelsea, & Rye, including also several other places in the vicinity ...* London: PM Powell

Storry, T nd *The Strangers and Visitants' Illustrated Pocket Guide to Scarborough*. Scarborough

Summerson, J 1949 *John Nash: Architect to King George IV*. 2 edn. London: George Allen & Unwin

Sutcliffe, S 1972 *Martello Towers*. Newton Abbot: David & Charles

Taylor, AF 1998 *Folkestone*. Stroud: Tempus

Telling, RM 1997 *English Martello Towers: A Concise Guide*. Beckenham: CST Books

Thompson, J 1839 *Historical Sketches of Bridlington*. Bridlington

Thoms, D, Holden, L and Claydon, T (eds) 1998 *The Motor Car and Popular Culture in the 20th Century*. Aldershot: Ashgate

Thornber, W 1837 *Historical and Descriptive Account of Blackpool and its Neighbourhood*. Poulton: W Thornber. (Facsimile edition *The History of Blackpool and its Neighbourhood*. Blackpool: Blackpool and Fylde Historical Society 1985)

Thorold, P 2003 *The Motoring Age: The Automobile and Britain 1896–1939*. London: Profile

Toll, RC 1974 *Blacking Up. The Minstrel Show in Nineteenth-century America*. New York: Oxford University Press

Torrington, John Byng, 5th Viscount 1934–8 *The Torrington Diaries: containing the tours through England and Wales ... between the years 1781 and 1794*. Edited, with an introduction, by C Bruyn Andrews. 4 vols. London: Eyre & Spottiswoode

Travis, JF 1993 *The Rise of the Devon Seaside Resorts 1750–1900*. Exeter: University of Exeter Press

Trussler, S 1994 *The Cambridge Illustrated History of the British Theatre*. Cambridge: Cambridge University Press

Turner, T 1979 *The Diary of a Georgian Shopkeeper*. 2 edn. Oxford: Oxford University Press

Turner, W 1562 *A Booke of the Natures and Properties, as well of the Bathes in England, as of the other Bathes in Germany and Italie, ...* Collen: Arnold Birckman

Utting, B 1846. *Guide to Great Yarmouth*. Yarmouth

Vicary, T 1587 *The Englishemans Treasure: With the true Anatomie Of Mans Bodie ... Also the rare treasure of the English Bathes: written by William Turner ...* London: Iohn Perin

Wales, T 1997 *Bognor Regis*. Stroud: Chalford

Wallis, J 1836 *Wallis's Royal Edition, Patronized By The Queen. Brighton as it is, 1836, exhibiting all the latest improvements in that fashionable watering place*. Brighton

Walters, JB 1968 *Splendour and Scandal: The reign of Beau Nash*. London: Jarrolds

Walton, JK 1979 'Railways and resort development in Victorian England: the case of Silloth'. *Northern History* **15**, 191–209

——1981 'The demand for working-class seaside holidays in Victorian England'. *Economic History Review* (May), 249–65

——1983 *The English Seaside Resort: A Social History, 1750–1914*. Leicester: Leicester University Press

——1992 *Wonderlands by the Waves: A History of the Seaside Resorts of Lancashire*. Preston: Lancashire County Books

——1998 *Blackpool*. Edinburgh: Edinburgh University Press; Lancaster: Carnegie Publishing

——2000 *The British Seaside: Holidays and Resorts in the Twentieth Century*. Manchester: Manchester University Press

——and Walvin, J (eds) 1983 *Leisure in Britain 1780–1939*. Manchester: Manchester University Press

Walvin, J 1978a *Beside the Seaside: A Social History of the Popular Seaside Holiday*. London: Allen Lane

——1978b *Leisure and Society, 1830–1950*. London: Longman

Ward, SV 1988 *The Geography of Interwar Britain: The State and Uneven Development*. London: Routledge

Ware, ME 1977 *Historic Fairground Scenes*. Buxton: Moorland Publishing Co

White, W 1850 *History, Gazetteer, and Directory of Devonshire, and of the City and County of the City of Exeter; comprising a general survey of the County of Devon, and the Diocese of Exeter, etc.* Sheffield: W White

——1855 *History, Gazetteer and Directory of Suffolk*. Sheffield: W White

——1867 *Directory of the Boroughs of Hull, York, Grimsby, Scarborough ....* Sheffield

Whitehouse, J 1986 *The Unfinished History of the Railway Convalescent Homes*. Portsmouth: The Railway Convalescent Homes

Whiteman, WM 1973 *The History of the Caravan*. London: Blandford Press

Whitney, CE 1986 *Folkestone: A Pictorial History*. Chichester: Phillimore

Whyman, J 1980 'A three-week holiday in Ramsgate during July and August 1829'. *Archaeologia Cantiana* **96**, 185–225

——1981 *Aspects of Holidaymaking and Resort Development within the Isle of Thanet, with Particular Reference to Margate, circa 1736 to circa 1840*. New York: Arno Press

——1985 *Kentish Sources. 8, The Early Kentish seaside (1736–1840): Selected Documents*. Gloucester: Sutton for Kent Archives Office

——1990 *Broadstairs and St Peter's in Old Photographs*. Stroud: Sutton

——1993 'The significance of the hoy to Margate's early growth as a seaside resort'. *Archaeological Cantiana* **111**, 17–41

Wigstead, H and Rowlandson, T 1790 *An Excursion to Brighthelmstone, made in the year 1789 ...* London

Wilkinson, WR 2002 *Salford by the Sea: 75 Years a City and its Children*. Salford: WR Wilkinson

Williams, J and Savage, A 1992 *A History of Margate's Winter Gardens*. Margate: Thanet District Council

Willsher, P 2003 *Fred Pontin: The Man and his Business: The Authorised Biography of Sir Fred Pontin*. Cardiff: St David's Press

Wittie, R 1660 *Scarbrough Spaw; or, a description of the nature and virtues of the Spaw at Scarbrough in Yorkshire*. London
——1667 *Scarbrough-spaw: or A description of the natures and virtues of the spaw at Scarbrough Yorkshire*. York
Wojtczak, H 2002 *Women of Victorian Hastings: 1830–1870: The Lives and Occupations of Women in Hastings and St Leonards in the Mid-19th Century*. Hastings: The Hastings Press
Wolters, NEB 1985 *Bungalow Town: Theatre & Film Colony*. Shoreham-by-Sea: NEB Wolters

Woods, M and Warren, AS 1990 *Glass Houses: A History of Greenhouses, Orangeries and Conservatories*. London: Aurum
Wyatt, M 1996 *White Knuckle Ride: The Illustrated Guide to the World's Biggest and Best Roller Coaster and Thrill Rides*. London: Salamander
Young, G 1983 *A History of Bognor Regis*. Chichester: Phillimore

Index